Northwest Coast
Archaeology as Deep History

Madonna L. Moss

SOCIETY FOR AMERICAN ARCHAEOLOGY

The SAA Press

The Society for American Archaeology, Washington, D.C. 20002
Copyright © 2011 by the Society for American Archaeology
All rights reserved. Published 2011
Printed in the United States of America

Printed on acid-free paper

Library of Congress Cataloging-in-Publication Data

Moss, Madonna L.
   Northwest coast : archaeology as deep history / by Madonna L. Moss.
       p. cm.
   Includes bibliographical references.
   ISBN 978-0-932839-42-8 (alk. paper)
   1. Indians of North America--Northwest Coast of North America--Antiquities. 2. Paleo-Indi-
ans--Northwest Coast of North America. 3. Excavations (Archaeology)--Northwest, Pacific. 4.
Antiquities, Prehistoric--Northwest Coast of North America. 5. Northwest Coast of North
America--Antiquities. I. Title.
   E78.N78M675 2011
   979.5--dc22
                              2011003707

Contents

Acknowledgments

I am grateful to Paul Minnis (SAA Contemporary Perspectives Series Editor) and the SAA Press Editorial Board for asking me to write a book on Northwest Coast archaeology. As usual, it has been a pleasure to work with John Neikirk, and I appreciate the ongoing support of Tobi Brimsek through production. The encouragement of David Anderson and Ken Ames, past and future SAA Press editors, is also deeply appreciated.

My greatest debt is to fellow archaeologists who have worked hard to accumulate the record synthesized here. Their names appear in the references, but I particularly thank these colleagues who have shared data, publications, and insights over the years: Bob Ackerman, Ken Ames, David Archer, Kitty Bernick, Pete Bowers, Virginia Butler, Scott Byram, Sarah Campbell, Aubrey Cannon, Roy Carlson, Risa Carlson, Tom Connolly, Debra Corbett, Gary Coupland, Dale Croes, Jennie Deo Shaw, Jim Dixon, Morley Eldridge, Jon Erlandson, Mike Etnier, Daryl Fedje, Terry Fifield, Knut Fladmark, Diane Gifford-Gonzalez, Greg Hare, Dennis Jenkins, Grant Keddie, Dana Lepofsky, Rob Losey, Mark McCallum, Iain McKechnie, Duncan McLaren, Alan McMillan, John McMurdo, Al Mackie, Quentin Mackie, Marty Magne, Andrew Martindale, Andrew Mason, Darcy Mathews, R.G. Matson, Charles Mobley, Trevor Orchard, Brian Pegg, Jane Smith, Martin Stanford, Martina Steffan, Julie Stein, Gary Wessen, Rebecca Wigen, and Dongya Yang. Other scholars who have contributed their disciplinary expertise include: Jim Baichtal, Susan Crockford, Susan Karl, and John Harper. The manuscript was improved by the careful evaluation by Colin Grier and one anonymous reviewer. Jon Erlandson, Ken Ames, and Paul Minnis also read the manuscript and made valuable suggestions.

I am grateful for the generosity of the following individuals and institutions who granted permission to use illustrations: John Harper, Coastal and

Ocean Resources, Inc.; Daryl Fedje; Valerie Nair of University of British Columbia Press; Ruth Kirk; Nancy Hammerslough, formerly of Pictures of Record; Don Mitchell; Ann Kaupp at the Smithsonian Institution; Charlotte Beck; Roy Carlson and Simon Fraser University Archaeology Press; Doug Glaum at the British Columbia Archaeology Branch, Sheila Greer from the Champagne-Aishihik First Nations, and finally to Daniel Leen, an authority on Northwest Coast rock art (http://danielleen.org/petroglyphs.html). Al Mackie, Tom Connolly, and Karl Hutchings also helped me arrange for illustrations. Dustin Kennedy, University of Oregon, prepared Figure 4.2 under very short notice. The substantial work of generating the six maps in this book fell to Jacob Bartruff, whose expertise is most appreciated.

At the University of Oregon, I thank Scott Coltrane and Larry Singell of the College of Arts and Sciences, Russell Tomlin of Academic Affairs, and Carol Silverman of the Department of Anthropology for their support of some time away from teaching that facilitated much of the writing of this book. Meg Conkey and Kent Lightfoot also contributed substantially to this effort, perhaps in ways they didn't intend. I thank my Eugene family for their unconditional love: Jon, who supports all my efforts in innumerable ways; Erik, who brings us great joy; and Patty, Tom, and Bridey, whose friendship is an ongoing gift. My parents, Rita and Harry Moss, have been steadfast in their unconditional support and encouragement.

Finally, I acknowledge all the indigenous groups of the Northwest Coast whose history and heritage it is a privilege to study.

1

Introduction: Shuká kaa, *"His Spirit is Looking Out from the Cave"*

In July 2007, Terry Fifield, US Forest Service archeologist, sent out an email to colleagues, "I feel like celebrating, and I wanted to share the good news." At the time, he and his family lived in the Tlingit town of Klawock, Alaska. Fifield worked on Prince of Wales Island for almost 20 years, but was not writing to announce a new archaeological discovery. He wrote to tell us that custody of the 10,300 year old human remains from archaeological site 49-PET-408 would be transferred to the local tribal governments: the Klawock Cooperative Association and the Craig Community Association. The tribes claimed custody under the Native American Graves Protection and Repatriation Act in February 2006. As Fifield explained, "this will be the first time a federal agency has transferred remains of this antiquity to a Native American tribe."

The bones from 49-PET-408 are the oldest human remains ever found in Alaska or Canada. Some archaeologists upon hearing the announcement of transfer of custody might be aghast. What about the data potential of such ancient remains? Remains this old should be available in perpetuity for future study. How can remains of this age be affiliated with a contemporary tribe? Why was Fifield happy at the prospect of this loss to science?

Archaeological site 49-PET-408 is known as "On Your Knees Cave" because the cavers who first explored it in 1993 had to squeeze through narrow passages on their knees. The site is located 125 m above sea level (asl) and a kilometer away from the current shoreline. The original entrance to the cave was obscured by rock-fall and forest vegetation, but the Tongass Cave Project cavers specialize in navigating dense forest and rocky wet slopes in their quest to find caves. The cavers recognized the site as a paleontological locality, and in 1994, caver Kevin Allred showed the site to Earth Sci-

ences professor Tim Heaton of the University of South Dakota. From surface exposures, Heaton collected the bones of brown bear, black bear, land
otter, and some fish. A brown bear femur dated to 40,700 cal B.P. (35,365
RYBP) and a black bear tibia to 46,150 cal B.P. (41,600 RYBP).[1] This meant
that the cave was available to land mammals during the last interglacial, and
that the fossil bones had survived the last glacial maximum (LGM). Later,
Heaton and his team excavated fossil bones of lemming, heather vole, mar-
mot, ringed seal—arctic species that no longer live in southeast Alaska. This
part of Prince of Wales Island was not completely covered by ice during the
LGM; ice-free refugia existed in southeast Alaska that would have been
accessible to some of the first people to come to the Americas.

In 1996, Heaton's colleague Fred Grady of the Smithsonian Institution
found a projectile point, considered then to be an isolate. A few days later,
Heaton found a human mandible, pelvis fragment, and vertebra, and a few
more tools. Excavation stopped and Fifield was notified. He, in turn, contacted representatives of the Craig, Klawock, and Kake communities. At
first, the Tlingit representatives were upset to hear of the disturbance to
human bones. In the words of Clarence Jackson, "[o]ne of the things that
people in the Tlingit world say we shouldn't do is to excavate where our people might be buried. I had a lot of mixed feelings when I heard about discoveries of caves and finding human remains" (Sealaska Heritage Institute
2005). Most Tlingit would prefer that human remains were left undisturbed
in the ground. They were reticent to allow archaeological study. But Fifield
had developed a strong working relationship with tribal members and continued to meet and talk with his Tlingit and Haida neighbors.

After intense negotiations, the tribes agreed to permit investigation, but
only if they were treated as full partners in the archaeological process and
kept informed of project results before the rest of the world learned of them.
They wanted to be involved in analytical decisions, especially those requiring destructive analyses. The tribes retained the right to approve any press
releases and were interested in reading reports and publications before they
were finalized. Fifield facilitated cooperation and the Tlingit approved the
initial request to radiocarbon date the bones. They would allow additional
excavation at the site by E. James Dixon, then affiliated with the Denver
Museum of Science. Tlingit students and community members would eventually participate in the fieldwork, supported by grants obtained by the
researchers, but also from the Regional Native Corporation, Sealaska. Tribal

representatives traveled to Dixon's labs in Colorado to see the facilities and meet laboratory personnel. Tlingit partners would later approve requests to conduct isotopic studies and extract ancient DNA from the bones of the man found at 49-PET-408.

Altogether the remains included a mandible, a few pelvis fragments, 5 vertebrae, 3 ribs, and 4 teeth. The pelvis was dated to 11,230 cal B.P. and the mandible to 11,150 cal B.P. (Dixon 1999; Dixon et al. 1997). These dates are statistically similar and corroborate the antiquity of the bones. The remains were identified as those of a man in his 20s, since his wisdom teeth were erupting. A few weeks later and about 1,000 miles away, the nearly complete remains of another ancient man were found along the Columbia River. Even though these remains are about 1,500 years more recent than those found on Prince of Wales Island, a firestorm of controversy broke out around "Kennewick Man" or "the Ancient One," as he is known to the Umatilla Tribe. While the Washington State tribes wanted to repatriate the remains, some scientists claimed that study of the Kennewick skeleton held the key to unlocking the mystery of the "First Americans." As Thomas (2000:273) pointed out in the Alaskan case, an "infrastructure of cooperation" was already in place between archaeologists, Native Americans, and agency officials prior to the unearthing of human bones at site 49-PET-408. The same was not true in Kennewick. A coalition of scientists sued the federal government to stop repatriation. Over eight long years of litigation was accompanied by a media frenzy, and over $3,000,000 of federal funds were spent in the Kennewick fight (Schneider 2002). Although the legal costs to the scientists and tribes have not been estimated, the case has taken an incalculable toll on the reputation of archaeology in Indian country. Over this same time period, investigation of site 49-PET-408 progressed.

In 1997, Dixon began NSF-funded excavation at the site. He and his team found a cultural stratum dating 10,150-9050 cal B.P., rich in burnt rock, charcoal, and ash, with hundreds of pieces of chipped stone and some microblades (Dixon 2002; Fedje et al. 2004). Beneath this, a few stone flakes were found and a bone tool dated to 12,070 cal B.P., one of the oldest artifacts in North America. The ^{14}C dates on the remains of the man, now known as *Shuká Kaa*, fall between these two dated cultural layers. Gnaw marks and punctures on some of the bones and their spatial distribution suggest that the man's body may have been transported into the cave by a bear or wolf. He may have died in a hunting accident. Shuká Kaa had

3

grooves in his canine teeth, indicating that he used them as tools, perhaps to hold lines, sinew, or cordage. Isotopic studies show that Shuká Kaa had a diet rich in seafood, not surprising in an island location. Genetic study of the mitochondrial DNA preserved in his teeth indicated he was a member of one of the five founding genetic populations that settled the Americas: haplogroup D (Kemp et al. 2007). Haplogroup D is most common in groups known from central California, the Great Basin, and the Columbia Plateau (Malhi et al. 2004), yet Shuká Kaa is one of the oldest of this group in the Americas. Through study of his Y chromosome DNA, Shuká Kaa has also been identified as a member of the Q-M3 subhaplogroup. Of the human remains in the Americas that have yielded ancient DNA, Shuká Kaa most closely resembles a ~1800 RYBP Illinois Hopewell person and two individuals from Tierra del Fuego (400–100 RYBP). Kemp and colleagues believe that the five founding populations are more diverse than previously thought, and estimated the earliest entry into the Americas ca. 13,500 cal B.P.

Although we do not know the life story of Shuká Kaa, we know that he and his people were skilled seafarers who used boats to travel the waters of southeast Alaska. They relied upon marine animals for food and acquired obsidian from non-local sources. He and his people are genetically related to other Native Americans in the Northwest, in the eastern Woodlands and in South America. But we only know these facts because the Tlingit and Haida agreed that the remains from 49-PET-408 should be studied. Director of Sealaska Heritage Institute (2005), Rosita Worl, said "the success of the consultation can be attributed to both the Forest Service and the Tlingit people themselves....They [the Forest Service] acknowledged that they were dealing with sovereign tribal entities ... they proceeded in a respectful manner." The story of Shuká Kaa illustrates the power of new scientific methods used by contemporary archaeologists, but it also shows what can be learned when archaeologists and Native Americans find ways to work together. Although such collaboration is not easy, it is essential for twenty-first-century archaeologists working on the Northwest Coast.

Study of his ancient DNA proved that Shuká Kaa is Native American. He was found in the aboriginal territory of the Tlingit tribe. On this basis, the Forest Service conveyed custody of Shuká Kaa's remains to the Klawock Cooperative Association and the Craig Community Association under NAGPRA. In their press release, the tribes explained:

One reason the tribes supported study of the remains was they believed it would scientifically prove what their oral histories have stated for millennia—that Native people have lived in this area since time immemorial and that they traveled here in canoes....The evidence collectively bolstered an emerging scientific theory that people first migrated to the Americas from Asia along the northwest coast in watercraft, perhaps during the last ice age. Tlingit oral histories also record coastal migrations into Southeast Alaska [Klawock Cooperative Association and Craig Community Association 2007:1–2].

Tlingit and archaeological views of the past will not always coincide. One aim of this book is to summarize the latest in Northwest Coast archaeological research in Alaska, British Columbia, Washington, and Oregon, in a way that connects with the needs and interests of contemporary people, Native and non-Native, professor and student, colleague and layperson, scientist and humanist. I point to new frameworks in which Northwest Coast archaeology relates to contemporary concerns.

Although I cannot incorporate all archaeological work on the Northwest Coast, I have tried to decouple the models that structure the story of Northwest Coast "prehistory" from the empirical records themselves. Although the region has compelling and rich ethnographic records, sometimes we archaeologists fail to use these as records of variability across the region or consider them within the historical context of colonialism. Portraits of Northwest Coast societies have influenced archaeologists working around the world; they have often been seen as the epitome of "complex hunter-gatherers." Complex hunter-gatherers have become a stereotype invoked in hundreds of journal articles and books. Even though the search for the origins and development of cultural complexity has driven a tremendous amount of valuable research, it may be time to consider other research directions. The essence of Northwest Coast social life both past and present is that these were fishing and food-producing societies.

Note

1. Throughout this book, I use both radiocarbon ages (RYBP) and calendar ages (cal B.P.). An age in radiocarbon years generally underestimates the calendar age by a few centuries for more recent dates, but by as much as 2,000 years for Late Pleistocene dates. Where original sources presented only RYBP dates, I used the Fairbanks et al. (2005) calibration curve to convert radiocarbon age to calibrated age, and rounded to the nearest 50 years to avoid false precision. Where the original source provided calibrated dates, I use these without RYBP dates. Because the offset is minor for the most recent 3,500 year period, I present calibrated dates only if the original investigator presented them. On the Northwest Coast, ancient trees can grow to be more than 1,000 years old, so charcoal dates can be affected by Schiffer's (1986) old wood problem. Shell dates are affected by both geographic and temporal variations in the marine reservoir effect; I rely on the sources for these corrections, as I do for dates on bone (calibrated with reference to carbon and nitrogen isotope ratios which reflect an organism's diet).

2

The Power of Northwest Coast Ethnography

The Northwest Coast of North America extends from southeast Alaska through British Columbia, Washington, and to southern Oregon and northern California. Northwest Coast peoples are famous for their spectacular artworks housed in some of the world's finest museums. Their magnificent totem poles, huge canoes, and elaborate masks can be seen on display in New York, Chicago, Berlin, Moscow, and Vancouver. Less well-known is that this was one of the most linguistically diverse regions in Native North America, where 45 distinct languages were spoken just 150 years ago. More than 30 distinct tribes have been defined, although the exact number is unknown. In each cultural group, people lived in semi-sedentary settlements that were mostly politically autonomous. Within a single settlement, related kin lived in extended family households where people were differentiated according to age, gender, reproductive and marital status, and rank. As in most societies, a person's social identity structured their relationships.

Archaeological investigations demonstrate that Native Americans have lived on the Northwest Coast for at least 12,000 years. The most recent centuries of Euro-American contact and expansion comprise a mere moment in the region's human history. In this book, I try to avoid using the term "prehistory" because some scholars believe it devalues indigenous sources of history and favors records written from outsiders' points of view (Echo-Hawk 1993; McNiven and Russell 2005:220). Many older anthropological works depicted Northwest Coast cultures as "dying" or "extinct," and tried to salvage knowledge of "traditional" cultures. Despite the devastating loss of indigenous lives due to European diseases and genocidal government policies, remnant groups survived and their descendants continue to persevere on the Northwest Coast today. Many indigenous people still live in towns their ancestors founded, and they fish, gather, and hunt in territories that

7

have been passed down. Their seafaring traditions live on through construction of old-style canoes and long-distance canoeing expeditions. Many are guided by indigenous social, philosophical, and moral codes they successfully incorporate into their daily lives. Resisting years of oppression, they have adapted social institutions including the "potlatch" to contemporary needs. Northwest Coast artists maintain and innovate in the realms of visual, oratorical, and performance arts. Despite changes, many practices and beliefs of contemporary indigenous people have deep historical roots.

Northwest Coast Societies in Geographic Context

The Northwest Coast "culture area" was once called the "salmon area," because salmon was such an abundant food that Native people relied upon as a year-round dietary staple. The region's immense biodiversity of marine, coastal, and forest resources allowed people to prosper and thrive. Although this large region shares many commonalties, at the time of European contact, it was characterized by remarkable cultural diversity. The language families include Athapaskan, Tlingit, Haida, Tsimshian, Wakashan, Chimakuan, Salishan, Chinookan, Alsean, Siuslawan, and Coos (Figure 2.1). Even with 68 languages and dialects (Thompson and Kinkade 1990:34–35), these groups were not culturally isolated from one another. People traveled and traded over long distances and some individuals were multilingual. Some elite Tlingit men were trained in two or three languages to facilitate alliance-building. Intermarriage between Oregon groups made it necessary for a young wife to learn the language of her husband. Children in such a household would learn their mother's and father's languages and daughters might acquire a third language upon their own marriages.

While group territories of the Tlingit, Haida, and Tsimshian were large, group territories in Washington, Oregon, and California were small. This pattern does not indicate political unity within territories; most groups were broken into local divisions who owned and managed their properties, and held their own names and identities.

The Northwest Coast extends over 2,500 km (~1,500 miles) of the Pacific coast from Yakutat, Alaska, to Eureka, California. One can travel along much of the more than 16,000 km (~10,000 miles) of shoreline because the irregular shape of coast helps protect "inside" waterways. From the Olympic Peninsula south, the outer coast faces westward and bears the

8

Figure 2.1. Distribution of linguistic groups on the Northwest Coast. Map by Jacob Bartruff.

brunt of the full force of Pacific Ocean swells. Estuaries punctuate the west coasts of Washington, Oregon, and northern California, but these are smaller than those to the north. The inland extent of this narrow coastal region is marked by mountains of the Saint Elias and Coast ranges in Alaska, the Coast Mountains in British Columbia, and the Coast, Cascade, and Klamath mountains in Washington, Oregon, and California. In the north, the terrain is rugged and active glaciers are still found at sea level. The mainland coast is indented by deep fjords and drainages including the Chilkat, Taku, Stikine, Nass, Skeena, Fraser, and Columbia rivers.

The region is famous for its heavy rainfall, but precipitation varies considerably in relation to rain-shadow effects caused by mountains, such as those on the Alexander Archipelago, Haida Gwaii (Queen Charlotte Islands), and Vancouver Island. Moist ocean air from the west rises up against the mountains producing heavy rainfall. During the year, up to 500 cm (~200 inches) of rain can fall on the west side of these insular mountains and the mainland positioned at the foot of the steep Coast Mountains. Topographic lowlands between these mountain ranges, however, often enjoy the rain shadow with as little as 100 cm (40 inches) of precipitation.

The Northwest Coast extends from 41° to 60° N latitude, over which terrestrial biodiversity and seasonal weather patterns differ. Terrestrial diversity is greatest in the south, where the moderate climate and longer growing season support an abundance of plants associated with western hemlock-Sitka spruce and western hemlock-Douglas fir forests. From the Gulf of Georgia south are patches of open prairie-like environments, with key economic plants not available to the north, including a variety of oak trees, hazelnuts, and the important starchy root, camas. Some of these prairies supported large populations of elk and were maintained by prescribed burning. Wapato, an edible tuber found in ponds, was also an important staple and trade food. In southern Oregon and northern California, redwood forests are supported by persistent coastal fog.

Western red cedar is the most widely known botanical species of primary importance to Northwest Coast Native people. Its range extends from 42° to 57° N. Cedar wood was used in the construction of houses, totem poles, canoes, furnishings, storage and food boxes, masks, and varieties of ceremonial regalia and utilitarian equipment. Cedar bark was used to make rope, cordage, baskets, clothing, and mats. Since the northern Tlingit did not have access to red cedar locally, they traded for it or used the wood, bark, and roots of spruce or other trees. Groups south of the range of red cedar used redwood lumber and found other sources of fiber.

The abundance and availability of land animals follow the trend of plant communities, with lower diversity in the north. From Vancouver Island south, subspecies of deer and wapiti (elk) are found, whereas only one deer species is found to the north. Different species of bear and small carnivores were found across the region, with rabbits and rodents more numerous in the south and furbearers and mountain goat found in the central and northern Northwest Coast. Archaeological data suggest that people depended more on terrestrial resources south of Puget Sound than to the north.

The spatial distribution and abundance of terrestrial resources are affected by latitude, precipitation, and island biogeography, but the distribution of marine resources is structured differently. Much of the Northwest Coast is affected by marine upwelling where nutrient-laden oceanic currents support highly productive food chains. This combined with estuary size and shape, the range and strength of tides, and the quantity and chemistry of incoming freshwater affect local marine productivity. The region is blessed with high numbers of marine mammals and fish, shorebirds and migratory waterfowl, intertidal invertebrates and seaweeds. The accessibility of these to people traveling in wood canoes varies. In the island archipelagos and fjords of Alaska and B.C., areas protected from ocean swells and storms might be accessible for fishing and hunting for much of the year, although limited by reduced daylight in the north during winter. In contrast, the outer coasts of the islands exposed marine travelers to greater risks, especially in stormy or fog-bound weather. The outer coast makes up proportionately more of Washington, Oregon, and California coastal environments, exposing these to heavy surf and more obstacles to offshore resource use.

Of the six (or seven) salmon species, the species present and their abundance in a river or stream depend on the size and gradient of the drainage. Individual species have their own requirements; for example, sockeye salmon must spend part of their life cycle in lakes. The timing of runs varies widely starting in the spring and continuing through late fall in some places. Salmon runs in large mainland rivers might last for weeks, while the run in a small island stream might be over in a matter of days. The different species and the different localities where fish are caught affect their suitability for different purposes. Oil-rich fish caught in saltwater might be superior in taste, but not as suitable as leaner fish caught upriver for smoking for long-

Table 2.1. Northwest Coast Ethnographic Groups (after Suttles 1990a, Heizer 1978)

First Nation	Geographic Territory	Language	Notes
Tlingit	southeast Alaska	Nadene	13-17 kwaans, matrilineal descent, avunculocal residence, 2 moieties
Kaigani Haida	southern 2/3s of Prince of Wales Archipelago	Haida	moved to Alaska from Graham Island sometime prior to European contact
Haida	Haida Gwaii (Queen Charlotte Islands)	Haida	world-renowned cedar dugout canoes; matrilineal
Nisga'a	Nass River	Tsimshian	matrilineal, with cross-clan names
Gitksan	upper Skeena River	Tsimshian	matrilineal, with cross-clan names
Coast Tsimshian	Prince Rupert Harbor, lower Nass and Skeena	Tsimshian	Nass eulachon attracted Tlingit, Haida, etc.; matrilineal with cross-clan names; avunculocal, 4 phratries
Southern Tsimshian	Kitkatla, Princess Royal Island	Tsimshian	matrilineal, with cross-clan names
Haisla	Kitimat River and Gardner Canal	Wakashan	northernmost Wakashans
Haihais	Milbanke Sound	Wakashan	matrilineages allied in three ceremonial groups
Heiltsuk (Bella Bella)	Fitz Hugh Sound	Wakashan	bilateral descent, crest groups functioned like matrilineages to north
Oowekeeno	Rivers Inlet	Wakashan	bilateral, but individual can choose crest group affiliation
Nuxalk (Bella Coola)	Burke and Dean channels	Salishan	isolated Salish speakers surrounded by Wakashans & Athapaskans; ambilateral descent, patrilocal residence, marriage within and between descent groups
Kwakwaka wakw (Kwakiutl)	north Vancouver Island & mainland along Queen Charlotte and Johnstone straits	Wakashan	local groups of 1-7 numayms, bilateral descent
Nuu chah nulth (Nootka)	80% of western Vancouver Island	Wakashan	whale hunters, ambilateral descent, with option to shift residence
Makah	northwest tip of Olympic Peninsula	Wakashan	whale hunters, ambilateral descent, with option to shift residence
Quileute	Olympic Peninsula, Hoh, Soleduck rivers	Chimakuan	bilateral descent, patrilocal residence
Quinault	Olympic Peninsula , Queets, Quinault rivers	Salishan	bilateral descent, patrilocal residence
Chemakum	Port Townsend, Admiralty Inlet	Chimakuan	

Table 2.1. Northwest Coast Ethnographic Groups (cont.) (after Suttles 1990a, Heizer 1978)

First Nation	Geographic Territory	Language	Notes
Coast Salish (>16 groups)	Strait of Georgia, Puget Sound, lower Fraser	Salishan	bilateral descent, with option to shift residence
Chehalis	Grays Harbor	Salishan	bilateral descent, patrilocal residence
Chinook	lower Columbia River	Penutian	bilateral descent, patrilocal residence
Tillamook	Tillamook Head to Siletz Bay	Salishan	patrilineal, with option to shift residence
Yaquina, Alsea	Otter Rock to Cape Perpetua	Penutian	patrilineal, patrilocal
Siuslaw	Siuslaw River	Penutian	patrilineal, patrilocal
Umpqua	Umpqua River	Penutian	patrilineal, patrilocal
Coos (Hanis, Miluk)	Coos Bay	Penutian	patrilineal, patrilocal
Coquille	Coquille River	Penutian	patrilineal, patrilocal
Tututni	southern Oregon coast	Penutian, Nadene	patrilineal, patrilocal, men & boys live separate from women & girls
Tolowa	northern California, Smith River	Nadene	patrilineal, patrilocal, men & boys live separate from women & girls
Yurok	Klamath River	Algic	mixed patterns of descent and residence
Wiyot	Humboldt Bay	Algic	patrilineal, patrilocal

term preservation. People positioned themselves on the landscape to take advantage of this variation, and intergroup trade allowed for redistribution of different types of salmon.

Table 2.1 summarizes the main cultural groups. The inlets, fjords, and estuaries of the Northwest Coast are the ecological settings that promoted the development of largely autonomous groups. Group territories usually encompassed a range of habitats. Some groups have origin stories that tie a distant homeland to the contemporary one. Groups reckoned descent in different ways and postmarital residence patterns varied widely. Some groups practiced lineage or clan exogamy, while others maintained village exogamy. Within and between related houses individuals held different social positions; these ranks changed over the course of one's life depending on age, sex, birth order, achievements, and an individual's relationships with title-holders. Although slaves might be considered a separate class, most ethnologists characterize Northwest Coast societies as having rank without class (Codere 1957). Houses and lineages were ranked within and between settlements. The size of the territories occupied by Penutians and others in the south was similar to that of Coast Salish dialect groups and to local divisions of the Nuu-chah-nulth, Kwakwaka'wakw, and Tlingit. In some areas, groups were divisions of a geographically widespread linguistic group; elsewhere, a few local groups comprised an entire linguistic group. This made for great variation in intergroup social relations across the coast.

Popular Conceptions of "Northwest Coast Indian Culture"

The variation among social groups often gets lost when people conceive of "Northwest Coast Indian Culture." Perhaps the most famous symbol of Northwest Coast "culture" to the general public is the totem pole. Some totem poles functioned as historical monuments or documents. Others display the origins of specific clans or lineages. Others recount supernatural experiences while still others mark heroic achievements. Some poles refer to specific territories or places of notable events. Most display crest animals that denote clan or cultural identities. Others were built to express extravagant wealth or claim social status. Even today, totem poles are raised in communities to mark special events or promote community healing.

Not all Northwest Coast groups carved and erected free-standing totem poles. Most historical accounts indicate that only the Haida, Tlingit, and

Nass River Tsimshian had indigenous traditions of free-standing totem poles at European contact (Barbeau 1929; Cole and Darling 1990:132; Drucker 1948). Some groups carved short interior and exterior house posts, and some carved less elaborate memorial poles or entry poles set up against houses. Archaeological evidence for the antiquity of totem poles is scarce since plant remains decay rapidly in most sites, but some likely predate contact. Totem pole carving exploded during the nineteenth century due to the introduction of iron fashioned into tools that made wood carving faster. With the influx of wealth stimulated by the fur trade, the Native elite commissioned more totem poles as symbols of their increasing social status after 1830 (Barbeau 1929). As intertribal exchange increased, totem pole carving spread southward to the Coast Tsimshian, Kwakwaka'wakw, Nuu-chah-nulth, Nuxalk, Coast Salish, and beyond. Later in the century, totem poles were in great demand by museum and private collectors, and the influx of travelers and tourists to the region fostered production of miniature totem poles.

Totem poles are a common sight in the Pacific Northwest today; they can be seen in museums, art galleries, parks, schools, hotels, playgrounds, and in front of homes. Very few nineteenth-century totem poles have been left in their original context, except for those that stand in a few remote villages on Haida Gwaii, in southeast Alaska, and up the Skeena River. Many poles have been transported from their original locations—with or without permission or payment—and set up elsewhere. Many poles seen today are replicas, while others are the product of recent revivals and innovations of ancient designs and traditions. Stewart (1990) provides an excellent review of some of the most accessible totem poles in the region. The twentieth-century revival of totem pole carving by aboriginal artists and its continuation into the twenty-first century is an exciting cultural development, but it is misleading to think of totem poles as archetypal symbols characteristic of the ancient peoples and history of the Northwest Coast. The totem pole illustrates the unfortunate habit of viewing the Northwest Coast as a culturally homogenous region. The historic tradition of carving and erecting totem poles, important as it is, cannot be projected onto the more distant, precontact past. This is why it's so important to understand the impacts of contact and colonialism.

Overview of Contact and Colonialism[1]

The history of anthropology is inextricably bound to colonial encounters and Western appropriation of non-Western material culture and intellectual property. Yet if George Emmons, Franz Boas, and others had not collected Northwest Coast art and artifacts, I (and many others) never would have seen the spectacular displays of the American Museum of Natural History in New York where my fascination with the Northwest Coast began.

The first documented contacts between Northwest Coast peoples and outsiders to the region occurred in the eighteenth century. European exploration and commercial expansion—the roots of economic and cultural globalization—were taking hold around the world. Russians, Spanish, French, British, and American explorers and traders converged in the region in pursuit of sea otter furs and geographic knowledge. The Russians had been moving east across Asia since the tenth century, demanding furs as tribute from indigenous peoples. As regions were hunted out, the Russians continued east, reaching the Pacific shore in 1638, eventually moving across the Bering Sea where they enslaved Aleuts and Kodiak Islanders in pursuit of sea otters. In 1741, a Russian expedition made landfall somewhere in Tlingit territory. At the time, Spain considered all the New World other than Brazil as its rightful domain, and in 1774, Juan Perez contacted the Haidas. Other European nations were also drawn to the abundant resources of the Northwest Coast. James Cook obtained sea otter furs from the Nuu-chah-nulth in 1778, and he and his crew made big profits selling these in China. By the end of the eighteenth century, new companies in Britain and independent Yankee traders were making fabulous profits from the maritime trade in sea otter pelts. George Vancouver's charting of marine waters and Alexander MacKenzie's overland expeditions helped determine that what we now call British Columbia was British, while the Russians set up colonies among the Tlingit, and the Spanish attempted a foothold among the Nuu-chah-nulth. Shortly after the turn of the century, Lewis and Clark explored the Columbia River and Simon Fraser "discovered" the Fraser River.

With first contacts, European diseases spread to the Northwest Coast. Aboriginal peoples of North America had no immunities to a number of infectious diseases, and smallpox, venereal diseases, tuberculosis, and other ailments were often fatal. Smallpox epidemics as early as the 1770s hit portions of the coast before some Native people had face-to-face contact with

Europeans. Diseases spread through indigenous networks of trade, intermarriage, and war. Boyd (1985, 1990) provides the most comprehensive treatment of the timing and impacts of disease epidemics during the contact period. Depopulation was an episodic process, with epidemics of the 1770s, early 1830s, and 1862–63 resulting in mortalities as high as one-third of the population.

The introduction of alcohol had long-term medical and social consequences. By the early 1790s, Natives indulged in wine and spirits when they came aboard ships to trade. Soon after, traders brought liquor to the coast to barter for sea otter furs. After 1800, American traders brought hundreds of gallons of rum to trade along with firearms. The land-based British and Russian traders recognized the danger that uncontrolled alcohol consumption posed to their trading posts and settlements, and prohibited the sale of liquor to Natives in the 1830s. Nevertheless, throughout the nineteenth century, alcohol played a part in violent intra-tribal and intertribal relations, as well as hostilities between Natives and non-Natives.

By 1825, sea otters were becoming extinct. Some groups spent more time hunting sea otter than before contact, reaping economic benefits in the form of iron, copper, glass trade beads, weapons, clothing, and exotic foods such as flour, tea, and rice. As sea otter numbers declined, the fur trade shifted away from the outer islands to the mainland coast where terrestrial furbearers such as beaver, mink, marten, and river otters were abundant. Power shifted from outer coast groups, such as the Sitka Tlingit and Nuu-chah-nulth of Nootka Sound, to groups positioned to take advantage of new Hudson's Bay Company posts on the mainland. Mainland coastal groups exploited their alliances with interior Athapaskans who provided another source of furs. The Chilkat and Stikine Tlingit controlled the trade with interior Athapaskans, as did the Tsimshian with the Gitksan, and the Nuxalk with the Carrier.

The fur trade disrupted seasonal cycles of food production long before anthropologists tried to describe subsistence practices and seasonal settlements. Sea otter hunting and furbearer trapping had occurred for centuries, but their scale intensified after contact. Aboriginal people also supplied explorers, traders, and colonists with fresh and preserved food, as the newcomers lacked local knowledge to provide for their own needs. While Euro-Americans introduced the potato to the Northwest Coast, it was the Tlingit and Haida who excelled in potato horticulture and supplied Russian and

British settlements with large quantities. These new activities changed indigenous patterns of land and resource use. Depopulation caused villages to be abandoned, and remnant groups consolidated in neighboring villages or near trading posts and Euro-American settlements. Such places became centers of exchange between indigenous groups and newcomers. Aboriginal diets changed as novel foods became symbols of status prized and potlatched by the elite. Old villages and forts were used for potato gardens.

During the fur trade, enormous amounts of wealth poured into the Northwest Coast. This influx stimulated ceremonialism and increased art production. With population decline, status positions were vacated, and along with consolidation of previously separate groups into new aggregations, competition for social positions and prerogatives escalated. The "nouveau riche" contracted with artisans to produce wealth items for display, and carving of masks and regalia had become easier and faster with iron tools. Items of Western manufacture were potlatched away, and new art forms developed including large shield-like coppers, silver bracelets, argillite carvings, and Hudson Bay Company blankets decorated with buttons, beads, and Chinese coins.

By the 1860s, the largest white settlements on the coast were Victoria, Seattle, Tacoma, Port Townsend, and Sitka. Victoria was a magnet for all groups in the area and those to the north. Many Natives spent winters in squalid slums where alcoholism and prostitution were chronic. To some, prostitution was not immoral or dishonorable; it was a way for Native women to make money and return to their villages with new goods for their families to distribute at potlatches.

When the United States took over Alaska in 1867, social chaos reigned in the absence of laws with the influx of miners and other white settlers. Yankee traders had always traded liquor, and now it was freely available in the new Alaska territory. Social relations between Natives and non-Natives and within and between Native groups were colored by rampant gambling, drinking, and prostitution. With the 1880s gold rush, Tlingit were drawn into the cash economy even more completely as laborers in the mines and in the new logging and fish canning industries. During this period, missionaries descended on Native communities to "save" them from their "heathen" ways, and the vices to which they had been exposed by the agents of "civilization." Missionaries judged most aboriginal customs to be morally wrong and everything from living in extended family households to customary ways of naming children was considered scandalous. Shamanism, potlatching, dancing, cremation, slavery, herbal medicine, polygamy, witchcraft, and the carving of "idols" were all condemned or outlawed. Children were sent away to Christian boarding schools where they were punished for speaking their own languages and schooled in "proper" modes of personal hygiene, dress, and comportment.

All this set the stage for the collecting and physical appropriation of Northwest Coast material culture by outsiders. Although collecting started in the eighteenth century with the earliest contacts, anthropological collecting intensified in the 1870s and 1880s. This coincided with the inflow of tourists to the region who were anxious to purchase baskets, wooden masks, miniature totem poles, and argillite carvings as curios. What Cole (1985) described as a "scramble" for Northwest Coast masks, totem poles, canoes, feast bowls, storage boxes, and even human skeletal remains, was fueled by international competition between North American and European museums. One of the earliest collectors was the American, James Swan, but competition by the Germans stimulated the U.S. and Canada to collect the remains of "their" Indian cultures for museums in New York City, Chicago, Ottawa, and Washington, D.C. Ironically, some missionaries were also avid collectors; even as the Presbyterian minister Sheldon Jackson condemned the use of masks in ceremonies, he collected them for his own enjoyment. Several Native individuals facilitated these exchanges in the hopes that some knowledge of aboriginal cultures would be salvaged. The most famous is probably George Hunt—born of a Tlingit mother and British father and raised as Kwakwaka'wakw. In his career as a mediator between cultures, he worked with the Jacobsens of the Berlin Museum, Franz Boas of the American Museum of Natural History and the Smithsonian, and with Edward Curtis, the famed photographer.

The colonial history of Washington and Oregon differs from that of B.C. and Alaska. Sometimes these more southerly areas are thought of as "cultural backwaters" and the material culture of these groups is not as visible in museums, due partly to accidents of geography and history. As in the north, early contacts here date to the eighteenth century when indigenous people were struck by epidemic diseases. In the 1840s, the trajectories of colonialism diverge. This is when white emigrants streamed into Oregon Territory where settlers and miners staked claims to Indian lands. In 1850, the Oregon Donation Act authorized the U.S. government to give huge tracts of land to settlers prior to any treaty negotiations. Treaty programs were initiated later in the 1850s, but no treaties were ratified for Oregon coast tribes. The Rogue River wars and other deadly conflicts led to the reservation era. The Coast Reservation (later known as Siletz) was established in 1855 and the Grand Ronde Reservation in 1857. Natives on the Oregon coast were forcibly removed (some by bounty hunters) from their traditional homelands to these reservations that lacked facilities. In 1866, the Oregon legislature prohibited intermarriage between Whites and Indians and Whites and "mixed-bloods," although such marriages had been common since the 1850s. Incredibly, this law remained in effect until 1951. By the 1870s missionaries had established boarding schools at Grand Ronde and Siletz, where children were taught "Christian" ways of life. Over time, reservations were reduced in size, and the General Allotment Act of 1887 divided them into allotments assigned to individuals in an effort to end communal living and destroy tribal integrity. Much of this land fell into non-Native ownership and in the 1950s the federal government launched a program to terminate Indian tribes. Restoration and self-determination of Oregon coast tribes has come only recently, with Congressional recognition of the Siletz in 1977, the Grand Ronde in 1983, the Confederated Tribes of the Coos, Lower Umpqua, and Siuslaw in 1984, and the Coquille Indian Tribe in 1989. The Clatsop, Chinook, and Tillamook are also represented among the Grand Ronde.

The tribes of western Washington fared somewhat better under American hegemony. In 1853, Congress established Washington Territory, where the treaties of Medicine Creek, Point Elliott, Point No Point, and Neah Bay were concluded with coastal Washington tribes. This led to a dispersed network of 19 reservations in western Washington. These tribes ceded most of their lands, but retained their rights to fish, hunt, and gather at "usual and accustomed places." The treaties also directed tribes to eliminate slavery, an aboriginal institution. In the 1870s, reservations were placed under direct control of Christian religious organizations that advanced government policies of forced assimilation. As in Oregon, after 1887, the allotment policy promoted the nuclear family, resulted in intra-tribal and intertribal divisiveness, and led to loss of Native lands. But western Washington tribes retained their rights to subsistence and commercial fishing through a long series of court battles that culminated in the 1974 Boldt decision. Today there are 22 federally recognized tribes in western Washington, five having achieved recognition since the 1970s. Seven tribes remain landless and nonfederally recognized because they did not move to reservations.

Although the British government did not declare war on the Indians of B.C., a number of villages were shelled or burned in the mid-nineteenth century including the Kwakwaka'wakw community of Nahwitti in 1850, a Halq'emeylem village on Kuper Island in 1863, a Nuu-chah-nulth village in Clayoquot Sound in 1864, and the Nuxalk village of Kimsquit in 1877 (Kew 1990). White settlement in B.C. was more confined geographically relative to the vast rural areas where most First Nations remained in their territories. By 1854, 14 Vancouver Island tribes had treaties. After B.C. joined Canada in 1871, the federal Indian Act defined the status of Indian individuals and limited their rights. Indian women who married non-Indians could not enroll as members of aboriginal Bands, severing their connections to home communities and reserves. This law, which remained in effect until 1985, meant to force acculturation and eliminate Indian identities, but also reflects the government's patriarchal notions of family. By the 1870s, 82 small reserves had been established, but aboriginal land rights had not been resolved. By 1916, there were 871 Indian reserves scattered across the coast, most of them small and isolated, but treaties with 90 of the constituent Bands had not been concluded. As elsewhere on the Northwest Coast, most of the first Indian schools were operated by Christian missionaries, even after the Canadian government took over school funding. Natives were treated as non-citizens, prohibited from homesteading, not allowed to raise money to assert their land rights, and Reserve Indians could not send their children to public schools. The potlatch and winter ceremonials were outlawed in 1885. Yet many individuals persevered fishing, hunting, and gathering wild foods (despite the outlawing of traditional fishing devices), subsidizing this with wage labor in the fishing, canning, logging, and shipping industries. During the twentieth century, organizations such as the Allied Tribes of British Columbia formed to assert Indian rights. It was not until the 1960s that the Canadian government made substantial financial resources available to Bands for welfare, education, and local initiatives. In the mid-1970s, 15 regional Band organizations or "tribal councils" were formed. Such groups have participated in the Assembly of First Nations attempts to settle land claims and establish sovereignty, but federal and provincial governments have yet to settle aboriginal land claims in British Columbia.

With the U.S. purchase of Alaska from Russia in 1867, small military garrisons stationed in Tongass, Wrangell, and Sitka allowed cultural misunderstandings to escalate into major assaults against the Tlingit. In 1869, villages near Kake and in Wrangell were destroyed by the U.S. Army, and the U.S. Navy shelled Angoon in 1882. By 1878 salmon canneries were operating all over Alaska, and many Tlingit worked in the commercial fishing and canning industries. In 1880, when some Natives led white prospectors to gold near Juneau, the Tlingit were not allowed to file mining claims because they were not U.S. citizens (Worl 1990). After the gold "discovery," miners flooded the region, and local Tlingit worked in the mines. In the 1870s, missionaries established the first schools, which were federally funded in 1884, but not taken over by federal authorities until 1895. Despite protracted legal battles waged by Tlingit and Haida organizations, Annette Island Reservation was established in 1891, the Tongass National Forest in 1907, and Glacier Bay National Park in 1925. The Alaska Native Brotherhood (ANB) formed in 1912, and asserted the rights of citizenship. Alaska Natives won the vote in 1922, two years before the Indian Citizenship Act was passed enfranchising Indians in the "lower 48." The ANB originally promoted the acculturative ideals of the time, suppressing Tlingit and Haida languages, fostering Christian morality, and encouraging formal education. In 1947, the ANB led the fight to eliminate the destructive commercial fish traps that had depleted salmon stocks, and these traps were outlawed in 1959. Tlingit and Haida land claims were finally settled in 1971, when the Alaska Native Claims Settlement Act established the regional corporation, Sealaska, and 10 village and two urban corporations, roughly following ḵwaan (geographic) divisions. While the corporations facilitate resource extraction following capitalist practices (Dombrowski 2002), culture and heritage committees, foundations, and other organizations work to promote and revive aboriginal languages, arts, and traditions.

Perils and Potential: Archaeological Uses of Ethnography

The experiences of contact and colonialism resulted in radical changes to Native American and First Nation societies during the nineteenth and twentieth centuries. Material culture, subsistence and settlement, population sizes and distributions, and the scale of social networks have all been transformed over last 250 years. Yet it is these historical societies that were documented by ethnographers and others. First Nations societies are products of their histories, as are all societies, and their responses to outside forces were varied. These societies should not be deployed by archaeologists as models for or simulacra of pre-contact societies. Understanding the history of colonialism is important because how we use ethnographic records affects how we interpret the past. Understanding colonialism is also a prerequisite for appreciating the politics involved in the contemporary practice of archaeology.

The powerful images of Northwest Coast societies seen in museum displays and contemporary art affect public perceptions, but also how archaeologists interpret and represent the past. Historic photographs serve as evocative images of past lifeways, but are themselves cultural products of specific times and places and the ethnographic gaze. The observers of the eighteenth, nineteenth, and twentieth centuries had their own biases and agendas. We cannot "reconstruct" the past in the same way a building can be reconstructed using architectural plans, old photographs, and information from the fabric of the building itself. Our understandings of the past are always partial, incomplete, and open for reevaluation. Ethnographic and ethnohistorical records on Northwest Coast can be invaluable, but must be used very carefully when interpreting archaeological data (Grier 2007).

The history of totem poles described earlier shows how nineteenth- and twentieth-century phenomena might mislead us about the more distant past. The rows of large houses in Haida and Kwakwaka'wakw towns in historic photographs were built with metal tools. Some were made of hand-hewn timbers, but others were made of lumber. House fronts were often painted with commercial paints. These characteristics do not make such houses less significant as cultural statements, but their large size may not represent ancient architecture. Many historic towns were aggregations of groups whose numbers had been diminished by disease and then drawn to white settlements. In archaeological contexts, house remains are often surprisingly unspectacular; one may find a pit from an excavated floor, or some decaying wood from an upright post or wall board, or a berm of shell midden that accumulated outside house walls. Although remarkable houses have been preserved at Ozette, the Meier Site, and elsewhere, the remains of Northwest Coast houses are often identified by a hearth or hearths, or a subtle difference in soil texture diagnostic of a house floor. In many archaeological sites, house remains are never identified, not because people did not live in houses, but only because house remains typically decay quickly in the forest soils of the Northwest Coast.

Many new art forms arose during the nineteenth century, including argillite carvings, silver bracelets, miniature baskets, canoe paddles, and totem poles. One early form was the "copper," large, shield-shaped emblems of chiefly power. Displayed as symbols of wealth and sometimes destroyed to emphasize the status of their owner, such coppers were rare before 1850, but are known from Tlingit, Haida, Tsimshian, Kwakwaka'wakw, and Nuxalk contexts. Jopling (1989) tested all the coppers in major museums and found that all were made of European copper. During the early fur trade, ships were copper-clad, and this was the source used by Northwest Coast copper artisans. The sheathing was removed from wrecked ships, but captains often packed extra sheets for repairs, and these became popular trade goods. Jopling argued that the Tlingit were the first to hammer and display coppers, and then these practices spread. Unlike coppers, most ethnographic art and material culture is made of materials that would perish in the typical archaeological site.

Archaeologists should not ignore ethnography in an attempt to avoid the pitfalls of projecting it onto the past. Even if we wanted to, we cannot bypass Northwest Coast ethnography and history because their influence is so profound. Archaeological data can do more than confirm what *we think* we know from ethnography. Too often, we use ethnographic information to write "just so" stories of the ancient past. In archaeological research focused on the Angoon Tlingit, I searched for evidence of the ethnographic model of Tlingit settlement, but did not find it (Moss 1989). In a study of shellfish, gender, and status, contradictions among ethnographic, oral historical, and archaeological data were found to reveal biases in the records and new interpretive possibilities (Moss 1993). Instead of expecting corroboration between data sources, more attention could be focused on the gaps between sources and the meaning of these. This will help us sort out what may be the result of historic change or observer bias, and what may result from spatial, geographic, temporal, or cultural variability. In some cases, we may identify long-term patterns of cultural continuity that extend into the deep past, and in others we may find discontinuities.

In his research on Nuu-chah-nulth history and archaeology, Alan McMillan routinely uses the work of ethnographers Philip Drucker and Edward Sapir. In his "tale of two ethnographies," McMillan (2009) noted that

Drucker presented a normative portrait of the Nuu-chah-nulth based on memory culture, while Sapir collected near-verbatim texts of stories and cultural knowledge. Drucker and Sapir represent contrasting ethnographic traditions on the Northwest Coast. Drucker (1951) is an authoritative, comprehensive, and easily comprehensible source of the type most often used by archaeologists. The "difficult and confusing primary sources" of Sapir (McMillan 2009:618) and others like him are less often used by Northwest Coast archaeologists. As McMillan explained (2009:639), "[i]n Sapir's texts and notes, we read the words of the Nuu-chah-nulth consultants who advised him and offered their knowledge. Histories, stories and reminiscences are recorded in the Native voice." Yet these texts have internal contradictions and lack chronological markers—they require patience to digest and sort out. McMillan (2009:639) mined these texts with admirable success, and considered them "indispensable in understanding the dynamic histories" of Nuu-chah-nulth groups. McMillan (2009:638) also showed how archaeology can anchor certain ethnographic details in time and provide more complete information on daily life, especially subsistence and settlement. Similarly, Andrew Martindale (2006) is grappling with difficult Tsimshian oral literature in the context of archaeological and paleoenvironmental research.

Such work requires understanding the consequences of colonialist histories, and recognition that the history of anthropology on the Northwest Coast is itself a product of colonialism. The vigorous collecting of the Museum Movement formed the basis of the earliest anthropological research in the region. Some of the first archaeological work was done by collectors and ethnologists. Although ethnological collecting of past centuries is different than archaeology today, most of the public sees these along a continuum. Much early collecting on the Northwest Coast was not ethical by today's standards, resulting in a legacy of suspicion and resentment on the part of some Native Americans and First Nations toward anthropologists.

The legacy of ethnographic collecting and uncontrolled archaeology can make life uncomfortable for archaeologists who want to work in indigenous communities. Since the 1970s, more archaeologists and museum professionals have collaborated with local communities pursuing shared interests. Recent repatriations through NAGPRA and other mechanisms have led to the return of human remains, funerary items, and objects of cultural patrimony, which include both archaeological and ethnographic materials. Issues of representation—how Northwest Coast peoples and cultures are depicted in museum exhibits, popular and academic literatures, and in classrooms, are sites of cross-cultural negotiation. The popularization and commodification of Northwest Coast art has resulted in a compelling set of images with profound implications for archaeological practice. As Sheehan (2004:163) wrote, "[f]or an archaeologist trying to 'reflesh' the figurative 'bones' of the archaeological record, ethnographic data can be very seductive indeed." I agree with Grier (2007:305) that we should move toward an archaeology that "works both in conjunction with and independently of the ethnographic record in a reflexive interplay."

Note

1. This section synthesizes information from Suttles (ed., 1990).

3

The "Complex Hunter-Gatherer" Stereotype

Archaeologists typically classify Northwest Coast societies as "complex hunter-gatherers," and invoke them as exemplars for prehistoric and historic societies such as the Calusa, Jomon, and Natufians. The Northwest Coast is seen as representative of "middle-range" societies of the last 12,000 years of human history around the world. Simultaneously, the Northwest Coast is often characterized as anomalous because complex social forms, such as hereditary inequality, slavery, and elaborate ceremonialism, evolved in the absence of agriculture.

The term "hunter-gatherer" is a misnomer because Northwest Coast peoples were first and foremost *fishers*. Fishing, by convention subsumed under the term "hunter-gatherer," was of such primary importance on the Northwest Coast that the term "hunter-gatherer" misses the point. Northwest Coast societies engaged in many different types of fishing, and social groups maintained control over fishing territories. They were not just fishers, but fisheries resource managers in contemporary parlance. They harvested a wide range of species, but their management and control of salmon was of special significance. Northwest Coast societies mastered the technologies of fish processing and storage, leading them to accumulate surpluses. They were food producers, even though this term is usually applied only to horticultural or agricultural societies.

In addition to fish, different Northwest Coast groups produced surpluses of other foods and products. The Makah and some Nuu-chah-nulth processed large quantities of whale and fur seal oil that they traded widely. Some Kwakwaka'wakw, Nuu-chah-nulth, Coast Salish, Nuxalk, and Haida cultivated plots of Pacific silverweed and springbank clover in estuarine gardens (Deur 2005). The Coast Salish maintained plots of camas. The Chinook intensified use of wapato-filled wetlands. The Haida selectively logged ancient cedar trees and manufactured seagoing vessels that they traded to others. The Tsimshian on the lower Nass River specialized in the production of eulachon oil. The Kwakwaka'wakw of the Broughton Archipelago practiced mariculture through the construction and maintenance of clam gardens. Ethnographically known societies of the Northwest Coast, and probably many of their ancestors, are more appropriately conceived of as fishing and food-producing societies.

Hunting for the Origins of "Hunter-Gatherers"

The term "hunter-gatherer" is an economic category, while the adjective "complex" usually refers to some threshold of social or political organization. Although hunter-gatherer studies did not evolve as a subdiscipline of anthropology until the 1960s, the notion of hunter-gatherers can be linked to seventeenth-century European ideas about "human nature" and social evolution (Barnard 2004:2). Humanity was thought to have moved through a series of universal stages, eventually progressing to "civilization." In archaeology, the study of hunter-gatherers has been a dominant theme since the 1966 "Man the Hunter" conference (Lee and DeVore 1968). The main attributes of hunter-gatherers defined at this conference included a mobile, nomadic way of life, minimal material possessions, and egalitarian social relations. Sahlins characterized hunter-gatherers as the "original affluent society" because they maximized their "free" time, not their wealth. The archetypal "simple" hunter-gatherers defined at this conference would become the counterpoint to the "complex" hunter-gatherers of the Northwest Coast.

In his paper in the "Man the Hunter" volume, Suttles (1968:56) stated that Northwest Coast groups "were not hunters so much as fishermen," a key point largely overlooked by later writers. Suttles did not use the term "hunter-gatherers," and refers to "simpler" hunters only a few times (e.g., Suttles 1968:68). He did suggest that Northwest Coast societies could be used as a source of analogies where archaeological evidence elsewhere in the world indicated cultural complexity. In the same volume, Murdock (1968:15) noted various societies that relied not on hunting and gathering, but on "fishing, shellfishing or the pursuit of aquatic animals." Where nomadic, Murdock (1968:15) classified these people with hunter-gatherers, but where they were sedentary, as in the case of Northwest Coast, Murdock said they "fall well beyond the range of cultural variation of any known hunting and gathering people." Despite these caveats, most archaeologists have classified Northwest Coast societies as hunter-gatherers, albeit complex ones.

Another problem with the term "hunter-gatherer" is that it sets up a dichotomy that evokes a strict division of labor: Man the Hunter, Woman the Gatherer. Over the last 40 years, feminist anthropologists have variously emphasized the economic importance of gathering, identified women's roles in hunting, reinstated the value of women's reproductive labor, and highlighted both women's and men's collaborative efforts in multistage activities.

Price (1981) coined the term "complex hunter-gatherers" in an article focused primarily on Mesolithic Denmark and the Jomon. From his passing references to "contemporary" Northwest Coast societies, Price (1981:55, 72) clearly considered them complex hunter-gatherers. He did not address any Northwest Coast archaeological data, however, or the antiquity of complex hunter-gatherers in the region. Kelly (1995:321–328) used ethnographic societies of the Northwest Coast as exemplars of non-egalitarian hunter-gatherers. Even though Kelly (1995:342) stated that the archaeology of hunter-gatherers was beyond the scope of his book, his portrait of Northwest Coast societies—living in large sedentary villages, with social inequality, ranking, owning slaves and warring on others—is routinely used by archaeologists working both within and outside the culture area. Following the work of Suttles (1968) and Riches (1979), Kelly (1995:321, 326–327) considered resource fluctuations more spatially homogeneous in the southern part of the area and more heterogeneous to the north, leading to a more rigid hierarchical structure ("reinforced" by the potlatch), and more slaving and warfare in the north. The variable effects of contact and colonialism on Northwest Coast societies were not evaluated. This portrait suggests that Tlingit, Haida, and Tsimshian were more advanced along the evolutionary scale than central and southern Northwest Coast groups. Kelly saw variability in Northwest Coast societies as part of a local response to environmental variation. The simple-to-complex progression has been projected onto a temporal scale in a way that assumes that over time where resources allow, "simple" hunter-gatherers on the Northwest Coast evolved into "complex" ones.

Cultural Complexity

The master narrative of cultural complexity assumes simplicity as a starting point. In North America, the story usually begins in the Americas, even though the first settlers came from Asia with hundreds of thousands of years of history behind them. The progression usually leads from simple hunter-gatherer to complex hunter-gatherer to horticulture to agriculture. Sometimes it leads from forager to collector; at other times, from band to tribe to chiefdom to state. Such concepts are linked to nineteenth-century ideas about cultural evolution wherein the "primitive" evolves into the "civilized." The trajectory of increasing cultural complexity provides a narrative upon which we judge what is more or less complex in a linear sequence that has come to be accepted as eminently logical.

A trajectory of increasing cultural complexity has become the scaffolding on which we hang scraps of evidence, some anchored in time, others not. This habit of thinking overwhelms the fact that the further back in time we look, the more fragmentary the archaeological record is, especially in coastal regions affected by postglacial sea level rise. The variables often tied to complexity among middle-range societies are population size, degree of population aggregation, and population density. The number of social roles increases with complexity because it's more complicated to organize and sustain more people in larger communities. But we do not have good techniques for estimating population size deep in the Northwest Coast past. We can use the number of sites, but we don't often have adequate chronological information. We can use the number of radiocarbon dates, but this is often more closely related to the histories of research and the practices of archaeologists than anything else. These measures are proxies that don't account for site loss due to rising sea levels and coastal erosion, or sites deeply buried or covered in concrete or asphalt. Not unexpectedly, more recent sites are more easily recognizable and better preserved than older ones.

As Quentin Mackie (2001:5–7) discussed, cultural complexity has usually been defined by employing abstract definitions or by developing trait lists. The trait list approach embeds comparisons to "simple" hunter-gatherers, so "complex" hunter-gatherers typically have *more complex* technology, *greater* sedentism, *larger* settlements, *more* trade, etc. Mackie (2001) noted that a virtue of the trait list is that it can be operationalized using archaeological data. He also identified the problem of interdependent traits, and of determining "how many, and to what extent, traits from a given list must be present in the archaeological record before a valid inference of complexity can be made" (Mackie 2001:6). For example, Matson and Coupland (1995:199) wrote that cultural complexity (the "Developed Northwest Coast Pattern") was "fully achieved" 2,500 years ago when the Gulf of Georgia record indicates people lived in large houses, stored salmon, and had ascribed social status. Using intensification of salmon fishing, Carlson (1998) argued for cultural complexity about 6,000 years ago at Namu. In a systematic assessment of a range of criteria, Arcas Consulting Archaeologists (1999) found evidence for complexity between 5,500 and 3,300 years ago in the Gulf of Georgia. Sites of this time period "suggest the existence of technical complexity and a social organization more sophisticated than previous authorities have ventured, but the exact pattern manifest within the society and its similarity to the later Northwest Coast ethnographic pattern is not yet fully understood" (Arcas 1999:80). By emphasizing different criteria, investigators have painted different portraits. We do not expect "complexity" to occur everywhere on the Northwest Coast simultaneously, but if we begin with an abstract definition of complexity referring to the amount of internal differentiation in a society or the number of interconnected parts, one eventually falls back on the trait list so as to recognize archaeological correlates. These approaches involve circular reasoning, as "the traits determine the presence or absence of complexity, which is a social phenomenon they cumulatively hope to define" (Mackie 2001:6-7).

Mackie (2001) and others (e.g., Fitzhugh 2003) noted that "complexity" has frequently been used as a synonym for social inequality; "the invariant linking of inequality to complexity has the effect of naturalizing equality within 'simple' societies, a category created by the unreasonable dichotomization of hunter and gatherers into two groups: simple and complex" (Mackie 2001:8). In this way, egalitarianism is undervalued and given little analytical attention. Mackie (2001:10) observed that studying the *emergence* of complexity "is clearly tied to the notion of most hunters and gatherers as the zero point on the complexity scale."

The trajectory of increasing cultural complexity has become the default model for conceptualizing culture change on the Northwest Coast. Archaeologists routinely use Northwest Coast societies as models for the development of cultural complexity elsewhere, in part to argue that our work has relevance beyond the Northwest Coast. As Rowley-Conwy (2001) pointed out, progressivist views of complexity embed a number of problematic assumptions: (1) the overall trend is from simple to complex; (2) the earliest settlers were "simple" hunter-gatherers; (3) the "emergence" of complexity occurred gradually; (4) change towards complexity was irreversible; and (5) the most interesting hunter-gatherers were the "complex" ones. As Rowley-Conwy (2001:64) has shown, there is no directional trend among hunter-gatherers and "[n]umerous examples reveal complexity coming and going frequently as a result of adaptive necessities."

Judgments as to what is simple or complex depend on the criteria chosen. Analyses have become more sophisticated as investigators have considered continuous, rather than dichotomous, variables (Chapman 2003:44–45). By convention, most archaeologists have chosen material culture, wealth, and hierarchical social relations. Certain characteristics of Northwest Coast societies have been valorized—social inequality, slavery, warfare—perhaps because of our contemporary fascination with these topics. But slavery and warfare on the Northwest Coast were fundamentally different in scale and content than slavery and warfare known in Western history.

Randall McGuire (1996) explained "why complexity is too simple," maintaining there were no simple societies. Developmental change can occur, populations grow, the number of social roles and the interconnectedness of those roles increases. Technologies can become more elaborate and societies organize themselves differently. McGuire (1996:24–25) prefers a historical and dialectical approach to developmental change, where the "motor for change" resides in relational contradictions. Ambiguities, complexities, and humanness of process means that we cannot predict what might happen or reduce it to general models. Culture change does not inevitably lead to hierarchy. Some have suggested that we "discard the term 'complexity' altogether to rid the discipline of imprecise unilineal and typological views of sociocultural variability" (Kantner 2002:94).

The Muddle in the Middle—
Problems with "Middle-Range" Societies

Feinman and Neitzel (1984) and Upham (1987) developed the idea of "middle-range" societies to focus research on the diversity of social systems in sedentary, pre-state societies. According to Rousseau (2006:21),

> Middle range societies have more complex technology and larger group size than do foragers, without having the same levels of political and economic control as states. The balance of constraints and possibilities in this phase allows for great variability and experimentation.

32

...The notion of middle-range societies is evolutionary: the systems that preceded them create contingencies, and internal factors bring about new developments. In turn, states appear out of middle-range societies.

Rousseau believes it is important to analyze middle-range societies, but not treat them as "mere stepping-stones in an evolutionary path between hunter-gatherers and preindustrial states," because "they display many social features that disappear or take on a new significance with state formation" (Rousseau 2006:21). Yet the moniker "middle-range" inevitably places such societies on a linear continuum between end-points, and the "statistically likely sequence of social forms" is from simple to complex (Rousseau 2006:37). In this way, the term "middle-range" embeds a clear unidirectional, evolutionary logic.

In a discussion of plant cultivation and domestication, Smith (2005) referred to Northwest Coast societies as "in-between" and "middle ground" societies. He explained that like the prehistoric Calusa, Hopewell, and Jomon, the economies of the Northwest Coast do not "fall comfortably under the heading of complex hunter-gatherers, but rather to also belong out in the middle, between hunting and gathering and agriculture...." (Smith 2005:38). By calling them "in-between" societies—neither hunter-gatherers nor agriculturalists—they link these two types in a linear evolutionary trajectory. Smith (2005:54) recognized this definitional problem:

> These diverse, vibrant, and successful human societies developed long-term solutions for deriving sustenance from a wide range of environments that combined low-level reliance on domesticates with continued use and management of wild species. So Northwest Coast societies like those of the middle ground in general, should not be viewed simply as reference points on the way to agriculture, as roadside markers of progress, but rather as stable and progressive solutions, as end points and destinations worthy of study in and of themselves.

Categorizing Northwest Coast societies as "middle range," or their food production as "low level," obscures the underlying assumptions that they exist somewhere between simple and more complex on a unilinear evolutionary path. Pluciennik (2004:17) noted "increasing recognition of the variability and historicity" of hunter-gatherer societies, but in my view, the hunter-gatherer moniker has outlived its utility on the Northwest Coast. The genius of Northwest Coast cultural achievements is not duplicated anywhere else and these accomplishments have grown out of deep attachment to and knowledge of the sea, landscapes, plants, and animals of the region.

Fishers and Food Producers

Ethnographically documented Northwest Coast societies were clearly food producers, and fishing and food storage technologies were central to life on the coast. Northwest Coast societies invested in infrastructure and altered some aspects of their physical environments to promote food production. They managed harvests through systems of territorial ownership and control. They restrained uncontrolled resource use through systems of social relations. Tribes, clans, and households were caretakers of particular watersheds, berry patches, fish streams, and stretches of ocean shoreline. They managed harvests as trustees who had established long-term relationships not only with resource territories, but with the plant and animal persons with whom they shared the world. As Atleo (2005:ix) explained, proper relationships had to be maintained between all life-forms.

> Since the salmon and human have common origins they are brothers and sisters of creation. Since the assumption of all relationships between all life-forms is a common ancestry, protocols become necessary in the exercise of resource management. If the salmon are not properly respected and recognized they cannot properly respect and recognize their human counterparts of creation. This historical process is neither evolutionary nor developmental in the linear sense. Changes are not from simple to complex, as a more modern world-view would have it, but from complex to complex, from equal to equal, from one life-form to another.

This ideology helps explain the ecological prudence of Northwest Coast societies and the restraint with which they managed resources. Traditional ecological knowledge also involved understanding relationships between species. Although my focus is on Northwest Coast archaeology, the worldview and philosophy described by Atleo provide a foundation for principles of resource management.

Fishing, Fisheries Management, and Fish Processing

Most Northwest Coast archaeological sites contain some evidence of fishing—particularly abundant are fish remains. Whereas salmon are the most widely known, Pacific cod and other codfishes, rockfish, lingcod, greenlings, herring, flatfish, surfperch, and sculpins are common. Fish typically account for 80–85 percent of the number of bones in the region's faunal assemblages (Moss and Cannon 2011). Isotopic studies of the bones of Shuká Kaa show that this man living in Alaska over 11,000 years ago had a diet rich in seafood that probably included fish. At The Dalles on the Columbia River, vast numbers of salmon were caught by site residents at 9300 cal B.P. (Butler and O'Connor 2004). From Namu, located on the central B.C. coast, Cannon and Yang (2006) studied the ancient DNA of salmon bones and found long-term reliance on pink salmon going back 7,000 years (Figure 3.1).

Since the mid-1980s, the remains of intertidal fishing weirs and traps have been found in water-saturated intertidal sites, where organic artifacts and features preserve. Over 1,200 wood stake and stone weirs and traps have been found in Alaska, B.C., Washington, and Oregon (Moss and Erlandson 1998a; Moss 2011). Fewer than 200 sites have been dated, but they range in age from ca. 6000 cal B.P. to the twentieth century. These numbers provide evidence of the scale of mass capture of fish on the Northwest Coast. At Little Salt Lake Weir, near Klawock, Alaska, Langdon (2006, 2007) mapped extensive features with an estimated 100,000 stakes found over a 75 hectare area, dating to the last 2,000 years. Based partly on salmon escapements, Langdon et al. (1995) estimated that between 75,000 and 80,000 fish could be caught in this weir annually.

Stevenson (1998) described three distinctive fishing technologies used along the lower Fraser River. Based on local geomorphological change and faunal data from the adjacent site, Stevenson argued that the Glenrose wet site was a tidal trap for salmon, sturgeon, flounder, and eulachon ca. 5400–4500 cal B.P. At Musqueum Northeast, 3,000-year old wood stakes were found to which nets were anchored. Based on the gauge of recovered cedar bark netting, Stevenson described these as gill nets used to catch salmon and starry flounder. At the Water Hazard site, the remains of 2,000-year old salmon trawl nets were found.

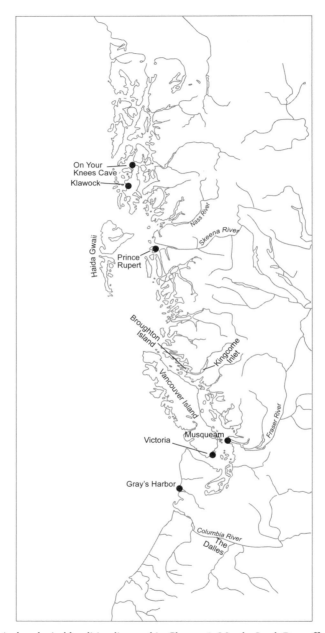

Figure 3.1. Archaeological localities discussed in Chapter 3. Map by Jacob Bartruff.

Figure 3.2. Intertidal fishing weir/trap on the Coquille River, Oregon. Photo by Madonna Moss.

Byram (1998, 2002) documented over 70 wood stake weirs and traps on the Oregon coast, several more than 3,000 years old. Most are in estuarine locations, where a variety of fish are available year-round (Figure 3.2). Byram believes such weirs and traps operated throughout the year, taking whichever species were available. His studies are an important caution against seeing weir and trap fishing as exclusively targeting salmon. On the southwest Washington coast, Schalk and Burtchard (2001) found a palimpsest of nineteenth-century commercial fish traps along with aboriginal traps dating as early as 1000 RYBP in Grays Harbor. Like most of the traps and weirs described above, these structures took advantage of currents and tides to strand fish.

Weir and trap fishing and the use of gill and reef nets required teamwork. Group fishing could result in large numbers of fish—processing quantities of fish for long-term storage also required well-organized labor. Some fish, including halibut, rockfish, and greenling, were caught by individuals with hook and line or gorges, but the capture of schooling salmon, herring, eulachon, and smelt were group activities. We know that Northwest Coast women fished (Barnett 1955:89; Boas 1921:181–182; Elmendorf and Kroeber 1992:63; de Laguna 1972:386; Olson 1936:29; 32; Singh 1966:58–59; Smith 1940:254; 257, 268; Suttles 1974:114, 188), even in societies that had an ethic precluding women from fishing. Children were also involved in fishing (Byram 2002:169; Smith 1940:268). Who actually catches fish is only a part of the process; women often gathered and processed the plant materials used to make the portable portions of fishing technologies, such as basketry traps, fish-baskets, latticework, netting, and nets (Byram 2002:167; Emmons 1991; Gunther 1973:28; Olson 1936:28; Paul 1944). In some groups, women helped build weirs (Hewes 1940), while in others, men made some or most fishing gear (e.g., Barnett 1937:164; Boas 1921:162; Drucker 1937:232, 1951:16). The rigid division of labor used to characterize Northwest Coast fishing breaks down under a close review of ethnographic sources.

Fish butchery is usually attributed to women, but the drying, smoking, and storage process likely involved mixed groups. Fish were processed in different ways depending on species and size. Weather also affected fish curing—sunny or windy conditions might allow initial drying outdoors, whereas rain required drying in the house or smokehouse. The number of sunny days and the amount of rainfall varies on the coast (Suttles 1968:63); Victoria, located in the rainshadow of the Olympic Mountains, enjoys over 2,000 hours of sunshine per year, while Prince Rupert gets half as much. Not all species of fish preserve equally well; Suttles (1968:63) wrote that his Salish informants said fatter fish (e.g., sockeye salmon) lasted longer than lean species, but elsewhere, Suttles (1990:25) stated that sockeye were the hardest fish to keep. Strategies of fish butchery, cooking, processing, and disposal are of great interest, and while some ethnographies provide important detail (e.g., Boas 1921), many do not. Capturing large numbers of fish is pointless without the technological knowledge and skilled organized labor to process them for storage.

Although many fish species contributed to the economic foundation of Northwest Coast societies, salmon were especially important. In their review of 63 Northwest faunal assemblages, Butler and Campbell (2004) found no evidence for the intensification of salmon relative to other fish over time, nor did they find evidence of resource depression. Ethnographically, salmon streams and spawning areas were owned by particular social groups: matri-lineages in the north, bilateral kin groups on the central coast, and families or households in the south. The antiquity of salmon resource ownership is difficult to document archaeologically, but may go back 7,000 years at Namu (Cannon and Yang 2006). While many archaeologists invoke salmon use as a driver of cultural evolution, Johnsen (2004:4-5) took a different tack:

> Given that Pacific salmon return to their natal streams to spawn and were beyond the tribes' ability to intercept prior to that time, tribal ownership of streams effectively included secure ownership of native salmon stocks, including the real option to take advantage of new growth opportunities. This gave the tribes the incentive to accumulate the stream-specific knowledge to husband these stocks. Rather than being the fortunate beneficiaries of a naturally rich environment, the compelling conclusion is that the NWC [Northwest Coast] tribes *created* the observed superabundance of salmon through centuries of pur-poseful husbandry and active management of other resources. In my view, they were not hunter-gatherers content to meet material subsis-tence needs, they were institutionally sophisticated salmon ranchers who actively sought and proudly achieved prosperity.

Although the argument for salmon ranching may seem radical, the idea that Northwest Coast groups enhanced conditions for salmon production war-rants more study. Deliberate stewardship of salmon and other resources would seem the best explanation for Butler and Campbell's (2004) findings.

Plant Cultivation

Douglas Deur and Nancy Turner's (2005) *Keeping it Living: Traditions of Plant Use and Cultivation on the Northwest Coast of North America* also chal-lenges the hunter-gatherer stereotype, by presenting a wide range of evidence supporting plant cultivation and landscape management on the Northwest Coast. The authors note that the orthodoxy of the non-agricultural Northwest Coast "became a part of most North American anthropologists' undergraduate training, a prominent observation within many introductory textbooks, and a cornerstone of later theoretical developments within the fields of anthropology, archaeology, geography, and ethnobotany" (Deur and Turner 2005:3). In retrospect, it seems remarkable that anthropologists ignored ethnographic and ethnohistorical evidence of plant cultivation and management for so long. Deur and Turner explained such ignorance as tied to European ideas of what agriculture "should" look like, and that the apparent absence of cultivation was one of several justifications used for the colonialist takeover of Native lands.

In the eighteenth century, Europeans reported cultivated plots of tobacco in some Haida and Tlingit villages. The tobacco was chewed with lime (from burnt shells) and planted from seed capsules. Tobacco plots were weeded and fertilized. A single herbarium specimen of "Haida tobacco" (*Nicotiana quadrivalvis* Pursh.) is known, a variety now extinct (Deur and Turner 2005:16). It appears to have been introduced from the dry B.C. interior or from further south. Turner and Taylor (1972) estimated its introduction to the coast 1,000 to 500 years ago, based on the role tobacco plays in Haida and Tlingit cosmology. The existence of this plant outside its natural range and its distinctive use suggest the pre-contact antiquity of tobacco cultivation. A related tobacco, *N. quadrivalvis* var. *bigelovii*, was grown in cultivated plots in southern Oregon (Deur and Turner 2005:17).

Other plants grown in owned, cultivated plots included Pacific silverweed, springbank clover, rice-root, and camas (Deur and Turner 2005:22). These were propagated by vegetative cuttings rather than by planting seeds, hence their tendency to have been overlooked. The best documented estuarine root gardens for silverweed and clover roots are from Kwakwaka'wakw, Nuxalk, and Nuu-chah-nulth territories. Silverweed and clover grow between the high marsh and the transitional salt-tolerant meadows at the heads of estuaries. People enhanced the productivity of these plants by removing rocks and boulders, churning, mounding, and supplementing soils, and using logs and rockworks to level the surface and enlarge the most productive zone within the estuary. Corporate groups owned large gardens—as many as 10 acres were under cultivation along Kingcombe Inlet—which were subdivided into family-owned plots; some were owned by individual women (Deur 2005:306; Turner et al. 2005:164). Plot boundaries were marked by corner posts, horizontal logs, or rock enclosures. The plots were weeded, plants were transplanted, and the starchy roots and rhizomes were dug in the fall. Roots were steamed or roasted and dried for winter or ceremonial use. The plants attracted geese and ducks, and people employed the "prey as bait" principle (Monks 1987) by setting up birding nets dropped from vertical poles (Deur 2005:307). Engineering of the tidal flats (Deur 2005) and purposeful landscape modification enhanced root production. Since these plants were important trade goods and feast foods, and because constructed gardens are grammatically distinguished from naturally occurring root patches, Deur believes estuarine root gardening has some antiquity. Using an experimental oxidizable carbon ratio (OCR) dating technique, he dated soils adjacent to rock walls in a garden in Nuu-chah-nulth territory to A.D. 1480–1575 (Deur 2000:236–250, 2005:319). Deur (2005:320) observed that the estuarine root-cultivation practices of the Northwest Coast are "remarkably similar to the 'wetland cultivation' methods" used by indigenous peoples in Oceania and the American tropics.

Camas is an edible lily of low elevation meadows amidst the drier Douglas fir forests of southern B.C., Washington and Oregon, but camas also grows in some tidal marshes (Turner and Peacock 2005:144). Some camas meadows were "burned over, weeded, cleared, selectively harvested, and sometime intentionally seeded" (Turner and Peacock 2005:140). The Coast Salish owned camas beds passed on to their descendents. Bulbs were harvested in the spring, steamed in large pits, and formed into brick-shaped cakes traded widely for winter use. Vancouver Island Salish traded camas to the Nuu-chah-nulth, Kwakwa̲ka'wakw, Ditidaht, Comox, and Halq'emeylem (Turner et al. 2005:175). Charred camas bulbs from interior Northwest archaeological sites date to 8900 cal B.P. (8000 RYBP; Cheatham 1988). Morphological domesticates have not been identified (Kramer 2000).

The Chinook of the Lower Columbia intensified production of wapato by placing villages near wapato fields, owning the fields, developing a specialized canoe that women used to harvest wapato in wetlands, and controlling the swans, ducks, muskrats, and beavers that ate wapato (Darby 2005). The Chinook produced large quantities of wapato for trade, bringing them great wealth (Darby 2005:208).

As many as 50 species of edible berries were used, including strawberries, salal berries, currants, blueberries, huckleberries, cranberries, soapberries, thimbleberries, and salmonberries. The Tsimshian, Haida, Haisla, Nuxalk, Kwakwaka'wakw, and Nuu-chah-nulth used fire to produce clearings to promote berry growth (Turner and Peacock 2005:127). Sometimes berry bushes were burned or pruned to control growth, enhance production, and ease collection. Some berry patches were fertilized with the remains of fish carcasses, hearth ash, and crushed clamshells, and cranberries were occasionally transplanted (Turner and Peacock 2005:106, 118). Some berry grounds were owned by chiefs, others by clans, families, or individual women (Turner and Peacock 2005:130–131, 165). The owner's responsibility involved harvesting, monitoring use, and granting permission to others to pick berries. Berries were eaten fresh but also processed in large quantities for storage: dried into cakes, covered in seal oil, or packed with eulachon grease.

The remains of elderberries are abundant in archaeological sites that have undergone paleobotanical analyses, including British Camp, Ozette, Hoko River, and Cape Addington Rockshelter. Losey et al. (2003) found more than 68,000 elderberry seeds at the Netarts Sandspit Village in Oregon. Because its seeds are somewhat toxic, elderberries were cooked and the seeds removed during processing. Unburned seeds preserve well in Late Holocene archaeological sites. Elderberries were processed in large quantities and were an important winter food.

For years, anthropologists have assumed that the cultivation of potatoes was introduced to Northwest Coast societies by outsiders in the eighteenth or nineteenth centuries (McDonald 2005; Suttles 1951). I argued that the pre-contact tobacco horticulture facilitated cultivation of potatoes after they were introduced (Moss 2005). Kunibe's (2007) genetic study of potatoes still grown by Tlingit gardeners links these potatoes to those grown by the Makah. Kunibe claims that these varieties originated in South America and do not have any of the genetic markers of European potatoes. Although this work remains unpublished, new research on the Northwest Coast is continually disrupting what we think we know. Conceivably, aboriginal trade of the potato within the Americas could have been more extensive than previously thought.

Although the Northwest Coast ethnographic record of plants and plant cultivation is robust, the archaeological evidence of pre-contact intensification and plant food production is limited. Despite systematic effort, Lepofsky et al. (2005) found no clear evidence of prescribed burning in soil charcoal or lake sediment records of the Fraser Valley. In Oregon's Willamette

Valley, the extent and antiquity of prescribed burning is contested (Boyd 1999; Knox 2000; Whitlock and Knox 2002). Archaeobotanical research on the Northwest Coast has significant, but still unrealized potential (Lepofsky et al. 2001). This may be due to misconceptions—that plant foods were unimportant on the coast, that they don't preserve well in archaeological sites, or cannot be distinguished from plant remains deposited naturally. Charred plant remains preserve as well in Northwest Coast sites as they do elsewhere. More paleobotanical study is clearly warranted in light of the importance of plants to Northwest Coast societies (Lepofsky 2004). The ethnographic evidence suggests people deliberately developed ways to increase the abundance and productivity of economically important plants.

Mariculture and Clam Gardens

Shellfish were (and are) important food resources across the Northwest Coast. The majority of the region's archaeological sites are shell-bearing sites, containing the remains of clams, cockles, mussels, sea urchins, chitons, and barnacles. Shellfish remains are known from some of the oldest sites, including Early Holocene components from Chuck Lake, Glenrose Cannery, and Kilgii Gwaay. Shellfish habitats range from protected estuaries that support quiet-water species to the wave-battered shores of the outer coast.

Shellfish are most available during the lowest tides of the month during the new moon and full moon phases. These "spring" tides occur about every two weeks, with about 4–5 low tides per cycle. During the 2–3 hour period around such tides, clam-digging and collecting gastropods and echinoderms can be very productive. Shellfish in the upper intertidal zone (e.g., some mussels and barnacles) can be collected more regularly, but the best time for clams, cockles, chitons, and sea urchins is when the tide is below mean lower low water.

Understanding the limited time clams are available per month helps explain why clam gardens are such a remarkable innovation. In the 1990s, geomorphologist John Harper began identifying remarkable rock walls in the intertidal zone during his aerial surveys of coastal British Columbia (Figure 3.3). In the Broughton Archipelago, Harper mapped 365 features he later called "clam terraces" or "clam gardens" (Harper et al. 2002). These were found along low energy beaches, near the 0-tide level. They are gravel and boulder ridges that run across small embayments along the mostly rocky shoreline. Alongside pocket beaches, these ridges create a sandflat extending

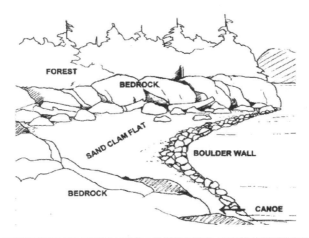

Figure 3.3. Clam garden in the Broughton Archipelago, B.C. Photo and drawing by John Harper, Coastal and Ocean Resources, Inc.

from the rock wall to the middle intertidal zone. These rock structures enlarge the intertidal area favored by two favorite clams: *Saxidomus* (butter clams) and *Protothaca* (littleneck clams). Clam gardens also make clam-digging easier. They qualify as mariculture, the cultivation, management, and harvesting of marine organisms in their natural habitat or in specially constructed rearing enclosures.

Clam gardens are known as "luxwxiwey" in the local Kwakwala language, or "place of rolling rocks together" (Harper et al. 2005). Elder Adam Dick

remembers clam gardens from his youth. Clam gardens also figure in Kwak-
wa̱ka'wakw stories, songs, and ceremonies. Clam gardens cannot be directly
dated, but more than 175 shell middens occur in the area, some ca. 2,000
years old (Harper et al. 2002). The Broughton clam gardens are found along
discrete pocket beaches, places well-suited for creating, managing, and controlling such features via ownership by specific social groups.

Like the estuarine root gardens and fishing weirs and traps, clam gardens
represent substantial investments in infrastructure that enhanced resource
productivity. They are part of the "built environment" of the Northwest
Coast. Clams were consumed fresh, but quantities were also dried, smoked,
and stored for future use—as feast foods, winter supplies, travel provisions,
and for trade. The clam mariculturalists of the Broughton Archipelago were
especially industrious, but clam gardens have also been found in Coast Salish, Nuu-chah-nulth, Haida, and Tlingit territories.

Dog Husbandry

Although not as geographically widespread as fishing structures and clam
gardens, some Coast Salish groups and the Makah of southern B.C. and
western Washington maintained two types of domestic dogs, one of which
was bred for wool. Crockford (1997) identified two dog types osteologically
from archaeological samples: a "village dog" and a smaller wool dog. Historically, wool dogs were kept on small islands to maintain reproductive isola-
tion. Their long hair was spun and woven into blankets. Deliberate breeding
apparently occurred at a finite number of locations, but has an antiquity of
at least 1400 RYBP (Crockford 1997, 2009).

Conclusion

I am not arguing that we should "search for the origins" (Conkey and
Williams 1991) of fishers and food producers, or try to identify archaeological signatures of hunter-gatherers vs. food producers on the Northwest
Coast. Such approaches would follow the same track without challenging
the normative evolutionary trajectory. The term "complex hunter-gatherer"
does not adequately characterize ethnographic societies of the Northwest
Coast. Conceiving of them as fishers and food producers recognizes their
reliance on fish and other resources that varied from place to place and time
to time. They were resource stewards, with vested interests in maintaining

the resilience of the ecosystems of which they were a part. This long-term stewardship allowed them to accumulate material wealth, so their economies achieved more than basic "subsistence." Some Northwest Coast groups were salmon ranchers, some were horticulturalists and mariculturalists, and at least some were dog breeders. Using these terms helps us better appreciate their achievements and ingenuity. Some of these practices have ancient roots, but clearly cultures changed over time.

Although no single theory of culture change can account for the variability we see in the Northwest Coast archaeological record, the coast's local and regional landscapes embed a complex mosaic of human history. Over time and in different ways, Northwest Coast groups transformed environments and their relationships with a range of species to enhance the biological productivity of key resources. In the spirit of Balée and Erickson's (2006:4) brand of historical ecology, I suggest that Northwest Coast environments "are in a sense adapted to the sociocultural and political systems that have coexisted with them" for long periods of time. We shall see that the reciprocal dynamic between people and their environments will play out differently in different localities.

4

First Peoples: Integrating Culture History and Paleoenvironmental History

Culture history is still fundamental to understanding Northwest Coast archaeology. Most archaeologists think of time as a continuum, and time and space are the primary dimensions of culture history. By convention, culture history compartmentalizes space and time into discrete units. This necessarily breaks up the continuity of time and carves up the archaeological landscape into analytical units that serve our research questions and interests. But these constructs have limitations, and one is that they are continually under debate. Another is that archaeological concepts of time are projected onto the past of peoples who may or may not conceive of history in the same way, so archaeology itself can be experienced as a colonizing practice.

On the Northwest Coast, culture history has operated on multiple scales. Cultural historical units have been defined for localities that vary in size and specificity. From north to south these "localities" have been: southeast Alaska, Prince Rupert Harbor, Haida Gwaii, central B.C. coast, "West Coast" of Vancouver Island, Gulf of Georgia, Puget Sound, Olympic Penin-sula, and Oregon coast (Figure 4.1). Not everyone would agree with these divisions, but culture historical units have also been defined at the regional scale. Fladmark (1982) was the first to successfully accomplish this, and all of us working in the region owe him a substantial debt for distilling regional patterns that retain utility 30 years later. He defined an early "Lithic Stage" and a later "Developmental Stage." The Lithic Stage was marked by stone tools and little else, and viewed as distinct from ethnographically docu-mented peoples. The "Developmental Stage" refers to the development of the "Northwest Coast Cultural Pattern," made manifest by shell middens where dependence on stored salmon and extensive woodworking and art were inferred. The Developmental Stage was recognized as ancestral to the

47

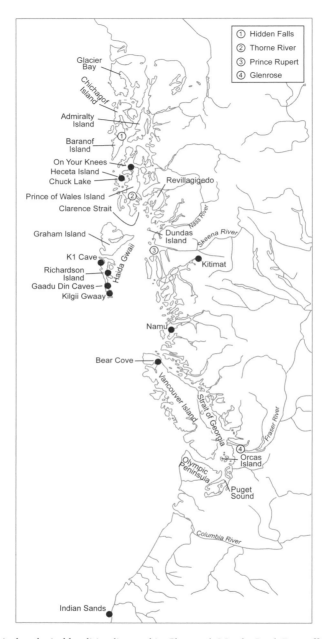

Figure 4.1. Archaeological localities discussed in Chapter 4. Map by Jacob Bartruff.

indigenous residents of the Northwest Coast, although without specific linkages to individual groups.

In their landmark *Prehistory of the Northwest Coast* (1995), Matson and Coupland tied Fladmark's trajectory to that of increasing cultural complexity. Although Matson and Coupland did not rely upon the Lithic Stage concept, their "Developed Northwest Coast Pattern" is similar to Fladmark's "Developmental Stage." Their chronologically ordered chapters trace initial colonization and then the "Emergence of Distinctive Coastal Cultures," the "Development of Cultural Complexity," the "Achievement of Cultural Complexity," and "Continuation of the Developed Northwest Coast Pattern." This unifying framework allowed the authors to bring order to the proliferating local culture historical units defined in different geographic areas of the Northwest Coast. Matson and Coupland successfully did this without requiring that these stages occurred synchronously everywhere on the coast. In 1999, Ames and Maschner termed Fladmark's "Lithic Stage" the Archaic Period. This was followed by the "Pacific Period," borrowing a framework Chartkoff and Chartkoff (1984) used for demarcating California prehistory. Few California archaeologists use the Chartkoffs' Early-Middle-Late Pacific sequence; instead, they refer to early, middle, and late Holocene. Ames's and Maschner's Early, Middle, and Late Pacific periods are consistent with units used by Fladmark (1982) and Matson and Coupland (1995), even though the onset dates of each period vary. The Lithic/Archaic and the Developmental/Pacific stages or periods are seen as distinctively different. The transition between these stages is thought to have occurred ca. 5000 RYBP (5700 cal B.P.), when sea levels were thought to have stabilized. Whether this marks a genuine turning point in the history of the Northwest Coast is addressed in Chapter 5.

Both discrete and continuous concepts of space and time are embedded in culture history, but our modes of presenting such information in culture historical units tend to be static, with arbitrary divisions. Certainly some environmental changes occur gradually over time (e.g., forest succession), while others occur at variable rates (e.g., seacliff erosion), yet others, such as earthquakes, are discrete events. Cultural changes undoubtedly also occur at different rates (e.g., variable birth rates led to differences in human population size), and sometimes abruptly (introduction of a new technology). Change in one part of the cultural system affects many others, and the boundaries of "systems" are permeable and in flux.

In this book, I use calibrated radiocarbon dates wherever possible and the geological time scale to encompass gross periods of time. The geologic time scale is helpful because it is widely used across North America and promotes comparability across regions. Along with calibrated radiocarbon dates, this provides more neutral temporal units that do not carry any cultural implications. I will not shy away from referring to the multitude of stages, traditions, complexes, periods, and phases employed in local sequences, but I hope to provide enough context that readers unfamiliar with the local units are not left in the dark.

The boundaries between geological time periods for the Holocene are arbitrary, but I try not to over-rely on these categories when cultural units span more than one period. The periods are:

Terminal Pleistocene	15,000–11,000 cal B.P.
Early Holocene	11,000–7,000 cal B.P.
Middle Holocene	7,000–3,500 cal B.P.
Late Holocene (pre-contact)	3,500–200 cal B.P.
Late Holocene (post-contact)	200 cal B.P. to present

Over the last 15 years, a tremendous amount of new archaeological data has been generated on the Northwest Coast. Understanding how space and time are intertwined in the archaeological record is a complex task. We will see ongoing tension between cultural continuity and change. For Terminal Pleistocene and Early Holocene periods, I focus on how the cultural record is a product of and embedded in the history of paleoenvironments. The Middle Holocene may be the most poorly known period, yet one previously thought to encompass a milestone in the region's prehistory. Late Holocene archaeological phenomena are the subject of most debates about cultural complexity, but for reasons explained in Chapter 3, I will emphasize other perspectives.

Earliest Settlement of the Americas

The Northwest Coast is a key region for understanding the first human settlement of the Americas. Since the earliest migrants came from Asia and because the Northwest Coast is strategically positioned along the Pacific Rim, it could be one of the earliest places these people moved through in settling North America. This is especially likely if early colonists used boats in coastal migrations to the Americas. Erlandson et al. (2007) argued that kelp forest ecosystems around the north Pacific, stretching from Japan to Baja California, facilitated coastal migrations. With sea levels rising more than 125 m since the end of the Last Glacial Maximum (LGM) at 21,500 cal B.P. (18,000 RYBP),[1] it's unlikely that the earliest coastal sites are preserved on what is now the Northwest Coast. Many sites may be drowned or destroyed. The oldest sites in the Americas are not found on the Northwest Coast, so we must look at surrounding areas to better understand how the coast may have figured into scenarios of early settlement. Recent research in western North America is shedding light on the complex process of colonization. Most archaeologists suspect that multiple populations migrated at different times following different routes. In this chapter I integrate new knowledge about the region's environmental history with the culture historical record of the Northwest Coast and surrounding regions.

Most archaeologists agree that people could not have traveled to the Americas from Asia during the LGM because of impenetrable ice, so the earliest migrants came either before or after. At the Yana RHS (rhinoceros horn site) in northeast Siberia, people in the high arctic were adapted to Beringian conditions similar to those they would find in what is now Alaska. At Yana, stone, horn, and ivory artifacts along with the remains of extinct fauna were found in a frozen cultural deposit dated to 32,000 cal B.P. (Goebel et al. 2008:1498; Pitulko et al. 2004; 27,000 RYBP). Yana residents used an unfluted bifacial technology lacking the prismatic blades diagnostic of Clovis. Beck and Jones (2010:102) suggested that the technology at Yana might be a precursor to the Western Stemmed projectile point tradition of the Interior West, to be described below. Although Yana RHS demonstrates that people were adapted to high arctic conditions prior to the LGM and were in a geographic position to stage movements toward Beringia, we have no occupational evidence from Beringia itself for this time period. Sea-level changes as well as the harsh and dynamic environment may have destroyed such evidence. The earliest dates from Meadowcroft Rockshelter in Pennsylvania (22,000 cal B.P.) and Monte Verde in Chile (33,000 cal B.P.), while provocative, are not widely accepted, whereas the post LGM dates are (13,400 cal B.P. from Meadowcroft, 14,000 cal B.P. from Monte Verde).

Archaeologists assumed that Clovis, now dated to 13,200–12,800 cal B.P. (Waters and Stafford 2007), represented the earliest settlers of the Americas. The most well-known diagnostic is the lanceolate fluted projectile point

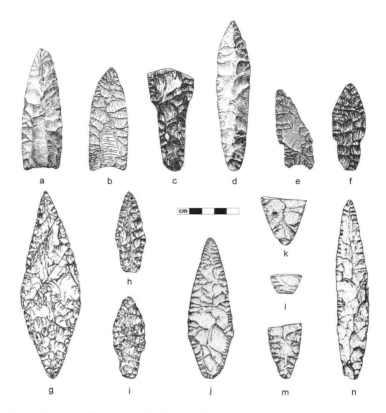

Figure 4.2. Early projectile points: a-b, Clovis; c-f, Western Stemmed (Cougar Mountain, Haskett, Windust, Parman); g-i, bifaces from On Your Knees Cave; j, m, n, bifaces from Gaadu Din 2 Cave; k-l, bifaces from K1 Cave. Illustration by Dustin Kennedy, adapted from Beck and Jones (2010), Dixon (2008:14), and Fedje et al. (2008:22).

made by removing broad thinning flakes from the faces of a large bifacial blank and then removing the "flutes" (channel flakes) from the center of the base (Figure 4.2). Other tools typical of Clovis assemblages are blades made from conical and wedge-shaped cores, end scrapers, cylindrical rods of ivory, antler, or bone (with beveled end(s) and used as fore-shafts or projectile points; Goebel et al. 2008:1499).

Clovis is the earliest continent-wide tradition in North America, but does it represent a migration of people or diffusion of technology? Could it represent both— does it indicate a migration of people into some regions but a diffusion of a weapon system elsewhere? Since Clovis has not been identified in Asia, it seems to have developed in North America: but where? By carefully reviewing the ages of Clovis assemblages, Beck and Jones (2010) found the oldest Clovis manifestations in Texas, Kentucky, and Tennessee, and more recent Clovis expressions to the northeast, west, and northwest. They contend that Clovis may represent the earliest settlement of some areas of North America, but that it was a later intrusion in the Great Basin, Plateau, and presumably the Northwest Coast, places where people unaffiliated with Clovis had already settled.

One such locality is Paisley Caves in central Oregon (Gilbert et al. 2008). Located about 200 miles from the coast, the Paisley Caves contain some of the oldest reliably dated evidence of the early residents of North America. At the time of their oldest occupation, the caves were positioned within a mile of the shoreline of pluvial Lake Chewaucan, which probably teemed with fish and wildlife. Fourteen human coprolites (desiccated feces) preserved in the dry, Pleistocene cultural deposit range in age from 14,340 to 12,000 cal B.P. in Cave 5. Some perishable artifacts, including cordage of grass and sinew, and a few undiagnostic stone tools have been found. The base of a stemmed projectile point associated with a date of 14,000 cal B.P. represents the Western Stemmed tradition. The evidence from Paisley Caves shows that people were in the Intermountain West 500–1200 years before Clovis.

At Paisley Caves, the remains of extinct camel, bison, horse, and goat have been found in association, but it is unclear if these bones are the result of human action or scavenging animals. Many animal bones within the caves are likely the results of wood rat (*Neotoma lepida*) activity. Wood rats accumulate large amounts of debris (branches, twigs, their own pellets, scat of other animals, coprolites, bones) into middens that become encased in their amber-colored crystallized urine ("amberat"). Over time, these remains were incorporated into the Paisley archaeological deposits along with rock-fall and windborne sediments. Although some human coprolites in the cave may be in their original position, others were probably moved by wood rats. Even so, the well-dated horizontal stratigraphy in Paisley Cave 5 shows that wood rats have not caused vertical mixing of the deposits. Bryan Hockett (2009, pers. comm.) is examining more than 400,000 animal bones for cut marks to identify which bones can be securely attributed to human activity.

The people who left the coprolites in Paisley Caves were members of Haplogroups A2 and B2. These are distinct from Haplogroup D, as represented by Shuká Kaa from On Your Knees Cave (Chapter 1). Haplogroup A is well-represented in groups that are often lumped as NaDene (Tlingit-

Eyak-Athapaskan). Members of Haplogroup B, like Haplogroup D, are founding East Asian lineages well-represented in Native Americans. Since the Paisley Caves were occupied before a viable ice-free corridor opened in the interior of North America, the site's age supports human migration along the coast ca. 15,000 cal B.P. This site in Oregon's high desert, located 200 miles from the Pacific Ocean, indirectly supports the coastal migration theory. This is consistent with geomorphological evidence that the Pacific coast was passable as many as 1,000–1,500 years before a route in the interior. From the Pacific Northwest, people could have continued to migrate south along the coast to South America and east along the receding margins of the Cordilleran and Laurentide ice sheets.

Thousands of Western Stemmed points (Figure 4.2) occur across the intermontane region, and Beck and Jones (2010:99) noted that these are invariably made on flakes of dacite, andesite, and other volcanic rocks, whereas Clovis points are typically chert. Another distinctive characteristic of the Western Stemmed tradition is the occurrence of crescents. The Western Stemmed tradition was thought to have evolved out of Clovis (e.g., Carlson and Magne 2008:356), but Western Stemmed may be earlier and contemporary with Clovis. Beck and Jones believe that the Western Stemmed tradition may be linked to an early coastal migration along the North Pacific.

Some of the earliest direct evidence of maritime peoples along the North Pacific coast comes from the northern Channel Islands of California, now positioned ~20–45 km from the mainland (Erlandson et al. 2008). These sites include Arlington Springs on Santa Rosa Island and Daisy Cave and Cardwell Bluffs on San Miguel Island. Using boats, people colonized these islands during the terminal Pleistocene at least 13–12,000 cal B.P. The bones of "Arlington Man" along with associated charcoal have been dated to 13–12,000 cal B.P. (Erlandson et al. 2008:2238). Daisy Cave was occupied about 11,500 cal B.P., as evidenced by a few chipped stone artifacts associated with a small assemblage of rocky shore shellfish remains (Erlandson et al. 1996). At Cardwell Bluffs, a large lithic scatter and shell midden complex dated to 12–11,500 cal B.P. are associated with two chert sources. Surface sites in the vicinity of the sources have produced chipped stone crescents and thin, delicate, stemmed Channel Island Barbed points, which look decidedly different from Clovis points. The presence of distinctive crescents and stemmed points in both southern California and the Western Stemmed tradition of the Intermountain West suggest a relationship between traditions or shared technology. Crescents may have been hafted onto darts with the convex edge serving as a blunt weapon to stun, but not penetrate birds, so as to avoid spoiling their skins and meat.

Bifacial traditions date back into the Upper Paleolithic of Eurasia more than 40,000 years ago. Distinct from the North American bifacial traditions discussed above—Clovis, Western Stemmed, and Channel Islands Barbed—are microblade traditions. The oldest microblades in the world are found in the Transbaikal region of Siberia, dated to ca. 21,500 cal B.P. (18,000 RYBP; Goebel et al. 2000). Microblades occur across east Asia; in Japan they date to ca. 25,000 cal B.P. and in Korea and China to ca. 29,000 cal B.P. (Ikawa-Smith 2007:190). In Siberia, some sites contain bifacial components stratigraphically below microblade components, demonstrating the temporal priority of the former. Along the shore of Ushki Lake in Kamchatka, small bifacial points, bifacial knives, and unifacial tools made on flakes and blades underlie a component with microblade and burin industries (Goebel et al. 2003). This is similar to interior Alaska, where bifacial industries known as Nenana (containing the tear-drop shaped Chindadn point) dated to 14,000–12,800 cal B.P. underlie microblade-bearing Denali[2] components dated to 12,500 cal B.P. (Goebel et al. 2003). The 13,800 cal B.P. age of the Swan Point microblade and burin industry and its co-occurrence with Chindadn points (Potter 2008) suggests that temporally and technologically, Nenana and Denali may not be as distinct as previously thought.

Does the emergence of microblade industries represent a radical change in technology, an adaptation to cooling climate during the Younger Dryas, or a specific migration of people from western Beringia into Alaska? The Younger Dryas (12,700–11,650 cal B.P.) was a Northern Hemisphere-wide "cold snap" that lasted more than 1,000 years.[3] In Beringia, it became colder and drier and the land bridge was flooded (Hoffecker and Elias 2007). Rapid flooding shifted settlement along the Bering Sea. Some authors suggest that microblade-using peoples came after the first migrants to the Americas and that these later groups were ancestral to the NaDene of the Northwest Coast (Carlson 1983:20, 1996a:217; Magne and Fedje 2007; Powers 1990). Alternatively, microblade technology had been part of the chipped stone tool-making repertoire of Northeast Asians for a long time, and was a functional adaptation used under certain conditions. Making and using microblades is a good way to take advantage of limited toolstone if access is restricted to small nodules. If toolstone is abundant, one does not have to invest effort in making microblades. But good source material can be scarce—during northern winters, snow is an impediment to collecting raw material on the ground, and adverse weather could limit travel to quarries. With the colder Younger Dryas climate, these conditions may have lasted for more of the year, prompting conservative use of toolstone. Another possibility is that as the landscape filled with people, specific groups might control quarries and deny access to others. Perhaps microblades were favored by people traveling long distances to reduce the weight of their belongings, or when traveling into a new territory, where the locations of toolstone sources were not yet known. It's not coincidental that microblades are found in northerly latitudes. Taking this view, the early dates on Swan Point microblades are not problematic, and microblade industries can be seen as an "insurance policy" to fall back on when toolstone is temporarily inaccessible in harsh, northern environments. Perhaps the Younger Dryas cooling period stimulated human groups to be more mobile, resulting in greater archaeological visibility of microblade users. Bifacial and microblade technologies can be considered complementary; bifaces can be used as cores to make other tools, and as general purpose knives and choppers, whereas microblades are more specialized (Magne 2001; Rasic and Andrefsky 2001).

Sea-Level Histories and the Earliest
Evidence on the Northwest Coast

To interpret the Northwest Coast archaeological record, one must consider how global climate change caused the advance and retreat of the world's ice sheets and how these affected patterns of oceanic and atmospheric circulation. Climate change affects sea-surface temperature and salinity, sea-ice cover, ocean wave conditions, and sedimentation (Hetherington et al. 2007). With volumes of the world's water tied up in glacial ice, sea levels were substantially lower than today during glacial periods. Under the massive weight of glacial ice, the earth's surface is depressed, but when this load lifts, the land rebounds upward (isostatic rebound). Adjacent to a glaciated area, the stress on earth's crust sometimes causes a forebulge, where its surface is forced upward. As the ice retreats, the forebulge moves with it in isostatic equilibrium, and when the ice is fully melted, the forebulge subsides. Sea-level histories vary based on the rigidity of the earth's crust, distance from retreating ice (roughly perpendicular to the coast) but also latitudinally because temperature and currents affect the rate of melting. Couple these variables with irregular bathymetry, and it's apparent why Northwest Coast sea-level histories are complex and must be reconstructed locally. The interplay of these forces determines the location of shorelines and the composition of floral and faunal communities. These are dynamic systems whose component species are variously affected by different types of climate and environmental change occurring at a variety of scales.

In the northern Northwest Coast, the outer islands and what is now the mainland coast experienced significantly different sea-level histories. During the height of the LGM, the islands of the Prince of Wales Archipelago in southeast Alaska were part of a large land mass, adjacent to ice-bound regions to the east. Haida Gwaii was part of a large landmass connected to the mainland by a narrow isthmus, with areas to the east covered in ice (Figure 4.3). Both these areas were elevated due to the forebulge, and were terrestrial refugia for bears, river otters, and cervids. The Prince of Wales and Haida Gwaii refugia were not contiguous land masses—even at the height of the last glacial, they were separated by ice blocking Dixon Entrance (Hetherington et al. 2007:123). The ice receded from Dixon Entrance between 16,300 and 14,650 cal B.P. (14,000–12,600 RYBP), and then they were separated by the rough waters of Dixon Entrance, a gap of up to 70 km. Vancouver Island was also connected to the mainland during this time, and the overland connection between Haida Gwaii, ice free areas along the fringe of the mainland, and northern Vancouver Island led to some similarities in endemic fauna. With retreat of the ice, sea levels rose, flooding huge tracts of land, and coastlines were substantially reshaped.

On the mainland of the northern Northwest Coast, isostatic rebound outpaced sea-level rise, stranding former shorelines as raised beaches now deep in the forest. At the heads of fjords, isostatic rebound has been particularly dramatic—at Kitimat, located at the head of Douglas Channel about 200 km east of Graham Island, the late glacial shoreline was 200 m higher than today. At Prince Rupert, located ~90 km from Graham Island, the late glacial shoreline was about 50 m higher than today. No early sites have been found on the B.C. mainland coast. On the southeast Alaskan mainland, the late glacial shoreline was ~190 m above present around Juneau. On the "inner islands" closest to the southeast Alaskan mainland, late glacial shorelines range from 35 to 170 m above present on Admiralty, Kupreanof, and

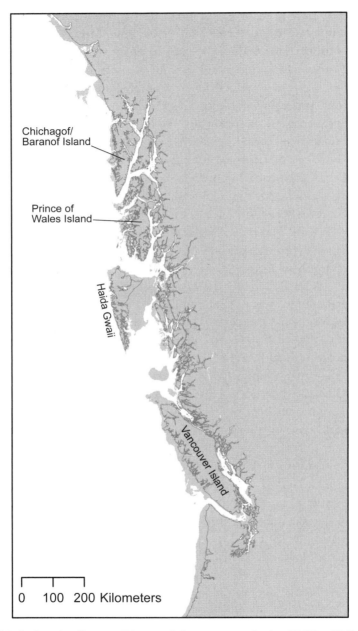

Figure 4.3. Ancient shorelines at -100 meters below current sea level at 15,000 cal B.P. (Masters and Aiello 2007:37). Map by Jacob Bartruff.

Revillagigedo islands (Baichtal and Carlson 2007; Baichtal and Karl 2009). Sea-level change in the Prince of Wales Archipelago is roughly parallel to that of Haida Gwaii. For the northern outer islands (Baranof and Chichagof) data are insufficient for identifying the elevation of late glacial shorelines.

Off the coast of southern B.C., relative sea levels reached between 50–200 m above present (depending on location) during the Late Pleistocene. Cordilleran Ice retreated by 13,800 cal B.P. (12,000 RYBP), but a reduced ice load persisted until 11,500 cal B.P. (10,000 RYBP) on the mainland (Hetherington et al. 2007:119). Some of western Vancouver Island was isostatically depressed just prior to the LGM, so sea level was close to modern (Ward et al. 2003). During the Late Pleistocene 13,800–12,700 cal B.P. (12,000–10,800 RYBP), bison (*Bison antiquus*), and other megafauna inhabited the lodgepole pine parklands of southern Vancouver Island, which was nearly contiguous with those of the San Juan Islands and mainland (Kenady et al. 2007; Wilson 2009). By 11,500 cal B.P. (10,000 B.P.), sea levels fell to present levels along the Fraser Lowland, and to −50 m at Victoria. By the start of the Holocene, bison had disappeared, probably due to expanding conifer forests.

If the first people to move to North America did so ca. 15,000 cal B.P., then a significant temporal gap occurs between initial entry and the earliest direct evidence of occupation on the Northwest Coast itself. At 15,000 cal B.P., sea level around Haida Gwaii was an estimated 150 m lower than today. The earliest well-dated archaeological evidence (12,900–11,500 cal B.P.) on the Northwest Coast is from Haida Gwaii: the Gaadu Din and K1 caves. There is still a gap of more than 2,000 years between the hypothesized first entry to documented occupation on the Northwest Coast. The elusive period between 15,000 and 13,000 cal B.P. was when sea level rose about 50 m. Hence, Late Pleistocene shorelines were quickly drowned, occupational evidence was likely ephemeral, and most sites were probably destroyed or their remnants are largely inaccessible today. At present, Haida Gwaii is the most remote archipelago on the Northwest Coast, located about 90 km from the mainland. But at 15,000 cal B.P., with lowered sea level, Hecate Strait was a terrestrial landscape, a "land bridge" connecting Haida Gwaii to the B.C. mainland.

Despite lack of direct evidence for watercraft dating to the Late Pleistocene, most archaeologists believe that the earliest people on the Northwest

Coast used boats. Although it is easy to conjure up images of the large nineteenth-century dug-out cedar canoes and those of today, the dense rain-forests for which the coast is famous had not yet developed. The early craft employed by the first migrants may have been canoes, but rafts of driftwood or skin boats are also possibilities. The oldest sites on Haida Gwaii were occupied about the same time as the onset of the Younger Dryas between 12,900 and 11,650 cal B.P. The Younger Dryas was a return to colder and drier conditions in interior Alaska, but on the Northwest Coast, it caused a reversion from forest to more open tundra in southeast Alaska and herb-rich parkland on Haida Gwaii (Lacourse and Mathewes 2005:55). Since Younger Dryas flooding of the Bering land bridge prompted movements of people along the Bering Sea coast, it seems likely that at least some people headed south to the Northwest Coast.

At the time people used Gaadu Din and K1 caves, Haida Gwaii was a large island, located about 60 km from the mainland. The landscape was more open tundra and parklands compared to today's dense coniferous forest (Fedje et al. 2008:33–34). The K1 and Gaadu Din caves are located inland from the present shoreline, at 40–45 m asl. Gaadu Din 2, a limestone cave on the east coast of Moresby Island, yielded the oldest dates (12,900–11,900 cal B.P.; 11,030–10,220 RYBP) of any site on the Northwest Coast, but K1 Cave on west Moresby (12,800–12,300 cal B.P.; 10,950–10,400 RYBP) and Gaadu Din (12,400–11,500 cal B.P.; 10,500–10,000 RYBP) are nearly as old (Fedje et al. 2008). At Gaadu Din 2, a bifacial industry is represented by a spear point, knife, and biface tips associated with a hearth. The foliate point has a broad stem and incipient shoulders (Figure 4.2). At K1 Cave, two simi-lar spear points were found with bear bones, suggesting people came to the cave to hunt bear in their dens (McLaren et al. 2005). One late-winter ethno-graphic hunting method used dogs to disturb a hibernating bear who would then impale itself on a braced spear at the cave entrance (Fedje et al. 2008:25). From Gaadu Din, two foliate points and a bone point tip were found associated with bear and deer bones. These Haida Gwaii bifaces were made of chert, thought to be from a local source (Fedje et al. 2008:20). Fedje and coauthors have christened this the "Kinggi Complex" (12,500–9750 cal B.P.; 10,600–8750 RYBP) on Haida Gwaii, but the points are similar to those previously defined for the Pebble Tool Tradition and Old Cordilleran complex (Carlson 1996b; Matson and Coupland 1995).

The bifaces in the oldest component at On Your Knees Cave (10,300 cal B.P.) are similar to the points found in the Haida Gwaii caves; they are foliate and some have incipient stems or shoulders (Figure 4.2). Dixon (2008:16) believes the bifaces from On Your Knees Cave are from weapons used to hunt and knives used to process brown or black bears that hibernated in the cave. These spear points, dart points, and knives were made on obsidian, rhyolite, chert, and other cryptocrystalline silicates. Altogether, 12 specimens from this earliest occupation have been found, but these were "spatially and temporally associated with microblades and microblade cores" (Dixon 2008:13). Dixon (2008:16) characterized the microblade technology at the site as "experimental," inferring it was added to an older, "extant and highly sophisticated" bifacial technology by 10,300 cal B.P. Dixon recognized the similarity between these foliate and stemmed bifaces to the Western Stemmed and Cascade traditions of the interior west. Stemmed and foliate points are found together at Ushki Lake, underlying the microblade component. Like K1 and Gaadu Din caves, On Your Knees Cave is located away from the current shoreline.

Carlson and Magne (2008) described a set of regionally clustered traditions, including the Foliate Biface and Intermontane Stemmed Point traditions. Foliate bifaces in other Early Holocene components include Groundhog Bay in southeast Alaska, Richardson Island and other sites in Haida Gwaii, and Namu on the central B.C. coast. Similar points have been found at Milliken, about 125 km from the coast in the Fraser Canyon and Sentinel Gap about 200 km from Puget Sound in the Columbia River basin. Carlson and Magne's Intermontane Stemmed Point tradition is essentially the same as Beck and Jones's Western Stemmed tradition. Despite the small sample sizes at the earliest Northwest Coast sites, the foliate and stemmed points are similar in shape and are found together at the Gaadu Din caves and On Your Knees Cave. They are also found together in pre-microblade components at Ushki Lake. For these reasons, I think it's a mistake to link these projectile point types to specific migrations, and suspect they are part of a single bifacial tradition.

Carlson and Magne described two types of fluted points in the Northwest, Peace River and Clovis. The Richey-Roberts Clovis Cache found in East Wenatchee, Washington (about 150 km from Puget Sound), is part of the "Clovis fluted" tradition. Large Clovis points (some >20 cm long), preforms, bifaces, scrapers, unifacial tools, debitage, along with bone and antler tools were found in a concentration suggesting intentional burial (Ames et al. 1998:103; Meltzer 2009:251). Some artifacts were sprinkled with red ocher indicating ceremonial activity. The cultural materials lay atop ash deposits thought to result from eruption of Glacier Peak in the North Cascades about 13,100 cal B.P. (11,250 RYBP). Yet we do not know how long after the volcanic eruption(s) the artifacts were buried, and questions have been raised about whether the ash was redeposited and is more recent. Except for this enigmatic find, most fluted points in the Northwest appear to be derivative of and more recent than the fluted points of the Plains, Southwest, and eastern U.S. (Carlson and Magne 2008:355). The relatively small Peace River fluted points and those in Alaska may represent a late Paleo-Indian migration north along what had become a completely ice-free corridor west of the Rocky Mountains by ~12,400 cal B.P. (10,500 RYBP; Dixon 1993). During the Younger Dryas, with the expansion of steppe habitat and increase in steppe bison numbers in interior Alaska, bison hunters from the Northern Plains migrated north to the Arctic with their Clovis-derived technologies (Hoffecker and Elias 2007:163; see also Dumond 2001).

What is the significance of different point and blade types for understanding the earliest settlement of the Northwest Coast? Archaeologists struggle to improve our typologies of artifacts thought to have temporal, geographic, and cultural meaning. But on the Northwest Coast itself and in near-coast areas, the number of projectile points securely dated to the earliest periods is very small, with foliate, stemmed, and Clovis points of comparable antiquity. Clear functional differences between point types are elusive. Recent studies of weapons technology from the ice patch sites of the Yukon indicate that multiple point types were in use simultaneously and that base type was unrelated to hafting technique (Hare et al. 2008). The temporal and functional context of microblades remains ambiguous. These observations challenge the essentialism that has dominated study of the earliest Americans—what has often been a search for discrete projectile point types or cranial forms that can be interpreted as signatures of specific groups (Dillehay 2009:976). By 13,000 cal B.P., material cultures in North America were diversifying in ways we have yet to fully document.

Sea-Level Histories and Transitions to the Early Holocene

The Younger Dryas ended abruptly, within a few decades of 11,650 cal B.P. (Hetherington et al. 2007:118). Then the Pacific subtropical high-pressure system expanded, with summer insolation at its maximum (Bartlein et al. 1998; Moss 2008a). Good summer weather persisted for longer each year and spring and fall were less stormy compared to today (Bartlein et al. 1998). Winters were drier, with weaker onshore flow and less rain. Although it is hard to extrapolate local conditions that would affect small boat navigation from climate models, long-distance small boat travel during this time may have been possible for more days during the year, relative to today. This period of ameliorating climate may have facilitated seafaring and long-distance travel on the Northwest Coast. This may be why the archaeological record improves with more evidence in additional places.

With this global warming trend, the tundra and more open parkland of Haida Gwaii and southeast Alaska gave way to the development of forests. Northwest Coast forests during the Early Holocene were more susceptible to fire during this period than anytime else during the Holocene (Gavin et al. 2003:198). In southeast Alaska, Jim Baichtal routinely finds charcoal in Early Holocene beach deposits dated between 10,800 and 9150 cal B.P. (9500–8200 RYBP); most is probably charcoal redeposited from forest fires (Baichtal et al. 2008). The incidence of large landscape fires (Gavin et al. 2003) may have also contributed to the mobility of human groups during the Early Holocene.

By 10,700 cal B.P. (9400 RYBP) on Haida Gwaii, relative sea level rose to the position of the modern shoreline (Fedje et al. 2005a:25). By 10,000 cal B.P. (8900 RYBP), sea levels rose above the modern shoreline to a height of 15–16 m asl (above sea level), dropping to modern about 2000 cal B.P. Kilgii Gwaay, in southern Haida Gwaii, was occupied between 10,700 and 10,600 cal B.P. (9450–9400 RYBP; Fedje et al. 2005b). The occupation was relatively short in duration—an unusual circumstance on the Northwest Coast where sites are often palimpsests occupied for long periods. When people camped at Kilgii Gwaay, the site was just a few meters above high tide. Today, its deposits extend 1–3 m below high tide. At 10,600 cal B.P., the sea rose above the site on its way to its maximum position 15–16 m higher than present, but local tectonic uplift since the mid-Holocene has raised the position of the land by 15 m, so Kilgii Gwaay is in the intertidal zone today.

About 4,000 chipped stone tools were excavated from Kilgii; most are unifacially worked or used flakes (Fedje et al. 2005b). A single biface fragment was found. The stone technology was focused on reduction of locally available cores and thus is hard to compare with bifacial and microblade traditions described earlier. Due to excellent preservation in the wet, intertidal deposits, bone tools and modified bones were found, including a unilaterally barbed point, a percusser, and an awl-like tool. More remarkably, over 100 wooden artifacts were found including braided spruce root cordage, wooden wedges, wrapped sticks, a composite haft, wood points, withes, and wood debitage. Cordage is used to make nets, lines, ropes, and other items that are fundamental components of maritime technologies. The cordage, wedges, and wood stakes are particularly striking because they resemble artifacts found in much more recent Northwest Coast wet sites such as Ozette (525–350 cal B.P.). These Kilgii artifacts suggest that technologies made of perishable materials have been important to Northwest Coast peoples for more than 10,000 years (Figure 4.4).

Kilgii Gwaay has yielded the most substantial faunal assemblage older than 10,000 cal B.P. from the Northwest Coast. California mussels (*Mytilus californianus*), characteristic of wave-swept rocky shores, were the most common shellfish. Of 39 vertebrate taxa, rockfish were most abundant, and bear, harbor seal, sea otter, dogfish, lingcod, Cassin's auklet, and albatross also occurred. Relatively large halibut (~20 kg) and lingcod (10–13 kg) were taken (Fedje et al. 2005b:201), suggesting fishing from boats using hooks and sturdy lines. The faunal remains show use of maritime and terrestrial habitats, comparing favorably to more recent assemblages. Fedje et al. (2005b:202) identified two differences between Early and Late Holocene faunal assemblages from southern Haida Gwaii; bear are more abundant at Kilgii than at more recent sites (dated within the last 2,000 years), whereas recent sites contain more salmon. Fedje et al. suggested that the more open vegetation of the time provided more favorable bear habitat than dense modern forests.

More than 100 intertidal lithic sites dating to the 10,800–10,600 cal B.P. interval (9500–9400 RYBP) have been identified on Haida Gwaii (Fedje and Christiansen 1999; Mackie and Sumpter 2005). The wide distribution of these lag deposits of stone tools across Moresby and surrounding islands

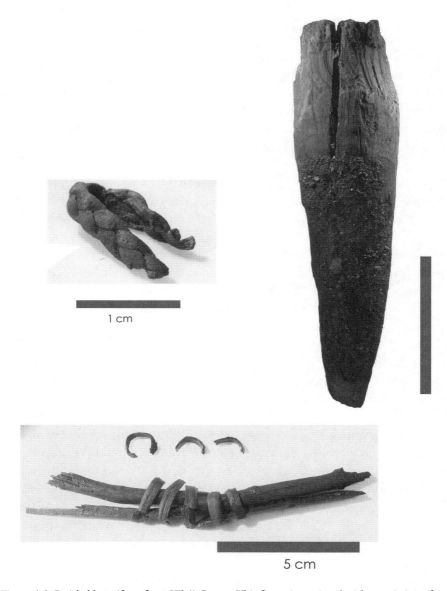

Figure 4.4. Perishable artifacts from Kilgii Gwaay. This figure is reprinted with permission of Daryl Fedje and the publisher of *Haida Gwaii: Human History and Environment from the Time of Loon to the Time of the Iron People*, by Daryl W. Fedje and Rolf W. Mathewes © University of British Columbia Press. All rights reserved by the publisher.

suggests a well-dispersed human population. The Richardson Island site is dramatically different from Kilgii Gwaay, but equally significant to understanding the history of occupation on the Northwest Coast. The site was occupied between 10,600 and 9400 cal B.P. (9400–8400 RYBP; McLaren and Smith 2008), during the last centuries of sea-level rise on Haida Gwaii (Steffen 2006:27). Careful study of the site's stratigraphy helped investigators unravel the sequence and timing of marine transgression and how people adjusted to sea-level change. A microblade industry was added to an older bifacial one, a general pattern previously noted in northeast Asia and interior Alaska. This well-stratified site contained 51 discrete depositional events, including 24 charcoal and artifact-rich cultural levels in a 5 m-deep sequence (Steffen 2006). The noncultural strata are alternating reddish levels of marine deposited beach gravels, and yellow and grey strata of silt and clay that moved downslope. As Steffen (2006:28) explained, people "revisiting the site from year to year or decade to decade would thus have occasionally found a 'refreshed' gravel surface capping earlier deposits."

The oldest cultural strata at Richardson Island contained tear-drop shaped (like Chindadn[4]) and other foliate bifaces, blade cores, scraper-planes, and flake tools. Sea level stabilized at 15 m above modern between 10,150 and 9850 cal B.P. (9000–8800 RYBP; Fedje et al. 2005c:236). This was when microblade technology was added to the bifacial technology in older strata. Bifacial and microblade technologies co-occur between 10,000 and 9400 cal B.P. (8900–8400 RYBP), which Fedje et al. (2005c) characterized as a transitional period. They suggested that toolstone may have become limited if sources were drowning with the rising sea—making microblades conserved precious raw material. By 8900 cal B.P. (8000 RYBP), bifacial technology was entirely replaced by microblade technology using tabular to conical cores of local stone (Fedje et al. 2005c:237, 240); these assemblages comprise the Early Moresby Tradition. Sea levels on Haida Gwaii would remain about 15 m higher than present for 4,000 years (Fedje et al. 2005c:242).

From the 16 hearths at Richardson Island, Martina Steffen (2006) screened the contents through 1 mm mesh and sorted through hundreds of thousands of burned bone scraps. No two hearth assemblages were alike, and each contained a distinctive vertebrate assemblage. From 2,000 identifiable bones from all hearths, rockfish was the most abundant taxon, making up 77 percent of the fish and found in 15 hearths. Spiny dogfish (a small shark), salmon, and Irish lords (a sculpin) were common. Rockfish, dogfish, and sculpin are not often recognized as important Northwest Coast fish, but they were to the people of south Moresby Island. The Richardson Island hearths were each used for a short period before burial, providing us some of the details of daily life during the Early Holocene. Reuse of the site over 800–1,000 years suggests it was a good place to camp and that fishing was reliable nearby. Most fish were probably available year-round and the site does not appear to have been a place where people dried or smoked fish for storage. The faunal evidence from both Richardson Island and Kilgii Gwaay confirms marine resource dependence during the Early Holocene on Haida Gwaii.

Other sites located on raised beaches 12–15 m asl on Haida Gwaii represent what Fedje and Mackie (2005:160) term "Late Moresby," dated between 8900 and 5700 cal B.P. (8000–5000 RYBP). Most lack good faunal preservation, but contain microblades, microblade cores, cores, and core tools ("pebble tools") and flakes. As sea level retreated further, sites were positioned accordingly; sites 4450 cal B.P. (4000 RYBP) in age are located on raised beaches 7–10 m asl, and more recent sites are even closer to current shorelines.

Although the history of sea-level change and human occupation on Haida Gwaii is not fully known, it is more complete than anywhere else on the Northwest Coast. In southeast Alaska, sea levels even within the Prince of Wales Archipelago are variable. On one of the outermost islands, Heceta Island, sea level was lower than present until 11,500 cal B.P. (10,000 RYBP), but then rose 15–18 m above present by 9500 cal B.P. (8500 RYBP). After 9150 cal B.P. (8200 RYBP) sea levels fell, retreating to close to the current position by 5700 cal B.P. (5000 RYBP) in many locales. On Prince of Wales Island itself, sea-level histories are variable, with marine transgression extending only a few meters to perhaps 6 m above present positions between 11,500 and 7800 cal B.P. (10,000–7000 RYBP).

The Chuck Lake Locality 1 site on Heceta Island dates to 9150 cal B.P. (8200 RYBP). The site is on a raised beach 15–18 m asl, almost a kilometer from the modern shoreline. During the Early Holocene, the site was near the head of an estuary (Ackerman et al. 1985). The microblade industry from Chuck Lake is similar to the Moresby Tradition on Haida Gwaii (Fedje et al. 2005c). Chuck Lake is one of the oldest shell middens on the Northwest Coast, with shell and the limestone bedrock counteracting forest soil acidity to help preserve cultural remains. Butter and littleneck clams were abundant, with lesser amount of blue mussels (*Mytlilus trossulus*)—all estuarine taxa common on the coast today. The fish were mostly bottomfish, with Pacific cod followed by greenling, sculpin, and rockfish (Ackerman et al. 1989). Steller sea lion, caribou, and beaver were also identified.

Carlson (2007) suggested that east of Clarence Strait in southeast Alaska, the response to glaciation can be characterized by isostasy, while to the west it was controlled by subsidence. Although this generalization is useful, it cannot be extended reliably to the north. To the south, McLaren (2008) has more precisely identified a "hinge point" on the Dundas Island Archipelago, located northwest of Prince Rupert, B.C. Here the sea-level curve is nearly flat, showing that relative sea level during the Late Pleistocene was only a few meters higher than today. The Dundas Islands occupy a geographic position between the region where sea-level change is controlled by isostasy (to the east) and that controlled by eustasy (to the west). McLaren found five Early Holocene sites on the Dundas Islands, the first of this antiquity to be found in Tsimshian territory. The oldest shell midden at Far West Point dates to ca. 7800 cal B.P. (7000 RYBP), and is underlain by a component that may date to 11,000 cal B.P. (9700 RYBP). No microblade industry was found, but the recovered artifact assemblage is small, and research is ongoing.

Other Early Holocene sites include Groundhog Bay II, near the entrance to Glacier Bay in mainland southeast Alaska, Hidden Falls on Baranof Island, Namu on the central B.C. coast, Bear Cove on northeast Vancouver Island, and Glenrose in the Fraser River delta. None of these sites is situated above 18 m asl, and all are positioned within 50 m of current shorelines. All these sites occur in places where isostatic rebound kept pace with or slightly outpaced eustatic sea-level rise and/or the sites were located not far from local "hinge points" such as the Dundas Islands. Groundhog Bay, Hidden Falls, and Namu have produced microblade industries (Figure 4.5), with an underlying foliate biface technology present at Namu (Ackerman et al. 1979; Carlson 1996c; Davis 1989). The oldest components at Bear Cove and Glenrose also contained foliate bifaces (Carlson 2003; Matson 1976). In 1996, Carlson (1996c:100–101) conceptualized this pattern as a coalescence of two distinctive traditions at Namu: (1) a foliate biface tradition (Pebble Tool Tradition) that originated to the south of the continental ice sheets and then moved north to Namu, and (2) a more recent microblade tradition (North Coast Microblade Tradition) that originated in the far north and

Figure 4.5. Microblades and microblade cores from Namu. Reprinted with permission of Roy Carlson and Simon Fraser University Archaeology Press.

moved south to Namu. Whether these represented migrating peoples or diffusion of technologies was left open. Carlson and Magne (2008) now see the ultimate origin of bifacial and microblade technologies in the far north. Of these five Early Holocene sites, none have produced substantial faunal assemblages that are temporally limited to the Early Holocene. Other Early Holocene sites of slightly younger age (8900–7800 cal B.P.) include Lyell

Bay and Arrow Creek on Haida Gwaii (Fedje et al. 2005c) and Thorne River in Alaska (Holmes et al. 1989). Along with Glenrose, the Arrow Creek and Thorne River sites are associated with salmon streams, as are Milliken on the Fraser River and the Roadcut site on the Columbia River (Butler and O'Connor 2004; Mitchell and Pokotylo 1996). Milliken and Roadcut are located 100 km or more from the coast.

The record of early human settlement along the coasts of Washington and Oregon is limited. The cultural origin of the Manis Mastodon site on Washington's Olympic Peninsula is not widely accepted, and no Early Holocene sites have been found on the Washington coast. The Late Pleistocene shoreline was far offshore the present coasts of Washington and Oregon and any occupation site from this era is most likely underwater. The Indian Sands site in Oregon dates to 8500 cal B.P., where a deflated shell midden was found on the surface of a sea cliff (Moss and Erlandson 1998b).[5] The dearth of Early Holocene sites from the southern Northwest Coast (and northern California) may be due to the geological dynamics of the Cascadia Subduction Zone (Erlandson et al. 2008). Very large earthquakes strike this region every 300 to 500 years, and these along with tsunamis, landslides, and coastal erosion provide the best explanation for the dearth of Early Holocene sites.

Early Lifeways on the Northwest Coast

The oldest Northwest Coast sites, On Your Knees, K1, and Gaadu Din caves, are all located on islands, some distance (.4–1.0 km) inland from present shorelines and at elevations above 40 m asl. Each of these caves is associated with bears; evidence for bear-hunting is strongest at K1 and Gaadu Din caves, while bear scavenging of human bones may account for the remains of Shuká Ḵaa. These sites were occupied during the Younger Dryas "cold snap," when the insular Northwest Coast was vegetated with tundra and open parkland. We can reasonably infer the use of watercraft, and the bones of Shuká Ḵaa show that this young man had a seafood-rich diet—his isotopic values are similar to those obtained from ring seal, sea otter, and marine fish (Dixon 2001:286). People made use of both coastal and terrestrial habitats. These sites provide a glimpse of the early occupation of the Northwest Coast.

Schalk et al. (2007:184) argued that during the Late Pleistocene, tundra and parkland fauna such as caribou and bison were broadly distributed in the refugia west of the glaciated Northwest Coast. They suggested that people migrating to this region found a terrestrial ecosystem more productive than today. The remains of what are thought to be butchered bison from Orcas Island, Washington, along with the Manis Mastodon site are marshaled as evidence for an ungulate hunting adaptation. This image of maritime peoples hunting bison, caribou, and bear in coastal tundra is one that has no precedent among documented hunter-gatherers, but the landscapes of the Late Pleistocene Northwest Coast were like none that exist today.

By the Early Holocene, the Younger Dryas cold snap had faded and forests were reclaiming terrestrial landscapes. With climatic warming some forests became susceptible to fire, and over much of the coast, sea levels were rising rapidly. This unstable landscape challenged Northwest Coast residents in new ways, and they appear to have been rather mobile in whatever watercraft they employed. The most complete views of life come from Kilgii Gwaay and Richardson Island, places where people camped for short time periods. Kilgii residents left evidence of perishable technologies that are remarkably similar to those from more recent times. Generations of people returned to a favored campsite at Richardson Island that must have been a well-known place to catch rockfish.

Obsidian was a valuable raw material to early residents of the Northwest Coast, but it also has been highly valued by archaeologists. Trace element geochemistry allows identification of chemical types that can be tracked back to places where the sources occur, and from this, archaeologists infer patterns of transport and trade in obsidian. Obsidian from Mount Edziza in interior B.C. has been identified at On Your Knees Cave, Groundhog Bay, and Hidden Falls. Obsidian from Suemez Island in the outer Prince of Wales Archipelago has been identified at On Your Knees Cave, Chuck Lake, Hidden Falls, and Thorne River. This suggests extensive travel and trade across southeast Alaska during the Early Holocene, but recent geochemical studies are revealing overlap between the chemistry of the Edziza and Suemez obsidians (S. Karl 2009, pers. comm.), raising doubts about these inferences.

Conclusion

The glacial refugia on the Prince of Wales Archipelago, Haida Gwaii, and Vancouver Island during the LGM were substantial enough to support bears, ungulates, and humans. Archaeological sites from the period are likely drowned, and the oldest sites on the Northwest Coast date to ~13,000 cal

B.P. The distribution of the earliest sites mandates a maritime adaptation and the use of watercraft by Shuká Kaa and his contemporaries. No Northwest Coast archaeological sites are any older than Clovis or Nenana, let alone Paisley Caves and Monte Verde. Sea-level histories clearly structure the Northwest Coast archaeological record, but must be reconstructed locally to efficiently prospect for early sites. Sites dating from the Early Holocene are more numerous than those of the late Pleistocene, or at least more archaeologically visible. These highly mobile people confronted a dynamic landscape in which sea levels were rising rapidly and forests were closing in. They had tremendous behavioral flexibility to survive, and probably explored quite widely. Also apparent from the Early Holocene record is significant continuity of some technologies—of wood implements and cordage, and of both bifaces and microblades—into more recent times. As will be discussed in the next chapter, older technologies do not disappear—they undergo modification while new technologies are added.

Notes

1. Hetherington et al. (2007:118–119) state that North American ice sheets reached their maximum extent at 21,500 cal B.P., but that the south end of Cordilleran ice reached its maximum at 16,900 cal B.P.

2. The Denali complex is related to the Dyuktai microblade culture of northeast Siberia. Both have been considered part of the Paleoarctic tradition as defined by Anderson (1970), Dumond (1977), and others.

3. The Milankovitch theory of ice ages views global climate change as a result of Earth's orbital changes and the inherent variability of and interactions between the ocean, atmosphere, and ice-sheet systems. The end of the Pleistocene is marked by the Bølling-Allerød interstadial at 14,600 cal B.P., when climate warmed and sea temperature rose. Global sea levels rose 20 m in less than 500 years. Between 12,700 and 11,650 cal B.P., climate cooled again with the Younger Dryas (Hetherington et al. 2007).

4. Chindadn points have also been found at two sites in the Bella Coola Valley and at Namu. Carlson (2008a) suggested that caribou hunters from the Yukon introduced this point type to the Northwest Coast when it was still tundra.

5. Claims for a Late Pleistocene occupation at this and another Oregon coast site have been made, but are not widely accepted (Erlandson et al. 2008:2237; Moss et al. 2006a).

5

The Middle Holocene:
Continuity, but Region-Wide Change?

Northwest Coast archaeologists have traditionally viewed the Middle Holocene period (7000–3500 cal B.P.) as a time of environmental and cultural change. It marks the break between Lithic and Developmental stages (Fladmark 1982), and between Archaic and Pacific periods (Ames and Maschner 1999). 5000 RYBP (5700 cal B.P.) has been viewed as the threshold of environmental stabilization and a major turning point in the region's pre-contact history. But Mid-Holocene climate change was initiated earlier than 5700 cal B.P., and on millennial time scales, Holocene changes were gradual (Moss et al. 2007). The variable effects of isostasy along the northern Northwest Coast and tectonism along southern Northwest Coast led to highly localized sea-level changes during much of the Holocene, suggesting that the littoral ecotone was rarely static. The Mid-Holocene archaeological record demonstrates cultural continuity with earlier periods. We lack evidence of a region-wide, simultaneous increase in the number and size of sites, in sedentism, and for significant technological change at 5000 RYBP. Cultural changes on the Northwest Coast cannot be tied directly to climate or environmental change. Yet the visibility of archaeological sites is a product of environmental factors, especially sea-level change. As in Chapter 4, sea-level history is key to understanding both cultural and natural processes in the formation of the archaeological record.

By ca. 7000 cal B.P. for most of the coast, climate was cooler and wetter than the Early Holocene, although warmer and somewhat drier than today. The late Pleistocene tundra and parklands gave way to pine, alder, and willow woodlands. During the Mid-Holocene, the intensity or duration of summer drought decreased compared to the Early Holocene, and western hemlock and mountain hemlock were established. Western redcedar survived south of the glacial margin at the end of the Pleistocene (Hebda and Mathewes 1984), but when abundant precipitation and moist conditions returned in the Mid-Holocene, it extended its range north. Between 6850 and 4000 cal B.P., redcedar increased in abundance from the Puget Trough to the north-central coast of B.C. in a time transgressive pattern (Moss et al. 2007:515). It spread to its northern limit at Frederick Sound in southeast Alaska by ~3000 cal B.P.[1] Hebda and Mathewes (1984:712) thought that Northwest Coast cultural developments were "environmentally constrained by limited occurrence and abundance" of redcedar before 5700 cal B.P. Based on cedar's ethnographic importance, they stated that the establishment of abundant redcedar stimulated the development of Northwest Coast material culture. But the relationship between western redcedar and culture change has received little systematic investigation. During the Middle Holocene, the composition of the coastal rainforests in various places approached their modern character, but at different times. The coastal rainforests of Alaska and much of B.C. thrived in the maritime climate in the near absence of fire since the Mid-Holocene, while Douglas-fir dominated forests in southern B.C., Washington, and Oregon are fire-dependent (Lertzman et al. 2002). By between 4500 and 3500 cal B.P., the cool wet conditions of the present day were established.

From Chapter 4, recall that both Richardson Island and Kilgii Gwaay are characterized by high temporal resolution. The more than 50 distinct strata at Richardson Island and the relatively short-term duration of Kilgii Gwaay's occupation make these two sites quite distinctive. In contrast, most Northwest Coast archaeological sites are palimpsests, with low temporal resolution (Stein et al. 2003). This is often true of shell middens which represent time-averaged accumulations of a broad range of activities. This makes detecting change over time difficult and accounts for the coarse-grained quality of cultural chronologies. This may also result from lack of attention to lithostratigraphic units and the differences between field observation of stratigraphy and laboratory analysis of sediments that permit recognition of post-depositional effects on that stratigraphy (Stein 1992:88–89; Stein et al. 1992). But the Middle Holocene is still conceived as the threshold of environmental stabilization leading to the "Developed Northwest Coast Pattern."

Re-Evaluating Fladmark's Paleoecological Model

Knut Fladmark's (1975) paleoecological model of Northwest Coast prehistory has profoundly influenced archaeological interpretations of the Middle Holocene period. The 11,400–5700 cal B.P. (10,000–5000 RYBP) period was understood as a time of environmental instability, changing sea levels, unstable river gradients, and fluctuating climate. Archaeological sites dating from this time were thought to contain only chipped stone artifacts and few features, reflecting a "sub-climax" generalized adaptation. Yet Kilgii Gwaay vividly illustrates a much broader material inventory than that limited to stone tools. But the model was developed long before Kilgii was investigated, and Fladmark's ideas are worth reviewing because they have structured how archaeologists have thought about the Middle Holocene:

> After 5,000 [RY] BP, with the stabilization of the land-sea interface and the attainment of climax salmon productivity, shell-midden sites begin to appear along the entire coast. Shell-midden accumulations are the result of dense winter population aggregates existing on the expenditure of stored energy derived from the fall salmon fisheries, and reflect a settlement type characteristic of the ethnographic Northwest Coast cultural pattern. Stone grinding, ornaments, and art work occur more or less simultaneously along the coast with the advent of shell-middens [Fladmark 1975:262].

Salmon was seen as the single-most important food resource on the Northwest Coast; "peak sockeye and coho (salmon) productivity could not have been achieved until major drainage systems developed stable run-off and sedimentation patterns. Optimum spawning and maturation conditions depend upon regular seasonal discharge and sedimentation rates; any fluctuations away from normal stream behavior are detrimental to climax salmon populations" (Fladmark 1975:198–199). Fladmark recognized that pink, chum, and chinook salmon were in the region during the Wisconsin glaciation and that these species would not have been as susceptible to fluctuations in run-off and stream gradients as sockeye and coho. But it was difficult to conceive "of any salmon, particularly sockeye and coho, attaining full productivity prior to the complete stabilization of stream gradients about 5,000 [RY] B.P." (Fladmark 1975:207). He interpreted the apparent increase in shell middens as a consequence of sedentism; "the advent of shell-midden build-up at 5,000

[RY] B.P. can be seen as not a function of preservation or increasing abundance of shell-fish, but instead <u>the result of a shift to the winter village settlement pattern following the development of peak salmon productivity</u>" (Fladmark 1975:253; underlining in original). A decade later, Fladmark (1986:54) suggested "all intertidal and anadromous resources were kept below climax productivity as a result of pronounced sea level instability which prevailed on the coast before about 4500 [RY] years ago."

In 1975, no shell-midden components older than 5700 cal B.P. (5000 RYBP) were known from the Northwest Coast. We now know of Early Holocene shell-bearing components at Kilgii Gwaay, Chuck Lake, and Indian Sands. As discussed elsewhere (Moss et al. 2007), more than a dozen other Northwest Coast shell components are older than 5700 cal B.P. (5000 RYBP), including the 6850 cal B.P. (6000 RYBP) Cohoe Creek site (Christensen and Stafford 2005; Fedje and Christensen 1999; Ham 1990), the 6850 cal B.P. (6000 RYBP) component at Namu in central B.C. (Cannon 1991; Carlson 1998), and the 5900 cal B.P. (5100 RYBP) shell layer at Tahkenitch Landing in Oregon (Minor and Toepel 1986) (Figure 5.1). At Far West Point on the Dundas Islands, shell midden deposits have been dated to 7750–7100 cal B.P. (6940–6185 RYBP; McLaren 2008:175). The lowest levels of the Boardwalk shell midden in Prince Rupert Harbor have not been excavated, but Ames (2005:293) estimated these may date to 8500 RYBP. Yet Fladmark's model retains appeal for Northwest Coast archaeologists, and is the basis for statements such as "maritime adaptations—evolved on the central Northwest Coast between 5000 and 4500 [RY] B.P." (Coupland 1998:50). Namu, Bear Cove, Saltery Bay, and Tahkenitch provide glimpses of life during the Mid-Holocene, and yield information about sea-level change, salmon productivity, and shell accumulation.

Namu

About 11,900 cal B.P. (10,200 RYBP), sea level at Namu was 17 m higher than current high tide (Sullivan 1993:60). It dropped rapidly to current levels between 8900 and 7850 cal B.P. (8000–7000 RYBP), then dropped even further to −3 to −5 m ca. 3750 cal B.P. (3500 RYBP). Sea level then rose again possibly covering some Mid-Holocene deposits to reach its modern level. Although the archaeological site is positioned along the Namu River mouth today, during the Early Holocene the river mouth was probably some distance away. The Namu River is an important salmon stream with large

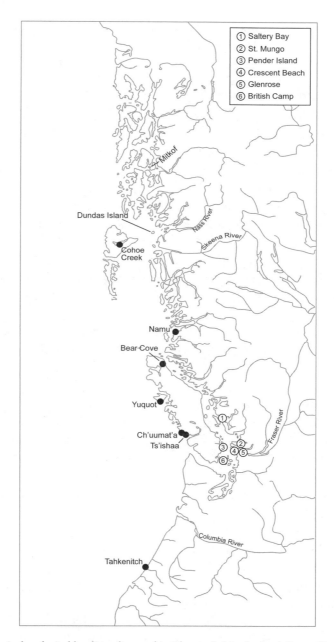

Figure 5.1. Archaeological localities discussed in Chapter 5. Map by Jacob Bartruff.

escapements historically, especially of pink salmon. A stone fish trap in the river has not been dated. The lack of shell remains in the oldest cultural deposit may be because Namu residents did not collect shellfish or shell refuse was deposited in a locality since destroyed. Middle Holocene faunal remains from Period 2 (6900–6000 cal B.P., 6060–5240 RYBP) came from discontinuous lenses of fragmentary fish and shellfish. Of nearly 7,000 bones identified, most were salmon, but samples of fine matrix suggest as many as 85,000 herring bones were lost through the 1/8 inch mesh screens used in recovery (Cannon 1991, 1996:104). Rockfish, cod, spiny dogfish, greenling, flatfish, and other fish were found. Deer and harbor seal were the most abundant mammals, and ducks and loons the most abundant birds.

Vertebrae are the most common salmon bones recovered in Northwest Coast archaeological sites, but cannot be distinguished to species. Ancient DNA studies of Namu salmon bones show use of five species, although Namu residents concentrated on pink salmon (Cannon and Yang 2006). The focus on pink salmon was sustained for almost 7,000 years at the site. Pink salmon are generally available in large numbers and are relatively small and lean, making them optimal fish to preserve for storage. During Period 2, salmon comprised 89 percent of the fish; after that, use of salmon intensified further during Periods 3 and 4 (5500–5250 cal B.P., 4775–4540 RYBP; 4950–4200 cal B.P., 4390–3825 RYBP) when they made up almost 97 percent of the fish. In Period 5 (3750–2200 cal B.P., 3500–2185 RYBP), salmon dropped in relative abundance (Cannon 1998:61), then dropped further in the first part of Period 6 (2000–1000 cal B.P.). The abundance of salmon recovered to near peak levels about 1,000 years ago (Cannon et al. 2011). Cannon interpreted this as evidence for periodic disruptions in the pink salmon fishery. Pink salmon spawn at two, and sometimes three years of age; today, largely independent populations of pink salmon across the Northwest Coast spawn in even and odd years. While this biennial pattern is unlikely to be recognized archaeologically, short-term environmental disturbances could have long-term consequences. Cannon et al. (2011) infer that the Namu pink salmon fishery was vulnerable to occasional failure over a 3,000-year period. People at the site responded to this uncertainty by catching more sockeye during bad pink salmon years, and relying on marginal resources such as ratfish, shellfish, and deer phalanges. They also may have reduced the number of dogs they maintained (Cannon 1995; Cannon and Yang 2006).

The vertebrate faunal record at Namu demonstrates that salmon provided the economic mainstay for the site's residents between 6900 and 6000 cal B.P., prior to the coast-wide model's threshold of sea-level stabilization at 5700 cal B.P. Between 4000 and 1000 cal B.P., periodic failures of the pink salmon fishery caused Namu residents to experience food shortages, but they developed ways to cope with the shortfall. This period (which spans the end of the Middle Holocene into the Late Holocene) cannot be viewed as a time when "peak salmon productivity" was "achieved," providing the basis for the "Developed Northwest Coast Pattern." Herring may have also been an important food (and bait?) throughout Namu's history, but because their bones are so small, they are underrepresented vis-á-vis other vertebrate fauna (as they are at most Northwest Coast sites).

Regarding shellfish, isolated lenses of poorly preserved shell are found in Namu Period 2, but during Period 3 (after 6000 cal B.P.), shell was more conspicuous in the midden. In Period 3, Namu residents focused on bay mussels, barnacles, and whelks, but after 4000 cal B.P., they used more clams. Shell deposition peaked between 3000 and 900 cal B.P. (2880–980 RYBP; Conover 1978:98). Cannon et al. (2008; Cannon and Burchell 2009) found no evidence for over-exploitation of shellfish (based on shell growth studies), but clams became more important when pink salmon were either less reliable or insufficient to support site residents. Cannon et al. (2008:19) inferred that either family or lineage groups at Namu exerted some regulatory control on shellfish harvest over the last 5,000 years. That the onset of "shell build-up" occurs after 6000 cal B.P., and that the site was probably occupied during the winter (indicating sedentism or semi-sedentism), is consistent with Fladmark's model. Yet Namu demonstrates that shellfish were used earlier and that species use changed over time. How these patterns relate to local environmental changes and broader culture change is not understood. The full record of shellfish use at Namu may not be represented in the excavated deposits since sea level was lower than present for much of the Middle Holocene.

Cohoe Creek

The Cohoe Creek site is located 50 km up Masset Inlet on Graham Island in Haida Gwaii. When the site was occupied in the Middle Holocene, the inlet was a much larger estuary supporting an array of shellfish. The site's oldest date (7800 cal B.P.; 6980 RYBP) is associated only with stone tools, but this portion of the site was not excavated (Christensen and Stafford 2005:252).

Four Middle Holocene components have been investigated. Component 1 (6850–6350 cal B.P.; 6000–5600 RYBP) contained "trace amounts of shell," Component 2 (6350–5950 cal B.P.; 5600–5200 RYBP) was largely shell-free, and Component 3 (5950–5750 cal B.P.; 5200–5000 RYBP) contained pockets and lenses of clamshells, in addition to a mound of fragmented shell and fire-cracked rock. This "low mound" represents a "discrete refuse pile...the initial large buildup of shell at the site, beginning about 5200 B.P." (5950 cal B.P.; Christensen and Stafford 2005:248–250). Much of Component 4 (4850 cal B.P.; ca. 4300 RYBP), described as "dense accumulations of shellfish remains," was bulldozed away, but some was sampled (Christensen and Stafford 2005:256).

The timing of the shell accumulation is consistent with Fladmark's model, but in this case, shellfish use is not associated with a focus on salmon. The site is adjacent to Cohoe Creek, where coho salmon spawn, but is also within 500 m of the outlet of the Yakoun River, the largest salmon stream in all of Haida Gwaii, which supports chinook, sockeye, coho, and pink salmon as well as steelhead (Christensen and Stafford 2005:245). The site's faunal remains are dominated by jack mackerel (1466 NISP; 85 percent of the fish), whereas salmon contribute less than 5 percent. Mackerel were found in deposits dating 6350–4850 cal B.P., but were particularly abundant ca. 5950–5750 cal B.P. (Christensen and Stafford 2005:254). The most abundant mammals were caribou and black bear. A pit feature contained a stockpile of caribou bone and antler along with hammerstones and abraders, indicating a place where bone tools were made (Christensen and Stafford 2005:270). Christensen and Stafford (2005:271) described the site as a "semi-sedentary camp or village" and noted cultural continuity in artifacts. The abundance of mackerel and caribou at Cohoe Creek make this a distinctive faunal assemblage; whether people lived here year-round is unknown, but the site does not fit the model.

Bear Cove

The Bear Cove site is located along Hardy Bay, on northeastern Vancouver Island. It lies within an inner coastal area, protected from the largest ocean swells, but open to Queen Charlotte Strait. Three major salmon streams occur within 2 km of the site. Here we focus on Components I and III. Despite one Early Holocene date, most of the Component I faunal assemblage dates to the Middle Holocene until ca. 4900 cal B.P. (Carlson 2003).

Component III is dated to 4900–900 cal B.P. Component I was described as "non-shell," while Component III contained substantial amounts of butter and littleneck clams.

The Component I vertebrate faunal assemblage, although small (2136 NISP), is unusual because of the abundance of delphinids (porpoises or dolphins). Deer, northern fur seal, northern sea lion, sea otter, and terrestrial furbearers were also found. Rockfish and taxa other than salmon are most abundant. In the larger Component III sample (24,301 NISP), the number of taxa increases, with deer the most abundant mammal, followed by delphinids, elk, and dog. Rockfish dominates the fish, but greenlings, ratfish, herring, codfishes, and sculpins are all more abundant than salmon.[2]

The Bear Cove faunal assemblage depicts an orientation to nearshore and offshore resources, without a focus on salmon, despite salmon streams nearby. Residents hunted dolphin and deer and fished for a variety of species. Carlson (2003:85) suggested that the scarcity of shell older than 4900 cal B.P. was because of erosion of older shell deposits at Bear Cove (as at Namu). She interpreted Component III as a winter-spring occupation with the accumulation of shell indicating semi-sedentism (Carlson 2003:81). This Bear Cove example decouples the model's link between sea-level stabilization and salmon exploitation from sedentism.

Saltery Bay

Although the archaeological site at Saltery Bay has not been extensively excavated, it is another case demonstrating the diversity of sites from the Middle through the Late Holocene. The site is located on the lower mainland of B.C., on the south-facing shore of Saltery Bay overlooking Jervis Inlet, a fjord that empties into the Strait of Georgia that runs between the mainland and Vancouver Island. Like both Namu and Bear Cove, Saltery Bay is protected from ocean swells, but the waters of the Strait pose their own challenges (Pegg et al. 2007:82). The site is adjacent to a small stream with a wood stake fish trap, but major salmon streams are located about 20 km west of the site, and several empty into Jervis Inlet. Other wood fish traps in the area have been described as "enormous" (Pegg et al. 2007:13). Because Saltery Bay is positioned at a constriction at the mouth of Jervis Inlet, many salmon ascending the inlet would swim past the site.

During most of the Middle Holocene (8500–4000 RYBP), sea levels here were as much as 3 m below modern, so sites positioned just above the shoreline then would be underwater or in the intertidal zone today. The non-shell earliest component dates between 7700 and 6000 cal B.P.,[3] with a small faunal assemblage (167 NISP), with mostly deer (Pegg et al. 2007). Harbor seal, porpoise, salmon, and other taxa also occur. Component II dates to ca. 3700 cal B.P., and contains "moderate" amounts of shell. The Component II vertebrate assemblage is also small (272 NISP), with porpoise, deer, and dogfish, and lower numbers of rockfish, salmon, dog, etc. Component III dates to 500 cal B.P. and contains "significant quantities" of shell, and roughly the same make-up of vertebrates (94 NISP), with proportionately more herring than in the older components. The site shows use of both terrestrial (deer) and marine (porpoise, seal, marine fish) resources throughout its 6,000-year history. Shell does not accumulate in the midden until 3700 cal B.P., and even then, the site is not a dense shell midden accumulation indicating sedentism. Substantial quantities of shell are found only in the Late Holocene component. Salmon are present in each component, but their numbers are low. Like Namu and Bear Cove, Saltery Bay was initially occupied during the Early Holocene and used repeatedly over time, but does not illustrate the pattern outlined in the coast-wide model.

Tahkenitch Landing

Tahkenitch Landing is today located along a freshwater lake, about 2 km inland from Oregon's ocean shoreline. When first occupied, it was positioned alongside an estuary emptying into the open ocean; the outlet to the estuary has since been cut off by dune building west of the site (Minor and Toepel 1986). The earliest "pre-shell" component contained small fragments of marine shell, but at low density, similar to the earliest cultural components at Namu, Cohoe Creek, Bear Cove, and Saltery Bay. The pre-shell component is dated to 8800–6000 cal B.P. (7960–5200 RYBP), but this broad range does not necessarily signify a long occupation—more likely it means uncertainty about its age. The most abundant cultural remains in the pre-shell layer were bones (971 NISP) with staghorn sculpin, tomcod, hake, flatfish, and ducks the most numerous, associated with a handful of stone tools. The oldest shell-bearing layer is dated to 5900 cal B.P. (5100 RYBP), and contained a low volume of estuarine clam shells. The fish remains (3029 NISP) were similar to those in the pre-shell component, with the addition of herring and surfperch. The main shell component, which produced most of the site's vertebrate faunal remains

(17,692 NISP), is dated to 3400 cal B.P. (3150 RYBP) and was interpreted as a village (Minor and Toepel 1986:106). Within a few hundred years, encroaching sand dunes blocked the estuary, and the "post-shell" component has not been well-dated. The 5900 cal B.P. shell layer cannot be considered a massive shell midden; not until 3400 cal B.P. did a large shell midden form. The Tahkenitch case illustrates how coastal environments continued to evolve in ways that structured human settlement through the Late Holocene.

Sea-Level Stabilization, Salmon, and Shell Middens—Variability across the Region

The records from Namu, Cohoe Creek, Bear Cove, Saltery Bay, and Tahkenitch Landing help dislodge the idea that Northwest Coast environments stabilized simultaneously at or around 5700 cal B.P. Although the magnitude of sea-level change since the Mid-Holocene has been less than that of the Late Pleistocene and Early Holocene, the relative position of the shoreline in most areas changed enough to have real effects on where people lived and the condition of the remains they left behind. On the southern Northwest Coast (Vancouver Island to northern California), sea levels have been affected by earthquakes for the last 2,000 or more years in the Cascadia Subduction Zone. Sea levels in the Gulf Islands have risen 1.5 m since the mid-Holocene (Fedje et al. 2009; Grier et al. 2009). On the northern Northwest Coast, isostatic rebound is ongoing, especially on the mainland. Even on the outer islands, Cape Addington Rockshelter was not available for human occupation until sometime after 2000 cal B.P. (Moss 2004a).

The generalization that sea-level stabilization is necessary for salmon populations to reach "peak productivity" is also problematic. Pacific salmon have been present on the Northwest Coast for over a million years (Montgomery 2003:24). The different species have overlapping ranges; pink and chum salmon can spawn in small streams near stream-mouths, sockeye require lakes (or lake inlets) to spawn, coho are found in small tributaries, and chinook occur in major rivers and tributaries. Although spawning salmon are famous for returning to their natal streams, a small percentage go astray, and these are the ones to colonize newly available habitats. Within 100 years of deglaciation, sockeye, pink, and chum salmon established themselves in streams emptying into Glacier Bay (Montgomery 2003:32–33). Salmon bones have been found in Late Pleistocene and Early Holocene paleontological and archaeological localities across the Northwest Coast (Moss et al. 2007:511–512). Certainly, the distribution of salmon species and their abundances have been affected by changing sea levels, the evolution of estuaries, and changing stream gradients, yet before the advent of industrial fishing, salmon were highly resilient to changing Northwest Coast environments.

Of the Mid-Holocene sites reviewed thus far, most illustrate use of a range of resources. Namu is the only site with direct evidence for long-term reliance on salmon, and this began prior to the 5700 cal B.P. threshold. At Namu, pink salmon abundance fluctuated over a 3,000-year period, during which people adjusted with multiple strategies. Fladmark thought salmon abundance was a result of Mid-Holocene sea-level stabilization and saw these as prerequisites for sedentism and the development of large shell middens. Salmon were a critically important resource, but many different fish species were used across the region (Moss and Cannon 2011).

The link between shell accumulations and sedentism was also considered characteristic of Mid-Holocene culture change. Shell-bearing sites are known from the Early Holocene. Namu, Cohoe Creek, Bear Cove, Saltery Bay, and Tahkenitch, all have "pre-shell" strata, in which shell occurs sporadically, at low density, or in thin lenses. The transition from these "shell-free" deposits to those that are "shell-rich" has attracted attention; Hebda and Frederick (1990:332) described the change as "abrupt," when "vast quantities of shellfish remains are deposited in massive shell middens." Dense shell deposits initially occurred at Namu at 5500 cal B.P., supporting Fladmark's threshold. The oldest substantial shell deposits at Cohoe Creek are a bit older (5950–5750 cal B.P.), but shellfish remains are found as traces, in pockets, in lenses, and in low mounds—suggesting spatial and temporal variation in the deposition of shell. At Bear Cove, the oldest shell-rich component dates to 4900 cal B.P., at Tahkenitch to 3400 cal B.P., and at Saltery Bay to 500 cal B.P.

Beyond sites described here, the main midden at Pender Island has been dated to 5150 cal B.P. (Carlson and Hobler 1993), but the Pender dates are on human bone that may not have been calibrated as marine or mixed samples, making these ages older than they should be. Despite this uncertainty, Pender is another case where sea-level history must be evaluated as a factor in site formation. As Carlson and Hobler (1993:30, 36) explained,

Sea level was much lower 9,000 years ago and rose 12.2 m between 8,000 and 2,250 years ago. The result is that any shoreline occupation earlier than 2,250 years ago would have been eroded by wave action during sea level rise, and inundated.... the pre–2250 B.P. midden deposits on Pender, and at other sites around the southern end of the Strait of Georgia are merely remnants of much more extensive settlements, and that those site features that remain from this period are only representative of those activities that took place at higher elevations.

The Glenrose and St. Mungo sites are today located along the Fraser River about 20 km up from the river mouth. At the time Glenrose was first occupied, today's massive Fraser Delta to the west of both sites had not yet developed. Glenrose was first occupied when sea level was at its lowest point relative today, about 8000 RYBP. A few lenses of mussel shell occurred during the 8000–5000 RYBP period at Glenrose. Sea level rose until about 5000 RYBP, and St. Mungo components were found at both sites. At St. Mungo (5100–4500 cal B.P.; 4480–4050 RYBP), located just a few kilometers downstream from Glenrose, massive shell deposits did not develop, with mussel shell (and that of other shellfish) making up only 8 percent of the matrix by weight (Ham et al. 1986:120). In contrast, the St. Mungo component at Glenrose (4800–3500 cal B.P.; 4240–3280 RYBP; Pratt 1992:16–17) contained large quantities of mussel shell. The original analyst considered mussels at least as important a food source as elk (Pratt 1992:47). At the Crescent Beach site south of the Fraser River mouth, some portions of the St. Mungo component were rich in mussel shell, whereas others were not. The variation in the nature of shell deposits at these sites occupied during the same time period is striking, and once again, argues against region-wide trends.

The earliest sites in Prince Rupert Harbor and on the west coast of Vancouver Island date from the Middle Holocene. In Prince Rupert Harbor, Kitandach, Lachane, and Boardwalk have initial dates between 5900 and 5500 cal B.P. Ames (2005:24) noted that some sites in the harbor have deposits as much as a meter below modern sea levels, suggesting occupation between 8500 and 5800 cal B.P. The massive shell deposits in Prince Rupert Harbor all postdate 3200 cal B.P. The oldest sites on west Vancouver Island all postdate ca. 5400 cal B.P., including Yuquot, Ch'uumat'a, Ts'ishaa, and Little Beach. On the West Coast, chipped stone microblades and bifaces have been found on raised terraces and other undated materials have been found in the intertidal zone, leading McMillan (1999:106–112) to reasonably suggest that changing sea levels have removed, destroyed, or "rendered inaccessible" substantial portions of the archaeological record. The massive shell midden at Yuquot is dated to 3200 cal B.P. (3020 RYBP; Dewhirst 1980) and that at Ts'ishaa to 4300 cal B.P. (McMillan and St. Claire 2005:77). Even though their sea-level histories differ, changing sea levels best account for the lack of Early Holocene sites identified in the west Vancouver Island and Prince Rupert records. People probably lived here, but the archaeological record of their occupations has been lost offshore or is covered in heavy vegetation some distance from modern shorelines. Like other sites on the Northwest Coast, initial deposits in these areas contain shell in low density, with more shell-rich deposits in later occupations.

The oldest shell middens and shell-bearing deposits in an area do not signal the earliest times when shellfish beds were established there. Instead, these sites provide clues as to where the shoreline was positioned at the time the sites were occupied. On the Northwest Coast, people disposed of shell in patterned ways—often in the intertidal zone or just above the high tide line. They deposited shell just shoreward of a living site tucked into the sheltering trees in what today's residents sometimes call the "beach fringe." Shell was tossed off seacliffs or outside the entrance of a rockshelter or cave to form a talus slope. Shell was deposited in berms around houses, perhaps to improve drainage or provide insulation in the wet climate. Northwest Coast residents apparently did not transport shell long distances to dispose of it.

The absence of shell in an archaeological component can be due to a number of factors. Site residents may not have consumed shellfish, and focused their efforts on other foods. When sea levels were lower than modern, most culturally deposited shell would be dispersed and reworked into beach sediments making it hard to identify as cultural. This may be the case for the earliest components at Namu, Bear Cove, and Pender Island; upland areas of the occupation site were preserved, but the places where most shell was deposited may be gone. Low volumes of shell may not preserve well in the acidic forest soils of the Northwest Coast. Some prerequisite volume of shell might need to accumulate before it can counteract soil acidity, improving the environment for subsequently deposited shell. The amount of shell deposited in a single episode and whether or not it is trampled by a few or many people will help determine the fragmentation of its constituent taxa and the likelihood it will be recovered archaeologically. Certain taxa have robust shells such as estuarine clams, whereas others such as blue mussel are thin-shelled. Shell can also be removed from a site post-depositionally as at British Camp, where Stein (1992) determined that with sea-level rise, groundwater inundated the lower strata of the site, leaching out the shell. The rise of sea level a mere one meter over the last 500–1500 years was enough to weather out much of the shell from the lower stratum of the site (Stein 1992:149).

Although the idea that shell-bearing sites provide information on the position of the shoreline when a site was occupied may seem self-evident, the tendency on the Northwest Coast has been to think about shell midden accumulation in cultural evolutionary terms. Development of shell middens has been interpreted as meaning that people: (1) figured out that shellfish were reliable foods, (2) were forced to use shellfish to avoid starvation, (3) relied on shellfish to support growing populations, (4) built up large shell deposits when they became sedentary, or (5) depended on shellfish during the winter when other resources were scarce or hard to procure. Another idea is that shell was accumulated, not as refuse, but as a building material. Site engineering with shell on the Northwest Coast was proposed by Blukis Onat (1985). At St. Mungo, crushed mussel shell was mined from middens and used as flooring material (Ham et al. 1986:95). At Cape Addington, people used shell to fill in the uneven surface of bedrock and expand their living space within the rockshelter (Moss 2004a:63). Shell midden material may have been used to create dikes to protect wetlands (Grier et al. 2009:274). Site engineering helped solve practical problems, some related to changing sea levels.

The Culture Historical Record: Do Artifacts and Technologies Change during the Mid-Holocene?

The Mid-Holocene is when Fladmark's (1982) Lithic stage changes to the Developmental stage, and when Ames and Maschner's (1999) Archaic transforms to the Pacific period. At the beginning of the Middle Holocene, Matson and Coupland (1995) see the "emergence of distinctive coastal cultures" and by its end, the "development of cultural complexity." In an earlier review, we found only 38 archaeological components dated between 6850 and 5000 cal B.P. (6000 and 4400 RYBP) over the approximately 1,500 mile (2,400 km) length of the Northwest Coast (from Yakutat Bay to the

California border; Moss et al. 2007). Like that of earlier time periods, the Northwest Coast archaeological record of the Middle Holocene is fairly sparse. Of the 38 components, 11 contained lithic artifacts only and 20 had shell midden components. Three sites (two wet sites and one sea cave) contained wood or basketry remains. Four sites did not fall unambiguously in one of these categories. Nine sites included evidence of microblade technologies, but these technologies persist into the Late Holocene (Moss 2004b). Other lithic sites contained cobble tools, bifaces, and other attributes of Carlson's (1996b) Pebble Tool tradition ("Old Cordilleran" following Matson and Coupland 1995). The lithic assemblages in both types of sites demonstrate cultural continuity with the Early Holocene. Of the shell-bearing sites, the amounts of shell vary. We argued that the range of shellfish use did not appear to represent a "sea change" in economic adaptation. At sites in Prince Rupert Harbor and at Glenrose, the Mid-Holocene shell deposits contained mostly mussels, while subsequent components at these sites contained proportionately more clams. We suggested this had more to do with the evolution of local estuaries than region-wide culture change (Moss et al. 2007:513). Change was not evident until 4900 cal B.P., when the number and size of sites across the Northwest Coast increased. This was a tentative conclusion because we did not analyze all sites and their contents that postdated this revised threshold.

C. Ames (2009) has systematically compiled information on assemblage composition of all well-dated cultural components in the Gulf of Georgia. Because the Gulf of Georgia sequence is the best known of the entire Northwest Coast, it has been the baseline for comparisons with sequences from other subregions. The Lithic to Developmental stage change is usually understood in culture-historical terms as a transition from assemblages made up almost exclusively of chipped stone to those comprised of ground stone and bone and antler tools (which Ames terms "faunal tools"). Looking at these three categories, Ames evaluated 75 archaeological assemblages and found that chipped stone technologies did not disappear during the Mid-Holocene even as ground stone and faunal tools became more abundant after ~4500 cal B.P. The highest proportions of ground stone and faunal tools occur in assemblages dated to 3000–2500 cal B.P., but after then, assemblage variability increases with all three categories of tool types occurring in low and high proportions (Ames et al. 2010). Assemblage composition in the Gulf of Georgia represents both environmental and functional variability. Ames found that the first ground stone artifact type added to Gulf of Georgia assemblages is the stone bead. Ames et al. (2010:19) wrote,

> The first substantial investment in laborious ground stone production was for beads and their appearance is relatively sudden. Subsistence and resource-based uses of ground stone gradually increased thereafter. Perhaps beads were the mechanism through which ground stone technology entered the technological tool kits of prehistoric populations in the Gulf of Georgia, after which the technology was harnessed for other purposes related to resource extraction.

When beads are removed from the quantitative analyses, the addition of ground stone is fairly gradual after appearing ca. 4500 cal B.P. in low proportions. Ames et al. also suggested that the addition of substantial numbers of faunal tools was because shell middens enhanced preservation. They suggested that archaeologists should reframe the Middle Holocene transition as the incorporation of ground stone into the existing chipped stone technological system. They dated the transition between 5000 and 4500 cal B.P., consistent with Moss et al. (2007).

By comparing proportions of chipped stone, ground stone, and faunal tools, Ames was working with closed arrays so that an increase in one category is necessarily accompanied by a decrease in one and/or the other category. Another problem is that these three categories of tools are not unrelated functionally—chipped stone tools were used to rough out bone tools or to pierce the holes for shell or ground stone beads. Ground stone tools were used to shape, abrade, and polish bone tools. Some varieties of ground slate tools were made by chipping (with chipped stone) and grinding. So these technologies are not separate and distinct. Yet Ames's findings are important because they help dislodge other assumptions about the meaning of Mid-Holocene transitions. Chipped stone wasn't entirely replaced by ground stone and/or bone tools. Cultural developments were more cumulative, and assemblage variability was greater than previously recognized. How the functions and manufacture of chipped stone tools changed over time requires more study. What the Mid-Holocene artifactual record from the Gulf of Georgia demonstrates is cultural continuity with the Early Holocene as well as technological innovation. The timing and character of such changes elsewhere on the coast has yet to be documented.

Wood and Fiber Technologies: The Largest of Data Gaps

Wood and fiber artifacts are perishable remains not often preserved in Northwest Coast sites. In the Great Basin and Southwest, such artifacts are commonly found in dry caves and rockshelters. In my experience, no cave or rockshelter in the Northwest is as dry as those of the interior west! Even though the preservation of faunal and paleobotanical remains from Cape Addington Rockshelter was very good relative to Northwest Coast settings, pre-contact perishable artifacts were not found (Moss 2004a) in this Late Holocene site. On the Northwest Coast, perishable remains are found in water-saturated contexts such as the intertidal zone. Understandably, for the Early and Middle Holocene, artifacts of wood and fiber have not figured into definitions of culture historical units because they are missing from most assemblages. The most famous wet sites—Ozette, Hoko River, Kwatna, and Qʷuʔgʷes—all date to the Late Holocene.

Kilgii Gwaay (Chapter 4) is the oldest wet site on the Northwest Coast (10,700–10,600 cal B.P.; Fedje et al. 2005b). In this remote location, braided spruce root cordage, wooden wedges, wrapped sticks, a composite haft, wood points, withes, and wood debitage were found, all of which would fit comfortably into material culture inventories of the nineteenth century. Kilgii shows that technologies made of perishables have been important to Northwest Coast peoples for more than 10,000 years. The artifacts show cultural continuity, even though modern forests had not yet developed.

The number of wood and fiber artifacts from the Middle Holocene is few. In southeast Alaska, a large fragmentary basket was found in the mud-flats of the Thorne River estuary on Prince of Wales Island. This Silverhole basket is a twined, cylindrical, spruce root basket, dated to 6200 cal B.P. Croes (1997:601) described it as similar to Tlingit and Haida baskets, except that the lean of the twine is up-to-the-right, whereas Tlingit/Haida baskets typically have up-to-the-left twining. Lean of twine is a subtle difference, but most basketry specialists consider it culturally prescribed, and this attribute has been used as an ethnic marker. Two other Middle Holocene baskets (5200–5000 cal B.P.) have been recovered from the Lanaak site on Baranof Island in Alaska. Bernick (1999:32) described these as "highly sophisticated artistic constructions that are stylistically like 19th century Tlingit manufactures." She documented four different types of twining, with the lean of the twine in both directions, raising the question whether or not the lean of twine is ethnically informative. Bernick also identified semi-rigid knotted netting as part of a dip net. A small sample of associated faunal remains was dominated by salmon. The remnants of a wood stake weir dated to the Late Holocene were driven into these older deposits. From the Wolf's Lair site in the outer Prince of Wales Archipelago, an unusual L-shaped implement of yellow cedar has been dated to 5000 cal B.P. (Moss and Erlandson 2000). The working end of the club is studded with the pointed spines of rockfish; it may have been used to club fish or process bark or other vegetal material.

As discussed earlier, the culturally important redcedar spread during the Middle Holocene from the southern Northwest Coast to Alaska. As redcedar became locally available, it was probably incorporated into the material cultures of the region in a south-to-north time transgressive pattern. In the absence of perishable artifacts, however, such evidence is lacking. Hebda and Mathewes (1984) suggested an increase in wood-working tools such as wedges, stone adzes, axes, and mauls might signal the use of redcedar, although a systematic review of such tools and their ages has not been conducted. Early Holocene wood-working tools are known from Kilgii Gwaay and Glenrose, although antler and bone wedges, celts, and mauls seem to increase in the Late Holocene (Mackie 1995:6–7).

By far, the most abundant wood artifacts on the Northwest Coast are found in the region's intertidal wood stake fishing weirs and traps. Over 1,200 sites have been found, but fewer than 200 have been dated. The oldest wood stake weirs and traps date to the latter part of the Middle Holocene. The ages of some of the oldest weirs/traps show continuing use during the Late Holocene: 49-PET–456 on Mitkof Island in Alaska (5650–1250 cal B.P.), Straight Creek (4350–2000 cal B.P.), and Thorne River (4100–1950 cal B.P.) on Prince of Wales Island (Moss and Erlandson 1998a; Smith 2006). Isostatic rebound in southeast Alaska has led to finding the oldest weir stakes highest in the intertidal zone, suggesting that weir builders shifted the placement of stakes as the sea receded (Moss and Erlandson 1998a:190–191). In areas controlled by subsidence (Cascadia Subduction Zone) older weirs may be found in deep channels currently unavailable to archaeologists surveying during low tides (Schalk and Burtchard 2001:41). The labor involved in yearly maintenance would differ based on an array of seasonal variables, but longer term shoreline changes would also affect how weirs and traps were engineered.

In 1998, we wrote that the antiquity of weir/trap fishing in Alaska and B.C. was consistent with Fladmark's paleoecological model of Northwest Coast prehistory (Moss and Erlandson 1998a:183), but I am less sure of this now. From Oregon, more than 70 weir/traps have been dated, but none are older than 3500 cal B.P. (Byram 2002). In 1998, we believed that earthquake-related subsidence and industrial practices in Oregon helped explain the more recent age of weirs and traps on the southern Northwest Coast. But what does the distribution of dated weirs and traps mean?

In some places, mass harvest of salmon (or other fish) began during the Mid-Holocene. The implications of this for labor organization, production of food surplus, distribution of surplus, population expansion, and trade are potentially far-reaching. But the archaeological record of weirs and traps is a product of coastal processes such as sea-level change, erosion, and deposition. These processes have combined to make the record of weir and trap fishing dated to the Middle and Late Holocene accessible to archaeologists. But weirs and traps are technologies known from around the world, and the oldest date to the late Pleistocene (Connaway 2007). Older weirs and traps on the coast have probably been destroyed, buried, and/or are now inaccessible. It does not seem coincidental that the multi-component sites dating back to the Early Holocene at Namu and Glenrose are spatially associated with weirs and traps. The Namu weir is made of stone and has not been dated, whereas the Glenrose weir/trap is one of the oldest on the Northwest Coast.

Despite their extensive areal distribution, not much has been done to document regional variation in weir and trap types. More detailed analyses (Byram 1998, 2002; Greene 2010; Langdon 2006; Mobley and McCallum 2001; Stevenson 1998) are crucial, but weir and trap technologies could be used to assess culture patterns at a larger scale. Wood and fiber technologies have not been incorporated into culture histories of the Middle Holocene, but the large number of weirs and traps in the region make such analyses possible. If wood stakes were also identified to species, this might shed light on the chronology of redcedar expansion.

Conclusion

There is little archaeological evidence for dramatic cultural change on the Northwest Coast at 5700 cal B.P. (5000 RYBP). The stone tool technologies present in the Early Holocene persist into the Middle Holocene. Mid-

Holocene shell-bearing sites demonstrate significant diversity in their size, shell density, and internal structure, and faunal inventories do not show region-wide trends. Subsistence change can be examined at Namu and Glenrose, but what we see at these sites is considerable continuity (see also Cannon 2003). The number of sites increases after 4850 cal B.P. (4300 RYBP), when ground stone and bone and antler technologies are better represented in the Gulf of Georgia (Ames 2009). Few technologies drop out of the record entirely. The representation of technologies that use organic materials (bone, antler, shell, wood, fiber) is related to sea-level change and preservation, even if we cannot yet quantify these effects.

By stressing cultural continuity, I do not mean to paint a portrait of cultural stasis. The Mid-Holocene period was not a time of environmental stabilization, but one of ongoing dynamism to which people made various adjustments. Sea levels rose and fell at different rates in different places, affecting where people built their dwellings and deposited their refuse. Human activities also affected shoreline features, for example through the construction of fishing weirs and traps that might have caused changes in sediment accumulation and drainage patterns. Salmon did not reach "peak productivity" simultaneously across the coast; each species was variously affected by the evolution of estuaries, changes in stream gradients, and fluctuations in climate and currents. Again, human activities may have affected patterns of salmon abundance and distribution in ways we do not yet appreciate. Namu helps show how people coped with fluctuations in pink salmon abundance; cycles of abundance in salmon and other resources required great flexibility on the part of the indigenous peoples of the Northwest Coast. Large shell middens did not appear simultaneously; the formation of shell-bearing sites always depends on local sea-level histories and may tell us more about coastal processes than culture change or sedentism. Dramatic region-wide culture change at 5000 RYBP has been the prevailing model for archaeological thinking about the Middle Holocene. It has been used to construct a narrative of Northwest Coast pre-contact history that views the Middle Holocene as a time of emerging cultural complexity, whether at 7,000 or 5,000 or 3,000 years ago. More research is necessary to understand the complexity of the Mid-Holocene archaeological record itself.

Notes

1. The pollen of yellow cedar (*Chamaecyparis nootkatensis*) and western redcedar (*Thuja plicata*) is difficult to distinguish, and the two species have different habitat requirements (Hennon et al. 2006). The abundance and distribution of the cedars at various times on the Northwest Coast remains uncertain.

2. Rockfish is also the most abundant vertebrate from the 7750–7100 cal B.P. component at Far West Point on the Dundas Islands (McLaren 2008).

3. The Saltery Bay radiocarbon dates derive from mammal bones; the oldest was identified as porpoise, but none of the other samples could be identified (Pegg 2009, pers. comm.). The calibrations performed by Beta-Analytic assumed these were terrestrial, consistent with the carbon isotope ratios (Pegg et al. 2007: Appendix II). The porpoise bone date (or others on marine mammal bones) are probably too old, since they have not been calibrated as marine samples.

6

The Late Holocene Mosaic

Across the Northwest Coast, the archaeological record of the last 3,500 years is more ample than that of earlier times. Sites are more numerous, with many that are larger and better preserved than older sites. Late Holocene sites are also more visible—especially shell middens where light-colored shell can be conspicuous in disturbed, dark forest soils. With more recent sites, modern environmental conditions are useful points of comparison. The relative increase in the number and size of sites leads archaeologists to invoke human population growth to explain this pattern. Growing populations are thought to have built larger settlements, vied for land, expanded their territories, over-exploited resources, established social hierarchies, accumulated wealth, intensified trade and exchange, and resorted to violence in competition for resources, land, and power. This is the overarching narrative of increasing cultural complexity on the Northwest Coast.

The narrative of developing cultural complexity is consistent with aspects of the archaeological record, but we know some of the increase in the number and size of sites is due to greater visibility and accessibility of sites located on recent shorelines. Paradoxically, the Late Holocene period is when ethnographic records are both most relevant and most hazardous to use. Archaeologists (including me) use ethnographic data to fill the gaps created by fragmentary archaeological data. Where archaeological data are ambiguous is precisely where we tend to use ethnographic data to support interpretations. Such interpretations rarely consider how post-contact histories have shaped the ethnographies on which we rely. Although Northwest Coast ethnographic data exhibit cultural complexity, its relative "absence" archaeologically may be a function of preservation and visibility, and complexity has been variously defined (or left undefined).

What is the alternative to tracing the development of cultural complexity? Paraphrasing Pauketat (2007:185), one could look for mutual, negotiated historical processes. But what might this mean on the Northwest Coast? No single alternative theoretical perspective can provide a master narrative that encompasses all of the Northwest Coast archaeological record. Such a quest is quixotic because the diversity in the record results from too many cultural and noncultural factors. At this stage in the history of Northwest Coast archaeology, the assumptions I can accept are:

- Late Pleistocene and Early Holocene populations were initially small;
- travel on the Northwest Coast was primarily by boat;
- population growth accelerated if/when/where people became more sedentary;
- as the number and/or sizes of groups expanded, some territories became circumscribed;
- with population growth, people could intensify resource use, increase storage capacity, fill open niches on the landscape, and/or cooperate or compete with others.

These assumptions are listed in sequence, but are not to be viewed as evolutionary steps. Any number of factors could affect or interrupt cycles of growth and expansion. Diseases spread, resources failed, habitats shifted, and groups fissioned. We cannot assume that people always depleted resources, exploited each other, aggrandized wealth and prestige, or established social hierarchies. These may have happened, but we should not project them region-wide in the absence of evidence. Principles of autonomy, communal decision-making, cooperation, decentralization, and communalism were also at work in most Northwest Coast societies (Coupland et al. 2009), leading to heterarchical forms of social organization (Angelbeck 2009), and heterarchical and hierarchical structural forms are not mutually exclusive. Cycles of interaction within subregions and across the larger region fluctuated. Many trajectories intersected with each other and webs of social relationships connected people in different places at different times, creating a mosaic with patterns that shift when illuminated by different questions. In this chapter, I explore some directions that lie outside the narrative of developing cultural complexity. Even though we still don't adequately control variability in Northwest Coast material culture over time and space, recent analyses help us reevaluate what we think we know.

Late Holocene Material Culture

Late Holocene material culture is expected to be "richer" than that of earlier periods as measured by increased taxonomic richness (more classes of artifacts) and more artifact types per class. The "development of art" on the Northwest Coast (most commonly indexed by decorated artifacts) is expected to increase over time with cultural complexity. Ames and Maschner (1999) believe that decorated artifacts were made by specialists, and that part- to full-time craft specialization reflects the evolving status system on the Northwest Coast. Such arguments for cultural complexity focus on numerically minor subsets of material culture: valuable items buried with people, including those made of exotic materials, decorated weapons or tools, or jewelry and ornaments. But humans have been decorating items of material culture and making and wearing jewelry since the Paleolithic.

The bulk of the Late Holocene archaeological record is comprised of undecorated utilitarian chipped stone, ground stone, and bone. This section outlines some culture-historical trends as a foundation for comparisons across the region with the benefit of recent technological and functional studies that complicate our understanding of these trends. Study of Ozette has shown that for pre-contact societies, botanical materials were the primary raw material made into artifacts. Extrapolating from Ozette, typical Northwest Coast sites may contain only 15 percent of the tools and artifacts made and used by site residents (Croes 2003:51; Samuels and Daugherty 1991:4). In the Early Holocene Kilgii Gwaay wet site assemblage, bone and wood artifacts outnumbered lithic artifacts (if flakes are excluded) indicating that conditions of preservation strongly structure the composition of artifact assemblages. Artifact densities tend to be low in Northwest Coast sites, especially in shell middens. This low artifact density is a result of poor preservation and the lack of perishables. Based on artifact densities in typical Northwest Coast sites, Lyman (1991:313) argued that 100 m^3 should be excavated per thousand radiocarbon years of a deposit to produce artifact and faunal assemblages of sufficient size to compare across the region. Even though few Northwest Coast excavations have approached this scale, the Gulf of Georgia region is the most intensively studied on the Northwest Coast.

Gulf of Georgia Artifacts

The term "Gulf of Georgia" is used here in an expansive sense to include the Fraser River watershed that drains into the Gulf of Georgia, the lower mainland, the islands in the gulf, and the adjacent eastern and southeastern shores of Vancouver Island (Figure 6.1).[1] The most famous phases of the region are the Charles/St. Mungo/Mayne, Locarno Beach, and Marpole[2] (Borden 1970; Mitchell 1971, 1990), followed by the more poorly known Gulf of Georgia phase. To achieve chronological control, early archaeologists focused on diagnostic artifacts thought to be time markers. Later, assemblage composition was systematically analyzed (e.g., Burley 1980; Pratt 1992; Thom 1992). Locarno ranges in age from 3500 to 2400 RYBP, while Marpole dates between 2400 RYBP and 1500-1100 RYBP (Matson and Coupland 1995; 154, 203). Table 6.1 presents some commonly used distinctions between these phases (Matson and Coupland 1995; Mitchell 1990). Locarno Beach components have clay-lined depressions, rock slab features, and midden burials. Marpole components have large postmolds and house outlines, midden and cairn burials, and head-shaping. Since these are not artifact differences per se, I've excluded them from this discussion. In the mid-1990s, Locarno Beach was known from 29 components and Marpole from 40 components in the Gulf of Georgia. The most diagnostic artifacts of Locarno Beach are thought to be microliths, labrets, faceted ground slate points, and the Gulf Island Complex (Figure 6.2), while the most diagnostic Marpole artifacts are leaf-shaped and triangular slate points, nipple-topped hand mauls, stone sculpture, and stone and shell beads (Figure 6.3).

Even though stone beads are diagnostic of Marpole, at 4500 cal B.P., "ground stone disc beads appear in considerable quantities suggesting they are the first formidable investment in ground stone technology" (Ames 2009:40–41). At Pitt River, 84 siltstone disc beads were attributed to the Charles phase (Patenaude 1985 vol. 2:147), with a date of 4390 ± 110 RYBP (Patenaude 1985 vol. 1:259). At Crescent Beach, 496 stone beads were found in the Charles/St. Mungo component, dating ca. 4000–3700 RYBP (Matson et al. 1991:126–128). Pitt River occurs upriver, while Crescent Beach is on the coast. Because of the labor involved, beads should be found in sites occupied during multiple seasons for some duration of time or with burials. Eighty-nine sets of human remains have been excavated at Crescent Beach, but their ages are not fully known. The beads at these two

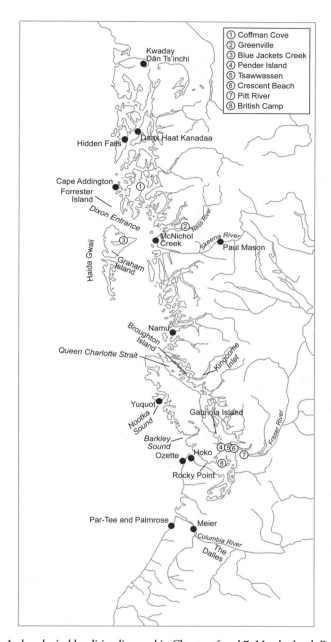

Figure 6.1. Archaeological localities discussed in Chapters 6 and 7. Map by Jacob Bartruff.

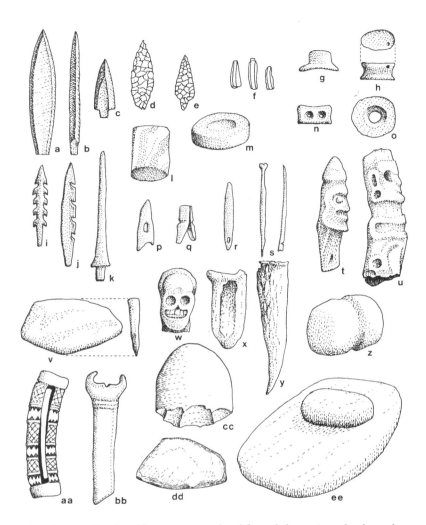

Figure 6.2. Locarno Beach artifacts, a-c, ground and faceted slate points; d-e, lanceolate and shouldered flaked stone points; f, microblades; g-h, labrets; i-k, bilaterally barbed antler point, unilaterally barbed bone point and antler composite harpoon shaft; l, stone celt; m and o, perforated stone disks; n, polished stone of Gulf Island complex; p-q, one-piece toggling harpoon head and paired composite toggling valves; r, bird bone awl; s, eyed and notched bone needles; t, carved anthropomorphic antler tine hook for atlatl; u, carved antler figurine; v, ground slate knife; w, human skull effigy carved on deer metapodial; x, bone wedge or chisel; y, antler wedge; z, grooved cobble sinker; aa, slotted antler dentalia purse; bb, bone knife with whale tail motif; cc, cobble chopper; dd flaked stone knife; ee, handstone and grinding slab; adapted from Mitchell (1990) and not drawn to scale. From *Northwest Coast,* Handbook of North American Indians, used with permission from Donald H. Mitchell and the Smithsonian Institution.

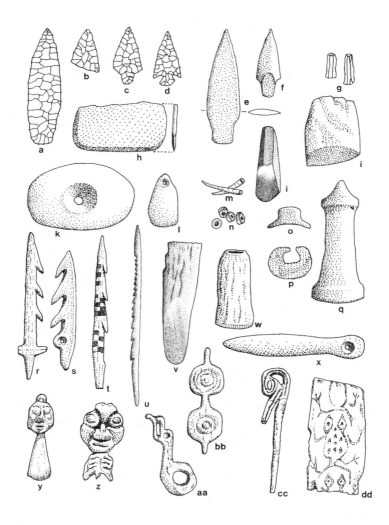

Figure 6.3. Marpole artifacts, a-d, chipped stone points; e-f, ground slate points; g, microblades; h, ground slate knife; i, ground stone chisel; j, ground stone celt; k-l, perforated stones; m, dentalia; n, disk beads; o, labret; p, crescentic copper object; q, nipple-topped stone maul; r-u, unilaterally barbed antler harpoon head, unilaterally barbed antler harpoon head with line hole, and unilaterally barbed antler points; v, antler wedge; w, antler adze haft; x, stone club; y, z, and bb, carved antler; aa, antler cord adjuster carved in bird form; cc, antler pin carved in bird form; dd, incised stone object; adapted from Mitchell (1990) and not drawn to scale. From *Northwest Coast*, Handbook of North American Indians, used with permission from Donald H. Mitchell and the Smithsonian Institution.

Table 6.1. Differences between Locarno Beach and Marpole Artifacts in the Gulf of Georgia

Locarno Beach	Marpole
medium, flaked basalt projectile points	more point forms; stemmed, unstemmed, small, triangular, barbed
microblades, microcores (quartz, obsidian)	in earliest subphase (Old Musqueum), not later
flaked slate, sandstone ovoids	not present
large faceted ground slate points	more forms, leaf-shaped, small triangular ground slate points
rectangular ground stone celts	more ground stone celt forms
ground stone & coal labrets	labrets in Old Musqueum, not later
Gulf Island Complex—ornaments, sliders, etc.*	not present
grooved, notched netsinkers	different sized perforated stones
handstones, grinding slabs	rare, but present
unilaterally & bilaterally barbed harpoon points	present
toggling harpoons	very rare
	nipple-topped hand mauls, shell & clam disc beads, stone sculpture bowls, copper & dentalia ornaments; more incised siltstone & decorated bone

*Keddie (2007) described items previously termed "Gulf Island Complex" as parts of composite labrets. These include ground stone items with drilled holes around which a cord could be attached to anchor the ornament to the teeth.

sites suggest possible year-round occupation or sedentism. Although such beads were wealth items found only in a few sites, beads are also easily lost in the absence of fine-mesh screening. The point is that even though beads are diagnostic of Marpole, they are found in deposits 2,000 years older.

In his study of 75 assemblages, Ames (2009) showed that the presumed shift from chipped stone to ground stone/bone tool assemblages is an over-simplification.[3] Ground stone and faunal tools did not replace chipped stone, and assemblage variability was found across the transitions between phases. Even though Ames (2009) considered assemblage composition in gross units, he found a marked increase in the proportion of assemblages with relatively numerous bone tools in Marpole compared to Locarno. This trend was intensified in the later Gulf of Georgia phase. Rahemtulla (2003) noted the economic importance of elk and deer, not just as food, but as sources of bone and antler used to make tools. Rahemtulla (2003:64) claimed that coastal dwellers hunted deer and elk primarily to satisfy their needs for raw materials. Some strong and dense deer bones are well-suited for points, awls, and knives; antler makes good wedges, adzes, and tool hafts.

Yet the reduction of bone and antler into tools is rarely studied on the Northwest Coast, and bone debitage is usually relegated to the category of "faunal remains" and not analyzed technologically. If sources of chipped or ground stone were limited on the landscape, it may have been easier for people to use food animal bones as raw materials rather than stone. The fact that Ames (2009) found some assemblages dominated by chipped or ground stone during the Gulf of Georgia phase may reflect uneven distribution of suitable lithic sources.

Labrets are considered diagnostic of Locarno, persist into the oldest subphase of Marpole (Old Musqueum), then drop out of the record after 2000 RYBP. Older labrets were found at Pender Canal and Helen Point. Labret wear (recognized by dental abrasion and/or tooth loss) was identified on Charles phase human remains at Pender Canal and Tsawwassen (Pratt 1992:293). The oldest labret wear from Pender is dated to over 5000 RYBP (Cybulski 1991:7), 500 years older than the age of the oldest known labret. At the other end of their temporal range, labrets occur within the last 1,500 years at Pitt River (Patenaude 1985 vol. 2:147), contradicting Keddie (1981, 2007) who stated that labrets fell out of use at the end of Old Musqueum. Remarkably, LaSalle (2008: Appendix G) found radiocarbon dates associated with only 8 of the 160 labrets she studied from the Gulf of Georgia region. This raises questions about using labrets as time markers here, especially where phase recognition rests on the presence of labrets (LaSalle 2008:18–19, 36).

Crescent Beach and two Pender Canal sites account for 55 of 160 labrets (LaSalle 2008:18). The Pender sites are shell middens used as cemeteries, and individuals were also buried at Crescent Beach. LaSalle (2008:29) could only identify five labrets in direct association with burials: two females, two males, and one person of unknown sex. From the burial populations at Pender Canal (n = 22) and Crescent Beach (n = 35), one male and one female had labret wear at the former site, and eight males and five females at the latter (Cybulski 1991:11). LaSalle (2008) identified seven of 10 types of labrets in the Gulf of Georgia, but the scarcity of contextual information precludes recognition of any relationship between labret type, material, size, or time period. Most scholars have interpreted labrets as status symbols, but LaSalle (2008:38–39) considered status itself as relational and situational. The meaning of elite status might be accepted in one context but contested in another. Labrets in the Gulf of Georgia show some regularity in size, but are diverse in forms and materials; as individualized ornaments, they indicated both social exclusivity and local group identities according to LaSalle.[5]

Ground stone celts are woodworking tools that encompass items used as adzes or chisels. Rectangular celts occur in Locarno Beach components, but a greater range of sizes and types characterize Marpole. In Q. Mackie's (1995) study of 1,496 celts from the Gulf of Georgia, he could not identify discrete morphological types, despite rigorous descriptive typology and cluster analysis. Instead, Mackie showed that because most celts were made of rare nephrite and serpentine,[6] were labor-intensive to make and used until exhausted, there was a "steady convergence of form to a generic, stubby, worn-out celt" (Mackie 1995:71). The main nephrite sources occur along the Fraser River, from about Hope (~150 km from the coast) upriver for another 200 km. Mackie showed how repeated resharpening changed the size and shape of the celt, with more economy of use further from the source; island groups conserved material more than those living along the Fraser delta who in turn were more conservative than upriver groups. Like LaSalle (2008), Mackie (1995:74) was unable to identify temporal change because most celts could not be assigned an age. This reinforces the idea that Gulf of Georgia culture historical units are best conceived as hypotheses to be tested.

Celts require valuable raw material, strategic flaking or sawing to create a preform, laborious grinding, and careful shaping and sharpening (Mackie 1995:39). Celts entail considerable investment in contrast to expedient pebble or cobble tools also used to work wood (Mackie 1995:44). Celts had long use-lives and were heavily curated. Like celts, tools that change gradually without breakage making them unusable include: ground slate knives, chipped stone knives, bone and antler wedges, bone and shell celts, and bone needles and pins (Mackie 1995:75). Other tools break episodically and become unusable, so their use history does not change form, including hand mauls, bone points and harpoon heads, harpoon valves and foreshafts, stone points, ground stone fishhook shanks, anchor and net weights, and ornaments (Mackie 1995:75). Mackie's study advances understanding of Gulf of Georgia culture history, but also of how to approach artifact variability across the larger region.

The history of slate grinding on the Northwest Coast remains elusive. Ground slate knives and points from Kodiak Island in south-central Alaska occur about the same time as they appear along the lower Fraser. Slate is a fine-grained, metamorphic rock with parallel cleavage that fractures along bedding planes, not conchoidally (Banahan 2000:2, 4). Ground stone knives, blades, points, harpoon heads, and whetstones can also be made on schist, phyllite, basalt, rhyolite, and andesite, and sometimes these are lumped together with ground "slate" because the end-products look similar. "Slate" is fairly widespread as a raw material across much of the Northwest Coast, but this category encompasses variability. Materials that *are* mineralogically slate can occur in forms ranging from beach cobbles to foliating sheets in outcrops (Graesch 2007:585). Harder slates are more difficult to work but retain their edges longer than easier-to-work softer slates that are more vulnerable to breakage (Banham 2000:7).

Slate-grinding was well-established during Locarno times, but ground slate tool types proliferated during Marpole, when they are thought to have been used to butcher salmon (Burley 1980; Mitchell 1990). Graesch (2007:582) claimed that slate knives were used for filleting and scoring salmon flesh, a point made earlier by Morin (2004:312), whose experiments led him to state that slate (and mussel shell) knives could not effectively cut through salmon skin. "If considerable force was applied, they could sometimes tear the skin, but could not cut or slice it in any controlled way" (Morin 2004:294). To judge efficiency, skill and experience matter, so such experimental observations may not be reliable. Another possibility is that Fraser Valley residents made ground slate knives for exchange to those with less optimal access to or lower quality slate. Graesch (2007) found that finished slate knives made up less than 1 percent of the slate tools at the Late Period/Contact Period site of Welqamex. Most of what he found was debitage and production errors (Graesch 2007:591), a result not inconsistent with craft specialization and trade. Graesch (2006, 2007) is one of the only Northwest Coast archaeologists to have systematically recovered slate debitage.

Chipped stone was also used in salmon butchery. Flenniken (1981) interpreted the hafted microblades from Hoko River as salmon-cutting tools. The function of chipped stone tools other than points or microblades isn't often addressed for the Late Holocene on the Northwest Coast. Angela Close suspects that the focus on biface reduction in North America ignores a substantial part of the record. Most Northwest Coast chipped stone studies have used projectile points as type fossils to construct culture-historical sequences, largely ignoring study of cores and debitage (Close 2006:2). Chipped stone debitage isn't always collected at Northwest Coast sites, even today. Using the *chaine operatoire* approach to identify reduction sequences and stone tool use, maintenance, and discard, Close (2006:11) tried to find the "people behind the artifacts" at English Camp on San Juan Island, occupied ca. A.D. 1600 (Stein 1992).

For chipped stone tools, English Camp (also known as British Camp) residents used nonlocal crystallized volcanic rock (CVR) that they brought to the site as unworked pebbles, via canoe. The pebbles were small (~4.2 cm long) and were worked by direct and bipolar percussion and bifacial thinning (Close 2006:35, 13). Close found two distinct areas of stone working at the site. Outside of the midden ridge, "triangles" were made on flakes without cortex; these comprised most retouched tools at the site, but many were abandoned during manufacture (Close 2006:145). Close suggested men made the triangles and used them as arrowheads. Within the midden ridge, women struck flakes from cores to use as tool blanks with a minimum of core preparation (Close 2006:161). The flakes they preferred had some cortex, but not much (Close 2006:142). Those flakes with a "natural back," i.e., a thick cortical edge with the cortex roughly perpendicular to the ventral face, made them well-suited for cutting, and they were used in processing animals, wood, and woven items (Close 2006:154). Close (2006:18) identified these as "scaled pieces," a type not previously described on the Northwest Coast. The scaling resulted from tool use, not retouch. The CVR material made initially sharp and fairly durable cutting edges, but could not be resharpened through retouch (Close 2006:154). Close's study illustrates the potential of lithic analysis on the Northwest Coast to show how a local group developed technology to serve their needs. The raw material may seem less than optimal, but not only was it available but it was socially constructed as acceptable (Close 2006:11). These are not "crude tools" irrelevant to the social lives of site residents; they may have been directly tied to fish butchery.

Graesch's and Close's work takes us into the Gulf of Georgia phase or Late Period, whose onset is between 1500 and 1100 RYBP. This phase is marked by "stylistic" changes in flaked stone, ground stone points, barbed bone points, hand mauls, and decorated items (Burley 1989:41; Mitchell 1990:347; Thom 1995). Ames (2009:19–20) found a decrease in the proportion of chipped stone from Marpole to Late Period, along with a concomitant increase in faunal tools, but the proportion of ground stone was about the same. Ames (2009:27) also found considerable intra-site and inter-site variability in assemblage composition in the Late Period, which can only be understood with more contextual information about how space was used at a site, seasonality of site occupation, and functional roles of sites within settlement systems.

Evidence of the bow and arrow is indirect and equivocal. Ethnographically, arrow points were made of chipped and ground stone, bone and antler, wood and shell, and later, iron and metal alloys. But distinguishing points as spear, dart, harpoon, or arrow points is not always done. With extraordinary preservation in Yukon ice patches, Hare et al. (2004) have clear evidence that the bow and arrow abruptly replaced the atlatl at 1250 RYBP. Their finds of intact wood arrows and barbed antler points set a minimum date for the bow and arrow in northwestern North America. In the Gulf of Georgia, is the relative abundance of unilaterally barbed bone and antler points during the Late Period a signature of the bow and arrow? Arrow points are not often explicitly identified, but Charlton (1980:56) is an exception; his narrow-necked side-notched arrow points date to A.D. 100–400 in the lower Fraser region, somewhat earlier than arrows in the Yukon.

In his study of the Gulf of Georgia, T. Clark (2010) redefined Marpole and Locarno Beach. Although widespread across the region ca. 3500 RYBP, he argued that by 2000 RYBP the spatial distribution of Locarno Beach was constricted to southern Vancouver Island and the southern Gulf Islands. Simultaneously, Marpole developed on the lower Fraser and northern Gulf Islands. These cultures are viewed as precursors to the Straits Salish centered in the former and the Halq'emeylem in the latter region. Clark proposed that Locarno persisted alongside Marpole, which was more spatially and temporally discrete than previously thought. In the Late Period (after 1100 B.P.), the two areas were knitted together through networks of trade and ceremonialism (Clark 2010:288). Clark has thus traced a more intricate pattern in the mosaic of lifeways in the Gulf of Georgia.

Artifact Trends beyond the Gulf of Georgia

Although I cannot be comprehensive regarding artifact types, assemblage composition, or technological variability, what follows is an attempt to demonstrate how geographic and cultural factors affect various archaeological questions.

West Coast of Vancouver Island and Queen Charlotte Strait

At Yuquot, the West Coast culture type endures for over 4,000 years, indicating a measure of cultural continuity. This culture type has been defined in relation to Gulf of Georgia units (Mitchell 1990); it differs from them in that chipped stone artifacts are nearly absent, ground slate points and knives are rare, and bone is the dominant material for tools. We have already seen that Gulf of Georgia assemblages dominated by faunal tools occur during the Charles and Locarno phases, and are more common during Marpole and Gulf of Georgia phases. Faunal tool dominated assemblages are not unique to the West Coast culture type, but perhaps people living here didn't enjoy access to good flaking stone. Because bone and shell were easily accessible, people made heavy use of them. Stone and bone fishhook shanks are distinctive of the West Coast culture type, dating within the last 2,000 years.

On northeast Vancouver Island, along the shores of Queen Charlotte Strait, Obsidian Culture Type assemblages are dominated by obsidian flakes reduced using bipolar techniques, some bone and shell tools, but few ground stone tools (Mitchell 1988, 1990). Almost all (99 percent) obsidian from these assemblages was identified as "Central Coast A" and "Central Coast B" because the source locations were unknown (Carlson 1994:315).[7] But Central Coast A has recently been identified in the vicinity of Kingcome Inlet (Skinner 2009), a fiord within the distribution of the Obsidian Culture. Even though it has taken archaeologists many years to locate this source, those who left behind the Obsidian Culture knew about the distribution of this raw material, suggesting they had been in the region for a while.

After 2400 RYBP, assemblages contain some ground slate points, stone celts, and a diversity and abundance of bone tools known as the Queen Charlotte Strait Culture Type. The affiliated group(s) could be people unfamiliar with local obsidian, or Kingcome (and Central Coast B) obsidian may have been insufficient for their needs. Animal bone and shell became major sources of raw material after 2400 RYBP. We saw a similar trend in the Gulf of Georgia (in Marpole and Gulf of Georgia phases). The faunal assemblages of the Obsidian Culture and Queen Charlotte Straits Culture are different, with deer the most abundant mammal in the former, and seals and sea lions more abundant in the latter. Perhaps bone tools were especially useful in hunting sea mammals, but it is also possible that increased use of deer bone for tool-making may have reduced the proportion of identifiable deer bone in the Queen Charlotte Straits Culture assemblages. Across the Gulf of Georgia, Vancouver Island, and Queen Charlotte Strait subregions, the increase in faunal tools appears as part of a widespread historical trend that results from various factors, including the availability of animal bone compared to more localized and restricted sources of stone.

Central B.C. Coast

Namu's Early Holocene deposits contain obsidian from more than 200 km away in the Rainbow Mountains in the interior that was traded down the Bella Coola Valley. Over the course of Namu's occupation, most obsidian is from the Anahim source (n = 109), followed by Mackenzie (n = 65), even though the Anahim source is farther away (Carlson 1994:314, 352–353). These connections to the interior point to the origins of Namu residents, the routes they explored, or the trade relationships they forged. The presence of Kingcome Inlet obsidian (n = 17) shows local knowledge of and access to the south as well.

Culture-historical trends on the Central Coast are not well-known. Chipped stone projectile points decline after 5000 RYBP (Carlson 2008b:76), when heavily used ground stone celts, mussel shell adzes, and an array of bone tools (barbed harpoon and fixed points, toggling harpoon parts, wedges, awls, barbs) were used (Luebbers 1978:66). This is parallel to trends in the other subregions discussed thus far. Chipped stone flakes continue to be used, and bipolar flakes and cores suggest conservative use of obsidian (Hutchings 1996:168–171). Like elsewhere by the Late Holocene, animal bone has become the most accessible source of material for toolmaking. At Namu and other sites, one can think of large shell middens as repositories of raw materials used to make tools.

Haida Gwaii

The Early Holocene bifacial (Kingii Complex) and microblade (Early Moresby) traditions of Haida Gwaii were followed by Late Moresby (8000–5000 RYBP), Early (Transitional) Graham (5000–3000 RYBP), and Late Graham (2000–200 RYBP) traditions (Fedje and Mackie 2005). The Kingii Complex employed local materials, emblematic of people with local knowledge who had settled in to their environment. Fedje and Mackie (2005:158) suggested that the lack of exotic materials indicated "little or no contact with mainland groups at this time." The shift to microblades was a way to conserve raw materials, as rising sea levels reduced access to toolstone (Fedje et al. 2005c). Early Moresby had tabular to conical microblade cores and microblades and fewer bifaces, all of local stone. Late Moresby had microblades, but not bifaces. In the Early (Transitional) Graham Tradition, bipolar technology replaced microblade technology, with similar blade end-products. Convex-edged retouched flakes were also found (Mackie and Acheson 2005:276).[8] The Early Graham Tradition was marked by an increase in ground stone. Mackie and Acheson (2005:288–289) noted that Early Graham assemblages resemble Late Moresby, especially if bipolar flakes were functional equivalents of microblades. In Late Graham, flaked and ground stone declined, with assemblages dominated by bone tools, especially bird bone. Mackie and Acheson (2005:299) noted widespread "if not universal" distribution of unilaterally barbed and composite toggling harpoons across the Northwest Coast contemporaneous with the Late Graham tradition.

The Graham tradition was defined from Blue Jackets Creek, a site not fully reported. Even though ground stone is thought to have increased, of the 2,500 artifacts from Blue Jackets, only 8 ground slate artifacts and 3 ground stone clubs were recovered (Sutherland 2004:232). Only one ground slate point type was described: a thin triangular one. Celts/adzes were more numerous ($n = 35$), as were celt/adze preforms ($n = 129$) of local cobbles (Sutherland 2004:232–233). Fedje et al. (2008:34) observed that "[i]n the later Holocene perhaps the most notable aspect of Haida Gwaii projectile technology is the relative lack of interest in ground stone. Slate and other suitable raw materials are abundant, however people appeared to focus on ground bone, antler and wood for their projectiles." These authors noted similarities between the Graham Tradition and the West Coast Culture of Vancouver Island.

Some of this culture-historical variation is based on geographic availability of raw materials, differential preservation, and different site functions. As sea levels transgressed Early Holocene shorelines, Haida Gwaii became isolated, leading to conservative use of stone (i.e., microblades and later, bipolar flakes). Although Haida Gwaii residents did not routinely grind stone to make points, they made celts, a primary woodworking tool. The occurrence of celts/adzes at Blue Jackets is not well-dated, but is roughly when bogs expanded and red-cedar became established by 3000 RYBP (3200 cal B.P.; Lacourse and Mathewes 2005:56–57). Increased celt usage suggests increased woodworking, perhaps of redcedar. Because large cedars provided the materials for building oceangoing canoes, long-distance travel across Dixon Entrance to Alaska or to the B.C. mainland across Hecate Strait likely increased after 3000 RYBP. This led to more interaction with various groups, including those of Vancouver Island (Mackie and Acheson 2005). The increase in faunal tools may also be part of a widespread trend discussed earlier.

The authors contributing to Fedje and Mathewes (2005) support the idea of cultural continuity on Haida Gwaii from at least the Middle to the Late Holocene. Mackie and Acheson (2005:287) identified a gap between 3250 and 2000 RYBP from which few components have been dated and none from well-excavated contexts. While the Late Graham tradition (2000–200 RYBP) is well-documented in southerly Gwaii Haanas, it is not well-known from Graham Island. In contrast, Sutherland (2004) sees cultural disconti-nuity between the Graham Tradition and the Haida. She found "little resemblance between the artifact assemblages from sites contemporaneous with Blue Jackets Creek and those from the past two millennia investigated by Acheson (1998) and thought to be ancestral to the Haida cultural tradi-tion" (Sutherland 2004:298–299). At Blue Jackets, 28 people were buried, and 17 measurable crania trend toward long-headedness, while historic Haida were more round-headed (Cybulski 2001:111; Mackie and Acheson 2005:288).[9] This sample is small, and Cybulski (2001:137) stated that the Blue Jackets burials may represent a single lineage, not archipelago-wide skeletal biology. Sutherland (2004:299) pointed to tooth abrasion suggestive of buccal labrets, whereas historically, the Haida wore medial labrets (as did Tlingit and Tsimshian). But tooth abrasion was found on only three individ-uals (male and female) and only one labret was found in the deposit.

The differences in artifacts between Blue Jackets and the Late Graham sites of Gwaii Haanas are more easily explained, not by cultural discontinu-ity and non-Haida identity, but by resource availability, site function, and the historical trend toward an increase in faunal tools. The prevalence of bird bone tools in Acheson's study is partly because Gwaii Haanas is an area of small rocky islands, where bird-hunting, fishing, and some whaling were important (Acheson 1998; Orchard 2007). Not surprisingly, abraders, most likely used in bone tool manufacture, are the most common stone tool in these sites (Mackie and Acheson 2005:290). The tool assemblage from Blue Jackets, a site located well up Masset Inlet in a protected locale, can be expected to differ from those of Gwaii Haanas. After 3000 RYBP, Haida

Gwaii residents interacted more with people living beyond the archipelago (MacDonald 1983a; Moss 2008a).

Prince Rupert Harbor

Prince Rupert Harbor is located along the mainland, near the outlets of Skeena and Nass rivers and sheltered by nearshore islands. The North Coast Prehistory Project (1968–1974) recovered substantial artifact assemblages from nine harbor sites occupied over the last 5500 cal years. K. Ames (2005) analyzed assemblage diversity and composition, correcting for assemblage size and volume excavated. Although the earliest period of occupation (Prince Rupert 3, 5500–3800 cal B.P.) is not well-represented, Ames compared the subsequent two periods: PR 2 (3800–1500 cal B.P.) and PR 1 (1500 cal B.P. to contact). Ames (2005:i) characterized Prince Rupert material culture as "remarkably stable" over 3,800 years. Aside from cobble tools, very little chipped stone occurs, similar to the West Coast and Queen Charlotte Strait cultures (Ames 2005:173). Although Ames subdivided bone tools into classes and types differently than other investigators, harpoon heads and parts, fixed points, awls, and barbs are common throughout PR 2 and 1. Land mammal bone was preferred over sea mammal bone in tool-making (Ames 2005:185), even to the point that land mammal bone not available on-island was brought to one site. Ames's density indices suggested abraders, celts, mauls, and percussers/hammerstones increased over time. Abraders were probably used to make ground stone and bone tools. Celts, mauls, and percussers suggested "increasing reliance on carpentry and increased use of large timbers" (Ames 2005:207). Such woodworking tools reflect house-building, boat-building, box-making—activities that would intensify with sedentism.

Ames (2005) analyzed 285 burials and funerary items from 12 harbor sites. He judged 34 burials to be associated with grave goods, estimating that 10 percent of the individuals were buried with artifacts (Ames 2005:230). Ames (2005:244) stated that "ranking existed in the harbour by 900 BC, and probably as early as 1600 BC. While males clearly had more access to high status than females, both males and females had high status." Yet of the 34 individuals reliably associated with grave inclusions, only seven were directly dated. Eldridge and McKechnie (2008) recalibrated the ages of the Prince Rupert burials incorporating a correction for the marine reservoir effect because these people had marine diets. Seven dated burials with grave goods ranged in age from 3000 to 1000 cal B.P., a long period of time for so few dates. The oldest burial associations (ca. 3000 cal B.P.), include a male with a hammerstone and quartz flake and a female with a bone point. More elaborate grave goods are more recent; a man buried with copper, amber beads, and shell gorget dates to 2200–2000 cal B.P., as does a man with a zoomorphic pendant. A man associated with copper, amber beads, and ankle bracelet dates to 1360–1200 cal B.P. Labret abrasion has been found on 19 males and three females (Cybulski 1992:72), but overall, the burial sample is skewed in favor of males (64 percent),[10] and the temporal contexts of these have not been published. While these data suggest wealth and/or rank differences of a 2,000-year antiquity, the social criteria for these are hard to establish.

Southeast Alaska

Few large artifact assemblages have been recovered in southeast Alaska. The Coffman Cove (49-PET-067; 5500–700 cal B.P.) assemblage contains ground stone and bone tools that have been compared to Locarno Beach (Clark 1979). A few bilaterally barbed harpoon points with tapering sockets are like those at Namu of the same age (Luebbers 1978: Figure 33k). Bone points and bipoints also occur, as do clamshell beads. A cache of chipped slate preforms, possibly the early stage of manufacture of ground and polished triangular slate points, are dated to 2000–700 cal B.P. A segmented stone similar to a few from Prince Rupert (MacDonald 1983b:113–114) was also dated to this recent period.

Most of the site's obsidian (86 percent) occurred in deposits dated to 5500–3500 cal B.P., and none after 2500 cal B.P. Of 25 obsidian artifacts tested, all were traced to Mount Edziza (Reuther et al. 2007), located ~320 km from the site via water route. This suggested that Coffman Cove residents (1) originated in the interior of B.C., (2) occasionally traveled to Mount Edziza, and/or (3) obtained Edziza obsidian through intermediaries (Moss 2008b). I thought the decline of obsidian use at Coffman Cove after 3500 cal B.P. was because of decreased access to this high elevation source due to Neoglacial cooling. While this remains plausible, the lack of chemical distinction between Suemez and Edziza sources (as mentioned in Chapter 4) renders these scenarios uncertain.

At Hidden Falls, the 5480–3360 cal B.P. component contains chipped stone of materials other than obsidian; most are flake tools, unlike the bifacial industry of Locarno Beach. Lightfoot (1989:265–266) noted that the ground slate points, celts, and labrets from Hidden Falls are within the range of those in Locarno assemblages. The segmented stone at Hidden Falls is older than that at Coffman Cove. Serpentine beads and debitage occur, indicating bead manufacture at about the same time as stone beads appear in Fraser River sites. The 3270–870 cal B.P. Hidden Falls component contains similar items, but not as many finely made ground slate points. Broad ground stone knives, shell beads, tooth pendants, small bone barbs and points, abraders, and a hand maul are familiar artifacts of this vintage.

At *Daax Haat Kanadaa*, dated to 1000–220 cal B.P. (Moss 1989), many of the same ground stone and bone tools occur (de Laguna 1960). Although a few artifacts from each of these southeast Alaskan sites and time periods show artistic investment, they do not signal craft specialization or great wealth. These assemblages are too small to substantively assess change through time.

Washington and Oregon Coasts

Par-Tee is the most extensively excavated (~550 m²) Northwest Coast site south of Ozette and is dated to ca. 2300–800 cal B.P. (Losey and Yang 2007:662–663). Sites of this age are not common on the southern Northwest Coast because of coastal erosion. This site occurs just south of the Columbia River where the shoreline is prograding, as does Palmrose (Connolly 1992; Losey 2010a). The Par-Tee assemblage includes more than 7,000 artifacts, but it is not well-known because it was dug by nonprofessionals. Well-preserved antler and bone tools and chipped stone dart and arrow points are represented. Although atlatls are rarely found in Northwest Coast sites (Fladmark et al. 1987), 23 whalebone atlatls were found at Par-Tee (Losey 2010a). Of 300 harpoon heads (fixed points with bilateral or unilateral barbs, also toggling valves and points), 90 percent are antler, and the remaining 10 percent are bone (Losey and Yang 2007:663–664; Losey 2010a).

While woodworking tools in the Gulf of Georgia include ground stone adzes and celts, Par-Tee woodworkers used basalt spall choppers, elk antler wedges, chisels and adzes made from elk metapodials, and some mussel shell blades (Losey 2010, pers. comm.). Elk antler was also used to make digging stick handles, a tool type not often found in Northwest Coast sites. The large number of awls and bird bone needles indicate mat-weaving, sewing, and/or basket-making. From the Palmrose site, bone harpoons decorated with incisions, and a number of pecked stones with anthropomorphic and zoomorphic motifs are similar to Marpole items (Connolly 1992). Par-Tee residents had good access to elk bone and antler, investing time making faunal tools. They also hunted whales and used whalebone, with ~350 modified pieces (Losey and Yang 2007:663). An elk bone point lodged into a humpback whale phalanx (1600–1300 cal B.P.) indicates whale hunting (Losey and Yang 2007). The manufacture of whalebone atlatls at the site is unique on the Northwest Coast; most atlatls were probably made of wood (Losey 2010, pers. comm).

At the 500–300 year old Ozette site, >30,000 wood artifacts and another 6000 of plant fiber were found (Kirk 1986:113; Wessen 1990).[11] Bows and arrows were well-represented; 1,534 wood arrow shafts, 5,189 wood arrow points, 115 wood bows, and seven stone arrow points were found (Croes 2003:58–59). Over 1,000 box fragments, >1,000 wooden wedges, 243 baskets, and 124 harpoon shafts were found, as were remains of clothing, sleeping mats, cradles, fishhooks, bowls, digging/prying sticks, tool handles/hafts, canoe paddles, spindle whorls, and loom parts (Croes 2003; Kirk 1986). The diverse inventory of perishable artifacts includes Makah artworks: carved wooden panels and planks, a sea otter tooth-studded effigy of a whale's dorsal fin, and bowls and clubs sculpted into zoomorphic and anthropomorphic figures (Figure 6.4). Over 800 whetstones/abraders used in tool manufacture were recovered (Kirk 1986:113). Although numerically rare in comparison, ground slate knives, mauls, line and net weights were also found, although chipped stone was absent (Wessen 1990:416). Over 500 mussel shell knives, harpoon blades, and adze bits are the functional equivalents of some stone tool types (Kirk 1986:113; Wessen 1990:414). Over 1,000 whalebone tools included 75 wedges (Huelsbeck 1994:284). Whalebone was also used for furnishings, cutting boards, chopping blocks, and to make clubs, bark-shredders, bark-beaters, wedges, spindle whorls, tool handles and hafts, and harpoon heads.

The artifact assemblage from the dry part of Ozette (A-trench) is important for comparison. A date of 2010 ± 190 RYBP is often associated with the trench, but derives from shell midden on an islet adjacent to the site (Samuels and Daugherty 1991:11). McKenzie's (1974:27) single date from the trench was 180 ± 22 B.P. Of 575 artifacts, 83 percent were faunal items, 12 percent were chipped stone, and 5 percent were ground stone (including fishhook shanks; McKenzie's 1974). Since the A-trench deposits were not screened, small items like chipped stone flakes are under-represented. Of the

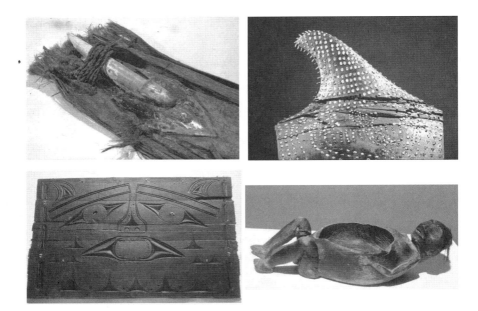

Figure 6.4. Ozette Artifacts. Top left: mussel shell-tipped whaling harpoon in cedar bark sheath; Top right: whale dorsal fin effigy cedar carving with >700 inlaid sea otter teeth; Bottom left: decorated bentwood box front; Bottom right: carved human effigy bowl for serving oil. Used with permission from Ruth Kirk and Pictures of Record.

bone tools, bipoints (40 percent), fixed points (20 percent), and harpoon heads/parts (9 percent) were most common, followed by awls, wedges, scrapers, chisels/gouges, hafts, bark-shredders, etc. Twenty major classes of bone artifacts were identified, similar to the bone tool types found in the West Coast Culture. A few wood artifacts were also found. The Ozette A-trench assemblage differs from that of Par-Tee, with the latter dated to a time when atlatls were still used. The Ozette trench assemblage probably dates within the last 1,000 years, by which time the arrow had replaced the atlatl. The trench assemblage fits well within the range of the West Coast culture type, and is consistent with a region-wide emphasis on bone tools for the late pre-contact period.

Some of the most spectacular finds at Ozette were the shed-roof houses, comprised of over 20,000 wood structural remains and drainage control features made of wood and whalebone. At this point, we shift focus from artifacts to houses and house features, to assess a crucial component of the built environment.

Houses—Physical Traces and Social Composition

The oldest house remains on the Northwest Coast date to the Middle Holocene, but even the earliest residents must have built dwellings to survive the Northwest Coast climate. Throughout pre-contact history, people occupied caves and rockshelters but they also may have used skin tents or shelters of pole frames covered with slabs of bark, layers of branches, sod, or woven mats. Even substantial wood houses decay quickly and can be hard to identify archaeologically. It is hard to decipher houses in areas that have been repeatedly occupied, where they may be obscured or filled-in with shell middens or later occupational debris. Older houses are unlikely to be identified from surface features, and may be impossible to recognize if excavations are limited.

The record of Northwest Coast houses is much slimmer than that of many areas of North America. Southwestern archaeologists routinely identify pithouses and puebloes. The circular houses in California, the longhouses in the Northeast, and tipi outlines of the Great Plains are well-known. Less well-known is the 9500 cal B.P. house found along Paulina Lake in central Oregon (Connolly 1999:230); yet this is one of the oldest houses in all North America. In arctic Alaska and Canada, ancient houses are identified from surface features. But along the Northwest Coast, organic structural remains decompose in the wet soils, and heavy vegetation conceals the ground surface. Falling trees churn up the ground, heavy rains saturate soils, and rivers erode their banks and ocean waves undercut seacliffs. Sometimes house features are recognized by surface features, but the remains of the oldest Northwest Coast houses are probably buried and retain only ambiguous traces. Compared to the rest of North America, the number of excavated Northwest Coast houses is surprisingly small, and few have been fully excavated.

In the archaeological literature of the Northwest Coast, investigators refer to "housepits" or "house depressions"; such surface features may be places where people excavated into the ground to either provide a level terrace or semi-subterranean foundation for a house. Other "housepits" result from the build-up of midden refuse outside the walls of the house. Midden berms around a house create an apparent "housepit," but the structure itself may have been entirely above ground, and the depression may result from the mounding of refuse outside of it.

Houses in the Fraser Valley

Lepofsky et al. (2009) described houses from several sites that range in age from 6000 cal B.P. through the historic period along the Fraser River. These are some of the oldest houses in the Northwest, although found between 50 and 75 km upriver from saltwater. The 6200–5400 cal B.P. house from X̱a:ytem (Hatzic Rock) was a semi-subterranean, rectangular structure 3.5 m by 4.5 m, and thought to have housed a "small family group" (Lepofsky et al. 2009:603). A larger (10 m by 11 m) semi-subterranean rectangular house was dated to 5700–4600 cal B.P. at X̱a:ytem and thought to have housed 35 people, or "at least two extended families" (Lepofsky et al. 2009:604).[12] Both houses were cut into the gravels of river terraces and recognized by post and stake molds.[13] The authors suggested that these two houses show a shift from nuclear to extended households. The Maurer House is a shallow, semi-subterranean, rectangular house (5 m by 7.5 m), dated to 4900 cal B.P. (Schaepe 2003). Large vertical corner posts supported the roof, while wood planks were lashed between smaller retaining posts set into the base of the walls, much like the houses at Ozette (Schaepe 2003:138). A single extended family is thought to have occupied the house. Lepofsky et al (2009:616) found no causal relationship between Mid-Holocene cooling or the establishment of redcedar and the construction of the X̱a:ytem and Maurer houses.

More recent Fraser Valley houses include semi-subterranean pithouses and plank-houses. The pithouses ranged from circular to rectangular to square, whereas the plank-houses were always rectilinear. Lepofsky et al. (2009:617) argued that by 2,400 years ago, the size of co-resident groups increased dramatically, with houses as much as four times the size of the Maurer house. A Qithyil house measured 11 m by 17 m, and several at Sxwoxwiymelh were 8–12 m a side. This signaled a shift to large co-residential groups that included "multiple nuclear families and potentially non-kin followers" (Lepofsky et al. 2009:617). Pithouses were limited in size (between 5–9 m across), whereas plank-houses could be larger. At the 300 cal B.P. to historic age Welqamex site, pithouses were connected with "possible" tunnels, suggesting they accommodated "both a certain degree of family autonomy and connections to the larger household group" (Lepofsky et al. 2009:617).

Houses Elsewhere on the Northwest Coast

Living in large houses was a diagnostic feature of Matson and Coupland's *Developed Northwest Coast* pattern and Ames and Maschner's (1999) *Middle Pacific* period. Houses indicate sedentism, extensive storage, and major changes in social organization. At the Paul Mason site (3000 RYBP), 10 houses of similar size (~62 m²) were found (Coupland 1996:124). These houses are located ~100 km up the Skeena River, and the early houses on the Fraser River are 50–75 km upriver. This suggests to me that shell midden formation has obscured the remains of houses on the Northwest *Coast* itself. Even though over 1024 m³ were excavated at Boardwalk (Ames 2005:181), and two house depressions were noted (Ames 2006:29), their architectural remains have not been described, possibly because they were not identifiable during excavation of the shell midden. Yet the two flat terraces at the site have been interpreted as remnants of a "two-row linear village" (Ames 2006:29).

On Vancouver Island, Marshall (1993, 2006) associated four categories of surface features with houses: terraces, back midden ridges, house depressions, and small ridges. Her analysis of Nootka Sound sites was based on mapped surface features, not excavation. Marshall (1993) and McMillan (1999:124) interpreted two clusters of superimposed hearths at Yuquot (2300–1900 RYBP) as the remains of permanent houses and the "curated placement" of firepits (Marshall 2006:43). House "outlines" or "platforms" were also identified at T'ukw'aa (McMillan 1999:68) and Ts'ishaa (McMillan and St. Claire 2005). Three large evenly spaced post-molds and large hearths in the Shoemaker Bay I deposit were evident of a house (McMillan 1999:76–77). In ethnographic villages, terraces are interpreted as flattened house platforms (McMillan 2009:627), but older house remains are difficult to identify in large shell middens covered in forest where houses certainly once stood.

At McNichol Creek in Prince Rupert Harbor, five of 15 house depressions were dated to 1800–1500 RYBP and partially excavated. The largest was 9 m by 11 m, with a surface area about 32 percent larger than the other four houses.[14] Coupland (2006) described this as a "chief's house" based on its larger size, clay floor, and a few artifacts of nonlocal nephrite, chert, and obsidian, including one labret. Even though the house did not have the central two-meter deep pit (*da-ak*) characteristic of historic chief's houses, Coupland (2006:94) described it as "monumental," communicating the "wealth, rank, and power of its owner." The largest house at McNichol Creek is more modest than the largest houses documented in Coast Salish, Makah, and Chinook territories. Excluding historic-aged houses built with metal tools, larger houses have been found at Tualdad Altu south of Seattle (135 m²; Chatters 1988), Ozette (160–250 m²; Samuels 2006:202), and Dionisio Point (200–400 m²; Grier 2003:178). The Meier House in Chinook territory was 35 m by 14 m (490 m²; Ames 1996), although its age extends into the historic period.

A main difference among Northwest Coast houses is that many plankhouses from the south were "longhouses" to which modular compartments could be added over time. The house frame, parallel rows of rafter support posts, and suspended rafter beams were permanent, while wall planks held between paired posts and the roofing could be taken apart and moved (Matson 2003:77). Because of the amount of labor to prepare wood to build houses, it makes sense that wall and roof planks could be recycled and used at more than one site. This house type has not been documented north of Vancouver Island (either ethnographically or archaeologically).

Mackie and Williamson's (2003) study of standing structural remains and house depressions at two nineteenth-century sites in Barkley Sound on Vancouver Island is instructive. In a single site, they found both shed-roof and gable-roof houses, and one house with both roof types. The long axes of some houses were oriented parallel to the beach, while others were perpendicular, depending on the curvature and width of the terrace on which houses were built. Some houses were rectangular, others were square, and others were rhomboidal or trapezoidal in shape. Mackie and Williamson (2003:150) showed that post-hole patterns in the absence of roof remains could not be used to distinguish shed-roof from gable-roof houses. This demonstrates great variation at a single site, raising doubt about the reliability of house outlines mapped from surface features alone.

At Ozette and Meier, evidence for status differences has been found between and within houses. At Ozette one house was slightly larger than the others (Figure 6.5), located in the beachfront row, contained a feasting hearth, and had more fur seal remains and dentalium shell than other houses (Samuels 2006:208). Within the Ozette houses, higher-ranked families had hearths in the corners, and controlled the central hearth (Samuels 1991). At Meier, the chief's position at the rear of the house has been inferred from

Figure 6.5. House 2 at Ozette during excavation. Gary Wessen in foreground, Sarah Fisken behind. Used with permission from Ruth Kirk and Pictures of Record.

abundant woodworking debris; most food processing occurred in the presumed lower-status area near the house entrance (Ames 1996).

Houses and Households

Extrapolations regarding social relationships—about whether a house or space within a house supported a nuclear family, multiple families, or "non-kin" are difficult to support. The variation in family structure across the region in the nineteenth and early twentieth centuries is a subset of many possibilities. For example, the Tlingit are matrilineal, but lived in avunculo-cal households prior to missionary intervention. Each matrilineage in a town occupied one or more houses. Children are of their mother's clan, but spent their earliest years (with their mother) living in the household of their father. When boys were 7–8 years old, they moved into the houses occupied by their maternal uncles, their fellow clansmen from whom they learned vital skills. Girls stayed with their mothers in their father's homes until marriage, when they moved to their husband's clanhouses. A mature woman who was widowed might marry one of her husband's brothers, but if not, she moved to her own clanhouse where her brothers had lived since childhood. Such women could gain considerable power and prestige in their later years, exerting influence over their brothers and sons. Clearly, the "nuclear family" model is not helpful in understanding Tlingit households and residence patterns because the personnel making up a household are in flux depending on age and life stage. The Tlingit clanhouse is eternal; it is the social unit that controlled crests, heirlooms, and resource territories, and held individual names, social prerogatives, songs and dances. The clanhouse is a social group that did not occupy a single physical structure.

Levi-Strauss conceptualized Northwest Coast peoples as "House societies" (Ames 2006; Marshall 1989, 2006), drawing from his understanding of Kwakwaka'wakw numayms. While some numayms were contained in single houses, others were represented in multiple houses (Codere 1990). A numaym is structurally analogous to a Tlingit matrilineage, controlling corporeal and non-corporeal property. Yet the composition of Kwakwaka'wakw houses was more variable than Tlingit houses because individuals could choose to affiliate with either their father's or their mother's kin at different times in their lives. A numaym held "a series of ranked social positions, plus children and adults who do not have one of the ranked positions but who may receive one as a relative of someone who has one to pass on or who may have held one and retired from it" (Codere 1957:479). Further south, residence was more likely to have been patrilocal. The Tolowa present an even greater contrast; the Tolowa "family house" was where a married woman or women married to the same man lived with their unmarried daughters and young sons. Adult men and boys past puberty lived in a semi-subterranean "sweathouse." Such gender segregation would involve entirely different social dynamics.

Taken together, these housing arrangements demonstrate substantial variability across the Northwest Coast during the nineteenth century. Life in an avunculocal household would differ for men and women and vary by age and life stage. Among the Kwakwaka'wakw, considerable energy would be devoted to recruiting household members. In nineteenth-century Northwest Coast societies, tensions existed between kin relationships and loyalty to clan and competition between household members and within clans for rank. Such conflicts functioned as dynamic sources of social change in more distant times as well. "House" and "household" have different meanings across time and space on the Northwest Coast and household membership was probably more dynamic and negotiated than conventionally conceived. Ethnographic variation helps guard against overly normative archaeological interpretations of houses and households.

The Built Environment Beyond the House

Shell Middens

Q. Mackie (2003:262) wrote that "[n]o one ever set out to create a shell midden" and viewed shell middens as "by-products of resource consumption." Some shell middens may be refuse piles, but purposeful human action has contributed to shell midden formation, especially in long-term settlements. People selected where to deposit shell, animal carcasses, hearth ash and rocks, whether on the beach, behind or between living structures, or some distance away. Some discards probably attracted gulls, crows, ravens, mink, raccoons—even bears—so the placement of middens required deliberation or periodic adjustment. Village dogs may have kept scavengers at bay, and patterns of refuse deposition may have differed at sites without dogs. People probably removed bone from its place of primary deposition for use in making tools, i.e., shell middens could thus be mined for raw materials. Shell midden constituents could also be used to fill in uneven or poorly drained landforms to prepare sites for houses. Some Northwest Coast shell middens served as burial grounds. These various uses involved trampling over and digging into shell middens, compressing, fracturing, and redistributing their contents.

R. Carlson (1999) suggested that during the Late Holocene, shell middens like that at Pender Canal were sacred sites, not mere trash deposits. Carlson cited ethnographic traditions that require deliberate disposal of animal bones in ways intended to insure animal reincarnation. Human burials with carved spoons placed near their mouths or clamshell bowls resting in their hands were interpreted as ritual feeding of the dead, dated to 3700–2500 RYBP (Carlson 1999:44). Between 2500 and 1000 RYBP, hearths associated with burials indicated the mortuary practice of burning offerings. Carlson (1999:44) explained that "a midden then becomes a food bank for the dead and placing the dead in this food bank then becomes a way of keeping them at peace. With a belief in the regeneration from bones it is a logical step to populate the places for dead people with the bones or shell of dead animals which are then reincarnated as food for the benefit of the human dead."

At Pender, the burials were contemporaneous with the developing shell midden, indicating that people buried the dead adjacent to where they lived.

At other Gulf of Georgia sites, shell middens accumulated, were abandoned, and only later served as burial places. At Somenos Creek on Vancouver Island, shell midden strata accumulated from 4000 to 1850 RYBP, but shortly after the midden was abandoned, the site was used as a cemetery for 50 or more individuals over a 300 year period (1850–1250 RYBP; Brown 2003:163). Almost all these Marpole individuals were buried in shallow pits, some capped with rock slabs or cairns. The remains of one individual were burned *in situ* (Brown 2003:160–161). Elsewhere in the Gulf of Georgia, people used abandoned shell middens as burial sites as many as 4,000 years ago (Brown 2003:163).

Burials in the Namu shell midden date to 5000 cal B.P. and appear contemporaneous with the shell deposits in which they were found. The re-dated human remains from the Prince Rupert Harbor sites (Eldridge and McKechnie 2008) also seem contemporaneous with the shell middens, as do those at Blue Jackets Creek (Sutherland 2004:230). At Coffman Cove, burials appear intrusive into older shell deposits, but analysis is not yet complete. Cybulski (1992:168) wrote,

> Because of the almost ubiquitous presence of human remains, one might wonder whether shell deposits were specifically sought out as cemeteries in the prehistoric past; whether in some cases, shell mounds may have specifically been built for the interment of deceased individuals; or whether the construction of shell middens was, in some cases, a by-product of a corpse disposal ritual.

Cybulski (1992) thought that the Greenville Burial Ground may be the latter type, i.e., a shell midden built in the process of carrying out mortuary rituals. For Northwest Coast people traveling via boat, shell middens were clearings that stood out along the forested shoreline. Once a shell midden became conspicuous and visible, its inscription on the landscape was a recognizable fixture of the built environment. If a shell midden were used as a burial place, it evoked ancestors and a range of social relationships that became important touchstones of social memory. A shell midden could become an anchor to the past and attach a social group to its territory and its history. Shell middens likely represent aspects of the built environment that changed over time and varied from place to place across the Northwest Coast.

Other Mortuary Sites

Sometime after A.D. 1200–1300, "above ground corpse disposal may have been initiated" (Cybulski 1992:165). Some individuals were interred in box burials placed in caves and rockshelters, others were buried in cairns or mounds, and others were placed in trees (Curtin 2002:1). A number of ethnographic groups cremated human remains and placed these in grave houses, mortuary poles, or canoes. In some cases, human remains were later collected and reburied, and the deceased's house might be abandoned or burned (e.g., Hajda 1990:512).

Curtin (2002:116) showed that for the Gulf of Georgia, there was no evolutionary sequence from midden to aboveground burial. During both the Locarno and Marpole periods on Gabriola Island, midden burials and cave/crevice interments occurred over a 2,000-year period. Curtin found no evidence for temporal, biological, or status differences between those buried in a midden and those placed in the caves and crevices in the nearby bluffs. The higher frequency of pathology among the cave burials led Curtin to infer that cause of death determined burial pattern. Yet the cave burials were not uniformly treated and displayed substantial variability (Curtin 2002:116–117).

Whereas burials in caves and rockshelters are hidden from general view, burial cairns and mounds were also built in the Gulf of Georgia region, and these are an important part of the built environment. Thom (1995) compiled information from over 150 burial mounds and cairns in the Coast Salish area. The Scowlitz site contained dozens of mounds and cairns ranging in age from 1600 to 1100 RYBP, about 1000 years more recent than the initial house occupations. The largest mound (12 m square and 3 m high) contained an inner cairn of hundreds of boulders covering an adult male buried with perforated copper disks, a copper ring, abalone shell pendants, and 7000 dentalium beads. This cairn is surrounded by a pair of concentric rock alignments. Mounds such as this were highly visible markers, manifesting a connection between those buried in the mounds (and their descendents) to owned territories (Thom 1995). Such mounds and cairns were built by groups of people working together and represent collective labor and group solidarity.[15] The mounds and cairns at Scowlitz mark this place as significant to people beyond the local group (Lepofsky et al. 2000). Positioned at the confluence of the Fraser and Harrison rivers, Scowlitz was visible to people moving up and downriver for fishing, trade, and communication. The people of Scowlitz conveyed a message of wealth and territorial permanence with their mounds and cairns to all who passed by. Features purposely constructed to reinforce land and resource ownership should be concentrated along heavily traveled routes.

Not all cairns and mounds in the Coast Salish region are monumental. Mathews (2006) documented a variety of burial features in the nearly intact Rocky Point Cemetery on Vancouver Island that are not visible from the water. Mathews (2006:214) argued that these features could only be viewed while walking across the landscape, possibly along specified paths. Presumably the intent of the cairn builders at Rocky Point differed from those at Scowlitz. Cairns of stone and whale bone were also used by Kwakwa̱ka'wakw and Nuu-chah-nulth (Marshall 2006:43), but do not approach the scale of those along the lower B.C. mainland.

Rock Art

Northwest Coast petroglyphs and pictographs are diverse in form, placement, and purpose, and rock art can be found along waterways that were important travel corridors (Figure 6.6). Like the mounds and cairns along the Fraser River, rock art enculturates the landscape and was meant to be seen by people traveling along a specific route. Rock art can commemorate significant events such as lives lost in a canoeing accident or battle. Rock art often marks places where mythical events occurred and is sometimes associated with named personages. Even though rock art surveys have been conducted on the Northwest Coast (Emmons 1908; Hill and Hill 1975; Lundy 1974), individual rock art sites demand intensive, careful analysis to understand their roles in ancient societies.

Fishing Weirs/Traps and Clam Gardens

Other components of the built environment represent investments in infrastructure that enabled intensification of resource use. As described earlier, fishing weirs and traps are found across the Northwest Coast, and while the oldest date to 6000 cal B.P., most date to the Late Holocene. These fishing features were tailored to local fish behavior and movements. Many weirs and traps were used to harvest salmon, although herring, smelt, eulachon, flatfish, and sculpins were taken from some weirs and traps (Byram 2002). In some places, the fish concentrated in the trap were also bait for other animals including birds and sea mammals (Monks 1987).

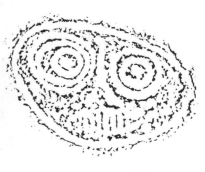

Figure 6.6. Face Petroglyph (possibly a seal), Saltspring Island, B.C. Photo and rubbing by Daniel Leen, used with permission. See http://danielleen.org/petroglyphs.html.

Losey (2010b) used emic perspectives to reveal the relationships between Northwest Coast communities and the fish on which they depended. Fishing weirs and traps were animate; they were spoken to and named. Weirs and traps were understood as analogous to the houses or forts occupied by people. In some areas of the coast, house posts were permanent, while house planks and roofs were taken down and moved to other settlements. Fishing weirs were built of stone and/or wood, and while some portions were largely permanent, lattice fences, portable traps, and sections of wood stakes could be removed to allow free passage of fish after harvest (Losey 2010b). To allow fish to pass through stone traps, walls were lowered or gaps opened up. Weirs and traps are thus salmon "houses" or "forts," and some had decorated trap stakes arrayed to attract the fish. Losey (2010b:28) noted that because portions of fish traps were durable, "many generations of fish encountered them." Thus traps and weirs on the landscape mark the long-term reciprocal interdependence between people and fish.

Clam gardens are not as widely known as weirs and traps. The highest density of clam gardens thus far is in the Broughton Archipelago in Kwakwaka'wakw territory, where 365 of them have been mapped (Harper et al. 2002). By building clam gardens, people enlarged clam habitat, increasing the quantities of clams that could be collected during low tides. Harper et al. (2002) found that clam gardens were not built adjacent to living sites. This may have reduced the chance that clam gardens would be polluted with the by-products of human occupation. Today we know of a variety of sources of shellfish toxicity, including paralytic shellfish poisoning (PSP) and domoic acid, but shellfish beds can also be contaminated by sewage. The Kwakwaka'wakw named beaches known for poisonous clams (Boas 1909), and they and other Northwest Coast societies were aware of shellfish poisoning (Moss 1993). People likely knew the hazards of sewage and inadequate circulation, and this may help explain why clam gardens were built away from villages in the constricted waterways of the Broughton Archipelago. As part of the built environment, clam gardens represent investments of labor into the landscape. They were probably owned and actively maintained, and were part of a social group's legacy.

While some of these constructed features represent economic investments that increase resource productivity, not all of them do. Features were built to communicate information; a rock art panel along a stream mouth may demonstrate ownership of the rights to salmon in the stream, but the beings depicted and their social affiliations may not be recognized by all viewers. Mounds and burial cairns can convey messages of status differentiation and long-term connection with a special place, even if the identity of those buried is not known to everyone. Other sites that held significant social meaning during the Late Holocene were defensive sites—also clearly part of the built environment. With the houses, fishing weirs and traps, clam terraces, mounds and cairns, much labor has been invested in the landscape and ownership has been claimed. Such investments and resource claims may be contested and require defense.

Warfare

A review of Northwest Coast archaeological evidence turns up cases of interpersonal violence dating to 2,000 years ago (Cybulski 1990, 1992, 1999), and many fort sites and some trench-embankments post-dating 1200 RYBP (Angelbeck 2009; Moss and Erlandson 1992). Concern with defense had become a significant factor in Tlingit, Tsimshian, and Coast Salish regions between A.D. 900 and 1400 (e.g., Martindale and Supernant 2009). Groups that produced surplus could be vulnerable to theft and attack, and as populations increased and the landscape filled, intergroup competition probably increased. Prince Rupert Harbor, with its seasonal concentrations of eulachon and salmon, may have been one of the first areas contested. Warfare became culturally significant to many Northwest Coast peoples by about 1,000 year ago. Northwest Coast warfare and slavery as documented for the nineteenth century, however, has probably led to exaggerating the scale of warfare in the more ancient past (Moss 2010).

For the Gulf of Georgia, Angelbeck (2009) identified two periods of warfare among the Coast Salish: between 1600 and 1200 RYBP and just prior to contact through the nineteenth century. Both periods followed phases of "increasing entrenchment of elite power and hegemony." Angelbeck views warfare as an anarchic practice individuals used to resist the elite power structures that had developed among the Coast Salish. Through warfare, non-elites gained wealth and prestige becoming *nouveau riche*, leading to a heterarchy of chiefs in which power was decentralized and continually contested. Thus warfare was employed not for the purpose of reducing inequality but to redistribute power among a broader base of elites. Local and individual autonomy (at household or village scale) was maintained, network forms of organization extended out from the household or lineage group, and persistent conflict kept the power of individuals in check, leading to a heterarchy of chiefs according to Angelbeck (2009:iii, 309–310).

Interaction across the Northwest Coast

It is easy to conceptualize ethnographic territories as static and bounded, and forget their origins as nineteenth- and twentieth-century anthropological constructions. While Western notions of political boundaries focus on land and its ownership, Northwest Coast societies were oriented to networks of waterways around island and coastal landscapes. Saltwater passages did not constrain relationships between social groups—they facilitated canoe travel between groups located on islands and the mainland. The interior mainland and the larger islands with their steep-sided mountains and dense forests were comparatively difficult to traverse on foot, although mainland rivers served as travel corridors. In the north, households and lineage groups maintained their autonomy, whereas village autonomy was the norm in the south.

Ethnographically, Northwest Coast people were enmeshed in social relationships beyond the local. Such relationships relied on long-distance travel made possible by seaworthy canoes, territorial knowledge, and expert navigation. Although the history of such interactions has yet to be traced archaeologically, it must depend on the development of canoe technologies and presumably, the availability of large cedar trees from which to carve canoes.

Although boats are inferred from the earliest period of coastal occupation, the frequency and extent of contacts must have fluctuated over time. By the Late Holocene, cedar was widely available south of Frederick Sound (Alaska), so extensive interaction probably occurred.

Across the North Pacific, changes in adjacent regions undoubtedly influenced the Northwest Coast. The Arctic Maritime expansion into southcentral Alaska ca. 1000 RYBP must have affected other groups on the Pacific Coast (Dumond 2009). If people were displaced into Tlingit territory, this may have increased conflict that affected groups to the south. The eruption of White River ash in the Yukon at 1200 RYBP stimulated Athapaskans to migrate south (Ives 2003), increasing pressure on groups in interior B.C., that in turn would have affected coastal groups. Some Haida moved from Haida Gwaii north to Prince of Wales Island during the protohistoric period causing territorial conflict, but the history of this fairly recent migration remains sketchy (Moss 2008a). These population movements likely contributed to an increase in warfare within the last 1,000 years.

Heterarchical models of Northwest Coast societies accommodate the dialectic between local structures of inequality within and between houses and extra-local relationships with people beyond one's village, town, or resource territory. These extra-local relationships could take the form of trade partnerships, marriage alliances, or reciprocal raids, and likely combinations thereof. Such relationships were probably not limited to local elites, but were open to anyone with the means to travel beyond the limits of their group. Angelbeck's (2009) application of anarchy theories holds potential for generalizing about this process; such practices also facilitate resiliency among Northwest Coast groups in times of environmental, resource, or social stress. Northwest Coast social systems were inherently dynamic—a mosaic of interlocking webs of social relationships in a continual state of flux.

Notes

1. It is also known as the Strait of Georgia or the Salish Sea.

2. Mitchell (1971) preferred the term "culture type" to phase, but as Ames (2009:6) pointed out, these terms are used interchangeably. I lump the phase designations for the Fraser delta and valley (Mitchell 1990) into those of the Gulf of Georgia, for the sake of simplicity.

3. In his study of 64 Gulf of Georgia artifact assemblages (using Burley's [1979] typology), Clark (2010:271) found a high proportion of chipped stone to be the best predictor of Locarno Beach assignment. Although this contradicts Ames on this point, both studies found that most artifact types could not be used as index fossils. Differences between the composition of Locarno Beach or Marpole assemblages are fairly subtle.

4. Keddie (2007) described items previously termed "Gulf Island Complex" as parts of composite labrets. These include ground stone items with drilled holes around which a cord could be attached to anchor the ornament to the teeth (such as shown in Figure 6.2n).

5. This pattern differs from the northern Northwest Coast, where ethnographically and historically, non-slave women wore labrets, and status was denoted by labret size (Moss 1999).

6. Of the total, 73 percent of celts were varieties of nephrite, 11 percent of nephrite or serpentine, while 16 percent were made of more commonly available slate or porphyry (Mackie 1995:46).

7. Relatively few artifacts from Queen Charlotte Strait assemblages have been geochemically traced. Carlson (1994:315) reported 87 items from 17 sites; the best sampled was the O'Connor site, with 39 items identified as Central Coast A (Kingcome) and 13 as Central Coast B.

8. Might these be similar to the scaled pieces identified by Close (2006) at English Camp?

9. Sutherland (2004:236) stated that 25 individuals were buried at the site, but I use 28 following Cybulski (2001:11, 2006:533).

10. The exact number of sexed burials in Prince Rupert Harbor has not been published; my estimate is drawn from Cybulski's (1992:70-72) text and tables.

11. No single source presents artifact counts from Ozette. I have pieced together the numbers presented here from various accounts; many are clearly estimates (e.g., "over 500" and "over 1000"), and not exact counts.

12. These figures derive from estimates of space per capita and the optimal size of housepits (Hayden et al. 1996).

13. The post and stake molds illustrated for both houses (Lepofsky et al. 2009:604-605) do not clearly outline rectangular structures, and numerous molds occurred outside both structures. Only one wall was excavated of the oldest house (Structure 1) and the position of the other three walls was extrapolated. The rectangular outline of Structure 2 seems more certain, since it was cut into the gravel terrace on three sides.

14. McNichol Creek house sizes were estimated. Although Coupland (2006:88) stated that House O was 105 m^2 and the other houses averaged 60 m^2, his data on p. 86 indicate that House O was 99 m^2 and the other houses averaged 67 m^2, a difference of 32 percent.

15. After about 1000 B.P., burial practices in the Gulf of Georgia become more individuated, with elites commissioning elaborately carved grave houses and boxes placed above ground behind the village (Thom 1995). Thom interpreted this as elites becoming more exclusive and competitive with one another.

7

Looking to the Future of
Northwest Coast Archaeology

In writing this book, I have tried to approach the archaeological record on its own terms. The pursuits of culture history and cultural complexity have produced valuable data on the pre-contact history of Northwest Coast fishers and food producers. Study of late Pleistocene environments has been incredibly productive over the last 20 years. Glacial refugia on the Prince of Wales Archipelago, Haida Gwaii, and Vancouver Island during the LGM were substantial enough to support bears, ungulates, and human settlers. The distribution of the earliest sites shows that Northwest Coast residents relied upon boats for travel and subsistence. Emerging data from the interior of western North America support late Pleistocene movement to the continent via a route along the Pacific coast at a time when ice sheets covered much of the north. Sea-level histories structure the archaeological record of the Northwest Coast, and Early Holocene sites are more numerous than those of the late Pleistocene. One of the most striking recent discoveries is how closely Early Holocene wood technologies resemble those of recent times (Kilgii Gwaay).

In previous synthetic treatments of region-wide patterns on the Northwest Coast, a temporal break at 5000 RYBP (5700 cal B.P.) was made between earlier "Lithic Stage" (Archaic) and later "Developmental Stage" (Pacific) periods. But older technologies did not entirely disappear—they underwent modifications while new technologies were added. Large shell middens didn't appear simultaneously across the coast. Formation of shell-bearing sites always depends on local sea-level and cultural histories. Shell midden formation may reveal more about coastal processes than culture change and sedentism. Region-wide cultural change at 5000 RYBP is not evident, even though this has been the basis of the prevailing narrative of Northwest Coast "prehistory" in which the Middle Holocene has been viewed as a time of emerging cultural complexity (7,000, 5,000 or 3,000 years ago).

In the Late Holocene, the number and size of sites increases, partly due to the greater visibility and accessibility of Late Holocene sites compared to older ones. The artifact patterning embedded in culture historical units can be treated as hypotheses requiring re-evaluation. Recent research raises questions about what we think we know about the archaeological record. Much variability in the record of the Northwest Coast results from the uneven distribution of obsidian, other sources of chipped stone, slate, serpentine, nephrite, mussel shell, and whale or cervid bones, leading to a mosaic of different assemblages. Shell middens, burial grounds, fishing weirs/traps, and clam gardens are not just site types, but are part of the built environment that resonated with people in the past. These same sites retain social meaning today because they represent cultural landscapes and mark aboriginal territories. In this chapter, I focus on new archaeological directions and how the future of Northwest Coast archaeology can be relevant to public concerns.

Landscapes and Seascapes: Beyond Coastal Sites and Assemblages

Across much of the Northwest Coast, most archaeological sites are found on the coast itself. Of the sites now located some distance away from the shoreline, many were closer to saltwater at the time they were occupied because of subsequent sea-level change. Exceptions are the numerous sites located along the Fraser River, an area where archaeologists have long focused their efforts. Surveys along the Skeena and Columbia rivers have also been conducted, but other large mainland river corridors have not been subject to systematic and intensive archaeological surveys.

A focus on the coast is justified by some ethnographic information. De Laguna (1960:30) wrote, "the Tlingit world is essentially the ribbon of the shoreline that winds along the indented coasts of the islands and fiords. Its parts are linked by boat routes across the open water." Saltwater passages facilitated canoe travel between social groups located on various islands and the mainland. The landscapes of the mainland and the larger islands with their steep-sided mountains and dense forests were comparatively impenetrable. De Laguna (1960:30) continued, the land was in a real sense only the back drop for the life which faced the salt water. Most of the village sites were small flats, cramped between the beach and the steep hillside.... Sites for settlements were chosen more for a good landing beach for canoes than for convenient access by trail to inland hunting or trapping grounds. Summer villages and camps might be far up the bays near the salmon streams, but for the winter village of permanent houses, the people prized a view of the more open waters across which the canoes of their friends or of their enemies might be seen approaching. The hunter went inland as little as possible, and tried to train his dogs to drive the deer to where he waited on the beach. Obviously, heavy timbers were cut near the water and were towed, not carried to their destinations.

To understand life of the island Tlingit archaeologists should turn our attention to seascapes that connect groups across water passages. Tlingit ethnographic data show how the spatial distributions of kwaan and clan territories encompass the waterways adjacent to portions of islands and sections of mainland (Moss 2004c). These straits, passages, channels, sounds, inlets, and canals flow between islands and mainland, connecting the social groups who lived across the region. The Tlingit were (are) seagoing people who depended on marine and intertidal habitats, whose social horizons reached beyond their home territories. The dense forests and steep mountains presented more of a barrier to social interchange than did marine waters. Such a portrait may not apply to all Northwest Coast groups, but it encourages us to think about seascapes. In the only study that tries to address Northwest Coast seascapes quantitatively, Q. Mackie (2003) argued that the basic transportation structure (i.e., routes of water travel between sites) of the coast's fjordland archipelago has an antiquity of at least 2,000 years. Mackie used location-allocation modelling to analyze the distribution of several hundred sites on the west coast of Vancouver Island. The water routes between sites form a network that comprised a "landscape of habit" or habitus (Mackie 2003:280).

Groups on the mainland whose territory encompassed riverine corridors that penetrate the interior may have been more terrestrially oriented than the island Tlingit. The Halq'emeylem (Salish) of the Fraser River undoubtedly used terrestrial landscapes and relied upon riverine and terrestrial resources. Recent studies have argued that the temperate forests of the region were actively managed and shaped by First Nations—such forests were not untamed wildernesses as popularly conceived (Oliver 2007). Based on historical records of First Nations using controlled fires to enhance plant growth (e.g., of berries, roots, and seed plants) and provide forage for deer and elk, Lepofsky et al. (2005) attempted to identify evidence for prescribed burning in the Fraser Valley before contact. From their extensive study of soil charcoal, Lepofsky et al. (2005) defined an era of frequent fires, christened the Fraser Valley Fire Period (2400–1200 RYBP). Although they were unable to distinguish evidence of culturally caused fires from natural fires, their research attempts to address the cultural contributions to landscape history at a broad geographic scale, going beyond the site or settlement pattern focus of most archaeological studies on the Northwest Coast.

Across the coast, use of forested uplands has been documented by identifying culturally modified trees (CMTs) (Figure 7.1). Despite de Laguna's supposition, people traveled away from the shoreline to find good cedar trees at elevations of 600 m or more in interior forests (Stryd and Eldridge 1993:200). Whole trees were felled, and "canoe blanks" or trunk segments from which planks were removed have been found. Cedars were stripped for their bark (used in weaving), leaving characteristic scars that usually healed over (Mobley and Eldridge 1992:97–98). Spruce, hemlock, and pine were also used; alcoves were chopped into trees to hold ritual items while some trees were hacked for pitch removal. Hemlock and spruce cambium were eaten and used as medicine. The oldest CMTs are about 500 years old, but historically scarred trees from commercial logging or from setting animal traps have also been found (Mobley and Eldridge 1992). Study of CMTs has potential to reveal forest use both before and after European contact. Using dendrochronology, Pegg (2000) documented an increase in cedar harvest after metal tools were introduced in the late 1700s. He correlated later trends in cedar harvest with a range of developments.

Although forest resources were available in most areas, "catcher" beaches in some locations collected driftwood that could be used as fuelwood. Cape Addington is located almost 400 km north of the range of Douglas fir, although substantial amounts of Douglas fir charcoal were found in paleobotanical samples from the site. We reasoned that Douglas fir was collected as driftwood from the beach and was preferentially selected because of its hot smokeless flame (Lepofsky et al. 2003). Such paleobotanical analyses can inform us about a range of activities conducted at a site. Driftwood distribu-

Figure 7.1. Barked-stripped western hemlock. From *Culturally Modified Trees of British Columbia, CMT Handbook,* used with permission from British Columbia Archaeology Branch.

tions changed over time, depending on shifts in the composition of forests, winds and storminess, and the strength and extent of ocean currents (Shaw 2008).

The Meier House stood for almost 400 years, and over its lifespan, it consumed at least 500,000 board feet of lumber to maintain (Ames and Maschner 1999:167). Assuming wood houses built across the coast required comparable amounts, impacts on forests near villages were not trivial, and sometimes may have resulted in erosion and soil loss, which in turn may have affected nearshore habitats. Other types of landscape modifications— weirs and traps, clam terraces, and estuarine gardens—could have unintentional impacts, e.g., if a fishing weir captured sediment rendering it ineffective. Similarly, clam terraces and root gardens may have affected coastal processes and drainage patterns. Yet emerging evidence suggests these modifications of intertidal and near-shore zones enhanced biological productivity beyond that of the "natural" environment. The unique Northwest Coast region is a product of its complex human histories embedded in its landscapes. How these landscape modifications were socially meaningful as markers of family, clan, tribal ownership, and social identity adds other dimensions to our studies.

The extent to which terrestrial landscapes away from the coast figure into Northwest Coast pre-contact history is an open question. Although de Laguna's portrait of the island Tlingit is valuable because it focuses attention on seascapes, all Northwest Coast groups probably made use of terrestrial landscapes. Current research by paleoethnobotanists and those studying cultural modified trees is revealing new information on the use of terrestrial resources, especially those of the forest. Documentation of traditional ecological knowledge and of traditional cultural properties is also contributing to more holistic approaches to the study of Northwest Coast landscapes. Even landscapes above timberline were used by Northwest Coast residents.

The Potential of Zooarchaeology

Although a great deal of zooarchaeological research on the Northwest Coast revolves around arguments about resource intensification, zooarchaeological data are also relevant to contemporary concerns.

Human Impacts, Climate Change, and Fish and Wildlife Management

Recent zooarchaeological studies of northern fur seal are revealing how changes in one part of the north Pacific affect others. Study of this species demonstrates how zooarchaeological data can expose new information about biogeography of relevance to fish and wildlife managers. While working on the Cape Addington project, we were surprised to find the remains of northern fur seal pups (Moss 2004a). Since most northern fur seals are born in the Pribilof Islands in the Bering Sea today, and pups don't swim before they are

4 months old, and because the Pribilofs are located ~2500 km away from Cape Addington, we reasoned that the fur seal remains were from animals migrating south in the fall, from stranded animals, or there was a breeding area located somewhere near Cape Addington in the past. We pursued this question with isotopic and ancient DNA studies of fur seal bones to see if and how they were related to Pribilof seals and where they foraged in the ocean. We confirmed that at least two Northern fur seal pups and two juveniles were present at Cape Addington, but the genetic evidence of their relationship to the Pribilof seals was ambiguous (Moss et al. 2006b).

Meanwhile Gifford-Gonzalez et al. (2005) had found abundant northern fur seal remains in California sites dated to the Middle and Late Holocene. Gifford-Gonzalez suggested that in the past, northern fur seals maintained breeding colonies in California. This was a radical idea that at least some biologists rejected, yet work by Lyman (1988), Etnier (2002), and Crockford et al. (2002) supports the idea that northern fur seals had breeding colonies along the coasts of California, Oregon, Washington, B.C., and locations other than the Pribilofs in Alaska. Crockford and Frederick (2007) suggested that the Pribilof Islands were not accessible to northern fur seals for breeding during the height of the Neoglacial between ca. 3800 and 2600 cal B.P. and that this is when they bred at more southerly latitudes. They proposed that winter sea ice on the Bering Sea extended to a more southerly position than it does now and that ice persisting longer into the summer blocked access to the Pribilofs at a crucial time in the reproductive cycle of fur seals. What biologists thought was a stable pattern of fur seal fidelity to the Pribilof breeding grounds (Gentry 1998) may be a result of post-Neoglacial warming after 2600 cal B.P. This suggests that northern fur seals are capable of significant behavioral flexibility over the long term. Not until fur seals were hunted in the early twentieth century were they in jeopardy. Understanding the longer-term history of this species that adapted not just to environmental change, but to human hunting pressure, is crucial for understanding how fur seals should be managed today.

Global patterns suggest that the long-term trend along the Pacific coast is toward warmer ocean temperatures that may be less biologically productive than in the past. The ranges and abundance of a variety of marine fish, birds, and mammals are expected to shift. With global warming, snowmelt will accelerate and stream runoff will increase in the spring. In summer, droughts will be more frequent, and low water levels may not adequately support salmon (Augerot 2005:110). Already, the decline in eulachon abundance is partially attributed to increased predation by Pacific hake, a species expanding to the north as water temperatures increase (U.S. Department of Commerce 2009:10869). Archaeological sites are important archives of data on animal abundance and distribution—when considered along with independent paleoenvironmental data and human use, these relationships can help us better understand the consequences of impending climate change. Ideally, this has the potential to yield information our society can use to plan accordingly.

Resource Conservation

During the nineteenth century, the maritime fur trade drove the sea otter to near extinction across much of its range in the north Pacific, and no populations existed on the Oregon coast for 100 years or so. In the 1970s, sea otters from the Aleutian Islands were transplanted to a few places in Oregon, but without success. In their study of ancient DNA extracted from sea otter bones from archaeological sites, Valentine et al. (2008) determined that precontact sea otters in Oregon were more closely related to California sea otters than to Alaskan ones. In the future, California sea otters should be the type introduced into Oregon. U.S. federal law requires that species or subspecies native to an area are the only ones that should be reintroduced to reestablish a population because these animals will be better adapted to and more successful in their new environment (Valentine et al. 2008). Zooarchaeological research has contributed information that can lead to more effective conservation of sea otters. The Confederated Tribes of Siletz and the Coquille Indian tribe are just two of the political entities supporting reintroduction of the sea otter into Oregon waters (Ecotrust 2009). Because sea otters are a keystone species, how they affect the structure and complexity of nearshore ecosystems is under investigation. Again, archaeological data may shed light on this relationship, as they have in other areas of the Pacific coast (e.g., Corbett et al. 2008; Rick et al. 2008).

Native American and First Nations Resource Rights

Archaeological analyses provide data on indigenous use of plants and animals. Today such resources provide more than food—they help define the identities and heritage of Northwest Coast tribes. Archaeological studies have shed light on the history of resource populations and how they have been used by tribal ancestors. In an era of environmental threats to several species, some archaeologists have argued that Native practices can provide a model for sustainable resource use. Perhaps the most famous and controversial example of archaeological data used to support assertion of Native American/First Nation resource rights is the case for Makah whaling. The Makah Tribal Council and Makah Whaling Commission (2005) explain:

> Whaling has been one of our traditions for over 1,500 years and is a right secured to us by treaty with the United States. We had to stop in the 1920s due to the scarcity of gray whales. Their full recovery to pre-commercial whaling levels and 1994 removal from the Endangered Species List made it possible to resume the hunt. There has been an intensification of interest in our own history and culture since the archeological dig at our village of Ozette in 1970, which uncovered thousands of artifacts bearing witness to our whaling tradition. Many Makah feel that our health problems result, in some degree, to the loss of our traditional diet of seafood and marine mammal meat. We would like to restore the meat of the whale to our diet. Many of us also believe that the problems besetting our young people stem from lack of discipline and pride. We believe that the restoration of whaling will help to restore that discipline and pride.

Excavations at Ozette establish the antiquity of whale hunting and resulted in the recovery of more than 3,400 whale bones, a range of tools made of whale bone, specialized equipment used in whale hunting, and numerous depictions of whales on artwork (Fisken 1994; Huelsbeck 1994; Monks 2003). Whales not only provided food, but were also processed for oil, a valuable trade item. Whales and whaling are the subjects of Makah songs, dances, and art. Whaling families play special roles in Makah society, and the whale hunt involves ceremonies and rituals that reinforce the social and spiritual relationship between Makahs and whales.

In today's society, one might think that indigenous use of seabirds is unnecessary; after all, any grocery store sells chickens and eggs. Study of the Forrester Islands, however, showed that collecting eggs and birds from this place was an important sociocultural practice (Moss 2007). Assemblages from five archaeological sites yielded identifications of 11 seabird taxa. Even though the Kaigani Haida, the Tlingit, and their ancestors had harvested seabirds during spring and summer on the Forrester Islands since 1600 cal

B.P., the Forresters, as part of the Alaska Maritime Wildlife Refuge, are off-limits to Native egg collecting and bird-hunting today. Even though it has been illegal for the Tlingit and Haida to take birds from the Forresters since 1912, in the 1910s through the 1920s, biologists shot large numbers of birds and collected quantities of eggs for museums, because this is the way field ornithology was practiced. This Forrester Island case is parallel to that of the Huna Tlingit, who traditionally collected gull eggs from the Marble Islands, now located in Glacier Bay National Park. Hunn et al. (2003) documented the traditional way the Huna collect eggs; if eggs are taken properly at specific times, the gulls will re-lay, and the number of surviving gulls every year will not be reduced by egg removal. Even though Huna are still prohibited from collecting gull eggs on the Marble Islands, biologists were allowed to remove eggs (following Huna protocols) to test the efficacy of this traditional practice. These ironies notwithstanding, zooarchaeology can support claims of aboriginal resource rights.

Pacific herring is the foundation of North Pacific marine ecosystems, and herring are key prey for a variety of animals. In southeast Alaska, the sac roe fishery is among the most lucrative in the region, with an enormous impact on the regional economy. Yet contemporary harvest levels are based on abundances of the late twentieth century, when herring were already depleted (Thornton et al. 2010). At the same time, Tlingit subsistence users of herring eggs have seen reductions in the quantities of eggs available for harvest. Long-term use of herring is not well-documented over space or through time, yet this archaeological information can inform us about pre-industrial patterns of herring abundance and distribution that should help us better understand the status of herring stocks today (Moss et al. 2011). Ancient DNA promises to reveal the genetic relationships between herring today and in the past (e.g., Lepofsky and Welch 2009).

Animals provide calories and nutrients, but on the Northwest Coast, contemporary uses of animals go beyond this. Traditional foods are consumed at social functions, presented as gifts, and traded widely. Animals provide a source of materials used to make regalia and artwork worn and displayed at social gatherings and in ceremonies. The many practices involved in obtaining and preparing animals for food and products are integral to the transmission of cultural knowledge and bonding between generations. Northwest Coast animals are central to artworks that help define the identity and heritage of families, clans, and tribes. Relationships between people and animals are characterized by respect, reciprocity, and cooperation. For these reasons, the archaeology of animals on the Northwest Coast is about much more than utility indexes or measures of intensification.

Confronting Stereotypes based in Ethnography

The ethnographic record of whaling by the Makah and the Nuu-chah-nulth of Vancouver Island is robust. These groups were specialized whale hunters, while other Northwest groups are not thought to have hunted whales systematically. Archaeologists working among the Makah and Nuu-chah-nulth understandably focus on the antiquity and character of whaling and whale use among these groups (e.g., Monks et al. 2001). When a whale bone embedded with a projectile point was found at Par-Tee in Oregon, the most likely explanation (based on ethnography) was that a whale injured by Makah or Nuu-chah-nulth hunters had drifted south and was scavenged by people living on the Oregon coast. But Losey and Yang (2007) identified the projectile point as elk (*Cervus elaphus*) bone, and its ancient DNA matched that of unmodified elk bone found at Par-Tee, indicating that local materials were used to make this weapon. Losey and Yang (2007) identified the whale phalanx as that of a humpback whale (*Megaptera novaeangliae*) and made a strong case for whaling by an Oregon group, ca. 1600-1300 B.P.

Another example is Drucker's (1951:46) categorical statement regarding the Nuu-chah-nulth that "[f]ur seal were not hunted aboriginally" (McMillan 2009:638). Drucker thought that his consultants' knowledge of fur seals was a product of their participation in the nineteenth-century fur seal industry. Yet fur seal bones are more abundant than those of any other marine mammal in most Nuu-chah-nulth sites (Crockford et al. 2002:152; Frederick and Crockford 2005:180; McMillan 1999:140, 2009:638). Here, a seemingly authoritative source led to a mischaracterization of pre-contact lifeways. Such archaeological studies open our collective minds to the possibility that past Northwest Coast peoples engaged in practices not adequately documented in ethnographic and ethnohistorical records.

Lessons from *Kwädäy Dan T'sinchi*, Long Ago Person Found

In 1999, the remains of an aboriginal man were found at the edge of a receding glacier 1600 m above sea level in northwestern B.C., in the traditional territory of the Champagne and Aishihik First Nations in Tatshenshini-Alsek

Park. The man was named Kwäday Dän Ts'ìnchi, or "Long Ago Person Found" in the Tutchone Athapaskan language. First Nations and Provincial representatives agreed to recover and study the remains. Over the last decade, aspects of this person's life have been revealed in astonishing detail.

In his late teens to early twenties, Kwäday Dän Ts'ìnchi lived sometime between A.D. 1670 and 1850[1] (Beattie et al. 2000; Richards et al. 2007). His stomach contents indicate that he ate meat, probably some crab, beach asparagus (*Salicornia* sp.), and berries during one of his last meals (Mudie et al. 2005). As Dickson and Mudie (2008:47) describe, "[f]or the last days of Kwäday Dän Ts'ìnchi's life it is very clear that he carried seafood, which he must have eaten well away from the coast, probably at high altitude." Even though Kwäday Dän Ts'ìnchi had recently been on the coast, he was found 1600 m above sea level in the mountains, about 50 km from the upper estuary of the Chilkat River (Dickson and Mudie 2008). Despite the harsh conditions at this elevation, Kwäday Dän Ts'ìnchi was traveling on foot across glaciers to the mountainous interior of B.C., not far from the Yukon. He was found with an interior-type robe made of ~95 Arctic ground squirrel skins, sewn together with sinew. He wore a coastal-type conical basketry hat made of spruce roots (Figure 7.2). He carried a beaver skin bag, a walking stick, an iron-blade knife and a throwing or snare stick. Fish scales found on his remains and clothing were identified as chum or sockeye salmon (Troffe et al. 2008). Through analysis of his tissues, molecular archaeologists found that Kwäday Dän Ts'ìnchi had spent much of his life on the coast eating marine foods (as indicated in bone), but that he had been living inland long enough (4–6 months) that a more terrestrially oriented diet had registered in his skin collagen (Dickson and Mudie 2008; Corr et al. 2009).

From oral history, we know that trails led from the coast to the interior, crossing glaciers. Kwäday Dän Ts'ìnchi made his last journey during late summer, and the carbonate mineralogy of the silt grains in his gut (from drinking water) suggest he traveled to the glacier up the Chilkat River basin (Dickson and Mudie 2008; Mudie et al. 2005). Kwäday Dän Ts'ìnchi's ancient DNA was compared to mitochondrial DNA from over 200 Native people. The results show 17 of the individuals tested—eight from Canada and nine from Alaska—are related to Kwäday Dän Ts'ìnchi. The Sealaska Heritage Institute press release (2008) stated,

Figure 7.2. Kwäday Dän Ts'ìnchi's hat, woven from split spruce roots. Photograph by Ruth Got-thardt, Yukon Government; used with permission from Champagne and Aishihik First Nations, ©CAFN.

It's not a huge surprise Long Ago Person Found is related to tribes from both Alaska and Canada. Oral histories and genealogical studies have shown there were migrations of Southeast Tlingits into the Interior and of Interior Natives to Klukwan. There were also intermarriages between the two tribes. It's also known that people from the Yanyeidí (Wolf) clan live in both Alaska and Canada.

Some Tlingit believe Kwäday Dän Ts'ìnchi was a person known from oral traditions as _Kaakaldeini_ (Sealaska Heritage Institute 2008). Kaakaldeini was injured while traveling in the mountains, and when caught in a storm, he told his companions to go on without him. His companions covered him in blankets before they left him for a certain death. In 2001, the remains of Kwäday Dän Ts'ìnchi were cremated, and his ashes scattered over the glacier where he perished.

A tremendous amount of research was conducted on Kwäday Dän Ts'ìnchi and his belongings. The resulting picture of his life is more detailed and intimate than that which emerges from a typical archaeological study. The story of Kwäday Dän Ts'ìnchi shows that the glaciers were not impassable and his last journey demonstrates the material reality of oral traditions. The lives of at least some coastal dwellers were not restricted to saltwater realms—aboriginal people traveled far and wide, and were attuned to glacial environments. J. Cruikshank (2005) documented how indigenous people of this area perceive glaciers as sentient beings who observe and respond to people. Traveling across glaciers requires special skill, knowledge, and attentiveness to avoid life-threatening hazards. The earliest migrants to the Americas must also have had experience with and knowledge of living with glaciers.

Kwäday Dän Ts'ìnchi's story shows the inter-connections of the Northwest Coast peoples to those of the interior, and hints at the influence of the Northwest Coast on the rest of North America. As does the story of Shuká Kaa in Chapter 1, collaborations between First Nations and archaeologists can be powerful and archaeology can benefit diverse stakeholders. In this case, collaboration of the Champagne and Aishihik First Nations with the B.C. Archaeology Branch and Royal British Columbia Provincial Museum insured that treatment of Kwäday Dän Ts'ìnchi was consistent with indigenous values and protocols. In 2008, Lawrence Joe, then heritage director with the Champagne and Aishihik First Nations, said, "[w]e want to be able to use the science to confirm our cultural knowledge, our beliefs and our family relationships" (CBC News 2008).

Not everyone sees the Kwäday Dän Ts'ìnchi case as one of post-colonial reconciliation. Wakeman (2008:173) maintains that unequal power relations characterized the relationship between Champagne and Aishihik First Nations and the Royal British Columbia Museum, with the museum retaining the power to preserve the remains and represent their meaning to broader audiences. In her view, "technoscience's fascination with using biological 'data' to authenticate or disprove Native identity" revivifies "racial taxonomization" (Wakeman 2008:166). Further, "[t]he case of Kwäday Dän Ts'ìnchi and its relation to broader debates about DNA testing on Indigenous populations therefore foregrounds how, under the guise of objective science, genetic discourses have reinvented colonialist preoccupations with biological essentialism, racial purity, and the body of the native other for the contemporary era" (Wakeman 2008:195). When Lawrence Joe expressed the desire to use science to confirm "our cultural knowledge, our beliefs and our family relationships" (cited above), is he merely looking to outside authorities for affirmation? If the results of the investigation of Kwäday Dän Ts'ìnchi helped settle First Nations land claims or regain access to resources protected within Tatshenshini-Alsek Park, then perhaps the benefits to First Nations stakeholders would be even more consequential.

The case of Kwäday Dän Ts'ìnchi demonstrates that while contemporary climate change causes increased vulnerability of archaeological sites and materials, we can work together to recover valuable information before it is lost. As climate change continues, more glaciers will recede revealing the remains of indigenous people's use of the uplands. As sea levels continue to rise, more coastal sites will be eroded into the ocean. These forces have the potential to destroy a great deal of the archaeological record, but simultaneously they present significant opportunities for collaborative research to uncover untold stories of the ancient history of the Northwest Coast.

Note

1. The radiocarbon dates on clothing suggest Kwäday Dän Ts'ìnchi lived between A.D. 1400 and 1490 (Dickson and Mudie 2008:31). The discrepancy between these dates and those on his body has not been resolved.

References

Acheson, Steven R.

1998 *In the Wake of Ya'aats' Xaatgaay [Iron People]: a Study of Changing Settlement Strategies among the Kunghit Haida*. BAR International Series 711. British Archaeological Reports, Oxford.

Ackerman, Robert E., Thomas D. Hamilton, and Robert Stuckenrath

1979 Early Culture Complexes of the Northern Northwest Coast. *Canadian Journal of Archaeology* 3:195–209.

Ackerman, Robert E., Kenneth C. Reid, James D. Gallison, and Mark E. Roe

1985 *Archaeology of Heceta Island: A Survey of 16 Timber Harvest Units in the Tongass National Forest, Southeastern Alaska*. Center for Northwest Anthropology Project Report No. 3. Washington State University, Pullman.

Ackerman, Robert E., Kenneth C. Reid, and James D. Gallison

1989 Heceta Island: an Early Maritime Adaptation. In *Development of Hunting-Fishing-Gathering Maritime Societies along the West Coast of North America*, edited by Astrida Blukis Onat, pp. 1–29. Proceedings of the Circum-Pacific Prehistory Conference, Seattle. Washington State University, Pullman.

Ames, Christopher

2009 From Chipped to Ground: The Spatio-Temporal Systematics of 9000 Years of Archaeological Change in Southwest British Columbia. Master's thesis, McGill University, Montreal.

Ames, Christopher, André Costopoulos, and Colin Wren

2010 8000 Years of Technological Change in the Gulf of Georgia: Is There a Major Transition at 4850 cal BP? *Canadian Journal of Archaeology* 34:32–63.

Ames, Kenneth M.

1996 Life in the Big House: Household Labor and Dwelling Size on the Northwest Coast. In *People Who Lived in Big Houses: Archaeological Perspectives on Large Domestic Structures*, edited by Gary Coupland and E. B. Banning, pp. 131–150. Monographs in World Archaeology No. 27. Prehistory Press, Madison, Wisconsin.

2005 *The North Coast Prehistory Project Excavations in Prince Rupert Harbour, British Columbia: the Artifacts*. BAR International Series 1342. John and Erica Hedges, Oxford. British Archaeological Reports, Oxford.

2006 Thinking about Household Archaeology on the Northwest Coast. In *Household Archaeology on the Northwest Coast*, edited by Elizabeth A. Sobel, D. Ann Trieu Gahr, and Kenneth M. Ames, pp. 16–36. International Monographs in Prehistory Archaeological Series 16, Ann Arbor.

Ames, Kenneth M., Don E. Dumond, Jerry R. Galm, and Rick Minor
  1998 Prehistory of the Southern Plateau. In *Plateau*, edited by Deward E. Walker, Jr., pp. 103–119. Handbook of North American Indians, Vol. 12, William C. Sturtevant, general editor, Smithsonian Institution, Washington, D.C.

Ames, Kenneth M., and Herbert D.G. Maschner
  1999 *Peoples of the Northwest Coast: Their Archaeology and Prehistory*. Thames and Hudson, London.

Anderson, Douglas D.
  1970 Akmak: an Early Archaeological Assemblage from Onion Portage, Northwest Alaska. *Acta Arctica* 16.

Angelbeck, William O.
  2009 "They Recognize No Superior Chief" Power, Practice, Anarchism, and Warfare in the Coast Salish Past. Ph.D. dissertation, Department of Anthropology, University of British Columbia, Vancouver.

Arcas Consulting Archaeologists, Ltd.
  1999 *Archaeological Investigations at Tsawwassen, B.C.*, Vol. IV, *Interpretation*. Prepared for Construction Branch, South Coast Region, Ministry of Transportation and Highways, Burnaby, British Columbia.

Atleo, E. Richard
  2005 Preface. In *Keeping it Living: Traditions of Plant Use and Cultivation on the Northwest Coast of North America*, edited by Douglas Deur and Nancy J. Turner, pp. vii–xi. University of Washington Press, Seattle.

Augerot, Xanthippe
  2005 *Atlas of Pacific Salmon*. University of California Press, Berkeley, Wild Salmon Center and Ecotrust, Portland, Oregon.

Baichtal, James F., and Risa J. Carlson
  2007 Raised Marine Data Set for Southeast Alaska. Appendix 1 in Current Models of the Human Colonization of the Americas: The Evidence from Southeast Alaska, by R. J. Carlson. Master's thesis, Cambridge University.

Baichtal, James F., Susan J. Crockford, and Risa J. Carlson
  2008 Possible Evidence of Warmer, Drier Climates During the Early Holocene of Southern Southeast Alaska from Shell-Bearing Raised Marine and Peat Deposits. Paper presented at the 35th Annual Meeting of the Alaska Anthropological Association, Anchorage.

Baichtal, James F., and Susan M. Karl
  2009 Pleistocene and Holocene Volcanoes, Obsidian Sources, and Shell-Bearing Raised Marine Deposits in Southern Southeast Alaska. Paper presented at the 36th Annual Meeting of the Alaska Anthropological Association, Juneau.

Balée, William, and Clark L. Erickson
  2006 Time, Complexity, and Historical Ecology. In *Time and Complexity in Historical Ecology: Studies in the Neotropical Lowlands,* edited by William Balée and Clark Erickson, pp. 1–17. Columbia University Press, New York.

Banahan, Joan
  2000 Ground Stone Tool Technology: an Experiment in Manufacturing Processes. *The Midden* 32:2–8. Archaeological Society of British Columbia, Vancouver.

Barbeau, Marius C.
    1929 *Totem Poles of the Gitksan, Upper Skeena River, British Columbia.* Anthropological Series 12, National Museum of Canada Bulletin 61, Ottawa.

Barnard, Alan
    2004 Hunter-Gatherers in History, Archaeology, and Anthropology: Introductory Essay. In *Hunter-Gatherers in History, Archaeology, and Anthropology*, edited by Alan Barnard, pp. 1–13. Berg, Oxford.

Barnett, Homer G.
    1937 Culture Element Distributions VII: Oregon Coast. *University of California Anthropological Records* 1(3):155–204. Berkeley.
    1955 *The Coast Salish of British Columbia.* University of Oregon Press, Eugene.

Bartlein, Patrick J., Katherine H. Anderson, Patricia M. Anderson, Mary E. Edwards, Cary J. Mock, Robert S. Thompson, Robert S. Webb, Thompson Webb III, and Cathy Whitlock
    1998 Paleoclimate Simulations for North America over the Past 21,000 Years: Features of the Simulated Climate and Comparisons with Paleoenvironmental Data. *Quaternary Science Reviews* 17:549–585.

Beattie, Owen, Brian Apland, Erik W. Blake, James A. Cosgrove, Sarah Gaunt, Sheila Greer, Alexander P. Mackie, Kjerstin E. Mackie, Dan Straathof, Valerie Thorp, and Peter M. Troffe
    2000 The Kwäday Dän Ts'ìnchí Discovery from a Glacier in British Columbia. *Canadian Journal of Archaeology* 24:129–147.

Beck, Charlotte, and George T. Jones
    2010 Clovis and Western Stemmed: Population Migration and the Meeting of Two Technologies in the Intermountain West. *American Antiquity* 75:81–116.

Bernick, Kathryn
    1999 Lanaak (49XPA78): a Wet Site on Baranof Island, Southeastern Alaska. State of Alaska Field Archaeology Permit 99-10. Report submitted to Sitka Tribe of Alaska, Sitka, and Alaska Office of History and Archaeology, Anchorage.

Blukis Onat, Astrida R.
    1985 The Multifunctional Use of Shellfish Remains: from Garbage to Community Engineering. *Northwest Anthropological Research Notes* 19:201–207.

Boas, Franz
    1909 *Geographical Names of the Kwakiutl Indians.* Columbia University Press, New York.
    1921 *Ethnology of the Kwakiutl.* Thirty-fifth Annual Report of the Bureau of American Ethnology for the Years 1913–1914. Government Printing Office, Washington, D.C.

Borden, Charles E.
    1970 Cultural History of the Fraser Delta Region: an Outline. In *Archaeology in British Columbia, New Discoveries,* edited by Roy Carlson. *B.C. Studies* 6:95–112.

Boyd, Robert T.
    1985 *The Introduction of Infectious Diseases Among the Indians of the Pacific Northwest, 1774–1874.* Ph.D. dissertation, Department of Anthropology, University of Washington, Seattle.

1990 Demographic History 1774–1874. In *Northwest Coast*, edited by Wayne Suttles, pp. 135–148. Handbook of North American Indians, Vol. 7, William C. Sturtevant, general editor, Smithsonian Institution, Washington, D.C.

1999 Strategies of Indian Burning in the Willamette Valley. In *Indians, Fire and the Land in the Pacific Northwest*, edited by Robert T. Boyd, pp. 94–138. Oregon State University Press, Corvallis.

Brown, Douglas

2003 Shell Middens and Midden Burials in Southern Strait of Georgia Prehistory. In *Archaeology of Coastal British Columbia: Essays in Honour of Professor Philip M. Hobler*, edited by Roy L. Carlson, pp. 153–164. Archaeology Press, Publication No. 30, Simon Fraser University, Burnaby, British Columbia.

Burley, David V.

1979 Marpole: Anthropological Reconstructions of a Prehistoric Northwest Coast Culture Type. Ph.D. dissertation, Department of Archaeology, Simon Fraser University, Burnaby, British Columbia.

1980 *Marpole: Anthropological Reconstructions of a Prehistoric Northwest Coast Culture Type.* Archaeology Press, Department of Archaeology, Simon Fraser University, Burnaby, British Columbia.

1989 *Senewélets: Culture History of the Nanaimo Coast Salish and the False Narrows Midden.* Royal British Columbia Memoir No. 2. Royal British Columbia Museum, Victoria.

Butler, Virginia L., and Sarah K. Campbell

2004 Resource Intensification and Resource Depression in the Pacific Northwest of North America: a Zooarchaeological Review. *Journal of World Prehistory* 18:327–405.

Butler, Virginia L., and Jim E. O'Connor

2004 9000 Years of Salmon Fishing on the Columbia River, North America. *Quaternary Research* 62:1–8.

Byram, R. Scott

1998 Fishing Weirs in Oregon Coast Estuaries. In *Hidden Dimensions, the Cultural Significance of Wetland Archeology*, edited by Kathryn Bernick, pp. 199–219. UBC Press, Vancouver.

2002 Brush Fences and Basket Traps: The Archaeology and Ethnohistory of Tidewater Weir Fishing in Oregon. Ph.D. dissertation, Department of Anthropology, University of Oregon, Eugene.

Canadian Broadcasting Corporation (CBC) News

2008 Scientists Find 17 Living Relatives of "Iceman" Discovered in B.C. Glacier. Electronic document, http://www.cbc.ca/canada/british-columbia/story/2008/04/25/ice-man.html, accessed March 17, 2010.

Cannon, Aubrey

1991 *The Economic Prehistory of Namu: Patterns in Vertebrate Fauna.* Department of Archaeology, Simon Fraser University, Publication 19, Burnaby, British Columbia.

1995 The Ratfish and Marine Resource Deficiencies on the Northwest Coast. *Canadian Journal of Archaeology* 19:49–60.

1996 The Early Namu Archaeofauna. In *Early Human Occupation in British Columbia*, edited by Roy L. Carlson and Luke Dalla Bona, pp. 103–110. UBC Press, Vancouver.

1998 Contingency and Agency in the Growth of Northwest Coast Maritime Economies. *Arctic Anthropology* 35(1):57–67.

2003 Long-term Continuity in Central Northwest Coast Settlement Patterns. In *Archaeology of Coastal British Columbia: Essays in Honour of Professor Philip M. Hobler*, edited by Roy L. Carlson, pp. 1–12. Archaeology Press, Publication No. 30, Simon Fraser University, Burnaby, British Columbia.

Cannon, Aubrey, and Meghan Burchell

2009 Clam Growth-Stage Profiles as a Measure of Harvest Intensity and Resource Management on the Central Coast of British Columbia. *Journal of Archaeological Science* 36:1050–1060.

Cannon, Aubrey, Meghan Burchell, and Rhonda Bathurst

2008 Trends and Strategies in Shellfish Gathering on the Pacific Northwest Coast of North America. In *Early Human Impact on Megamolluscs*, edited by Andrzej Antczak and Roberto Cipriani, pp. 7–22. BAR International Series. Archaeopress, Oxford.

Cannon, Aubrey, and Dongya Y. Yang

2006 Early Storage and Sedentism on the Pacific Northwest Coast: Ancient DNA Analysis of Salmon Remains from Namu, British Columbia. *American Antiquity* 71:123–140.

Cannon, Aubrey, Dongya Yang, and Camilla Speller

2011 Site-Specific Salmon Fisheries on the Central Coast of British Columbia. In *The Archaeology of North Pacific Fisheries*, edited by Madonna L. Moss and Aubrey Cannon. University of Alaska Press, Fairbanks, in press.

Carlson, Catherine C.

2003 The Bear Cove Fauna and the Subsistence History of Northwest Coast Maritime Culture. In *Archaeology of Coastal British Columbia: Essays in Honour of Professor Philip M. Hobler*, edited by Roy L. Carlson, pp. 65–86. Archaeology Press, Publication No. 30, Simon Fraser University, Burnaby, British Columbia.

Carlson, Risa

2007 Current Models of the Human Colonization of the Americas: the Evidence from Southeast Alaska. Master's thesis, Cambridge University.

Carlson, Roy L.

1983 Prehistory of the Northwest Coast. In *Indian Art Traditions of the Northwest Coast*, edited by Roy L. Carlson, pp. 13–32. Archaeology Press, Simon Fraser University, Burnaby, British Columbia.

1994 Trade and Exchange in Prehistoric British Columbia. In *Prehistoric Exchange Systems in North America*, edited by Timothy G. Baugh and Jonathan E. Ericson, pp. 307–361. Plenum Press, New York.

1996a The Later Prehistory of British Columbia. In *Early Human Occupation in British Columbia*, edited by Roy L. Carlson and Luke Dalla Bona, pp. 215–226. UBC Press, Vancouver.

1996b Introduction to Early Human Occupation in British Columbia. In *Early Human Occupation in British Columbia*, edited by Roy L. Carlson and Luke Dalla Bona, pp. 3–10. UBC Press, Vancouver.

1996c Early Namu. In *Early Human Occupation in British Columbia*, edited by Roy L. Carlson and Luke Dalla Bona, pp. 83–102. UBC Press, Vancouver.

1998 Coastal British Columbia in the Light of North Pacific Maritime Adaptations. *Arctic Anthropology* 35(1):23–35.

1999 Sacred Sites on the Northwest Coast of North America. In *Bog Bodies, Sacred Sites and Wetland Archaeology*, edited by Bryony Coles, John Coles and Mogens Schou Jorgensen, pp. 39–46. WARP (Wetland Archaeology Research Project) Occasional Paper 12. Short Run Press, Exeter, U.K.

2008a The Rise and Fall of Native Northwest Coast Culture. *North Pacific Prehistory* 2:93–121.

2008b Projectile Points from the Central and Northern Mainland Coast of British Columbia. In *Projectile Point Sequences in Northwestern North America*, edited by Roy L. Carlson and Martin P. R. Magne, pp. 61–78. Archaeology Press, Publication No. 35, Simon Fraser University, Burnaby, British Columbia.

Carlson, Roy L., and Philip M. Hobler
1993 The Pender Canal Excavations and the Development of Coast Salish Culture. *BC Studies* 99:25–52.

Carlson, Roy L., and Martin P. R. Magne
2008 Projectile Points and Prehistory in Northwestern North America. In *Projectile Point Sequences in Northwestern North America*, edited by Roy L. Carlson and Martin P. R. Magne, pp. 353–362. Archaeology Press, Publication No. 35, Simon Fraser University, Burnaby, British Columbia.

Chapman, Robert
2003 *Archaeologies of Complexity*. Routledge, New York.

Charlton, Arthur S.
1980 *The Belcarra Park Site*. Department of Archaeology Simon Fraser University Publication No. 9, Burnaby, British Columbia.

Chartkoff, Joseph L., and Kerry K. Chartkoff
1984 *The Archaeology of California*. Stanford University Press.

Chatters, James C.
1988 Tualdad Altu (45KI59): a 4th-Century Village on the Black River, King County, Washington. First City Equities, Seattle.

Cheatham, Richard D.
1988 *Late Archaic Settlement Pattern in the Long Tom Sub-Basin, Upper Willamette Valley, Oregon*. University of Oregon Anthropological Paper 39, Eugene.

Christensen, Tina, and Jim Stafford
2005 Raised Beach Archaeology in Northern Haida Gwaii: Preliminary Results from the Cohoe Creek Site. In *Haida Gwaii: Human History and Environment from the Time of Loon to the Time of the Iron People*, edited by Daryl W. Fedje and Rolf W. Mathewes, pp. 245–273. UBC Press, Vancouver.

Clark, Gerald H.
  1979 Archaeological Testing at the Coffman Cove Site, Southeast Alaska. Paper presented at the 32nd Annual Northwest Anthropological Conference, Eugene.
Clark, Terence N.
  2010 *Rewriting Marpole: The Path to Cultural Complexity in the Gulf of Georgia.* Ph.D. dissertation, University of Toronto. Electronic document, http://hdl.handle.net/1807/24713, accessed September 21, 2010.
Close, Angela E.
  2006 *Finding the People Who Flaked the Stone at English Camp (San Juan Island).* University of Utah Press, Salt Lake City.
Codere, Helen
  1957 Kwakiutl Societies: Rank without Class. *American Anthropologist* 59:473–486.
  1990 Kwakiutl: Traditional Culture. In *Northwest Coast*, edited by Wayne Suttles, pp. 359–377. Handbook of North American Indians, Vol. 7, William C. Sturtevant, general editor, Smithsonian Institution, Washington, D.C.
Cole, Douglas
  1985 *Captured Heritage: the Scramble for Northwest Coast Artifacts.* University of Washington Press, Seattle.
Cole, Douglas, and David Darling
  1990 History of the Early Period. In *Northwest Coast*, edited by Wayne. Suttles, pp. 119–134. Handbook of North American Indians, Vol. 7, William C. Sturtevant, general editor, Smithsonian Institution, Washington, D.C.
Conkey, Margaret W., and Sarah H. Williams
  1991 Original Narratives: The Political Economy of Gender in Archaeology. In *Gender at the Crossroads of Knowledge, Feminist Anthropology in the Postmodern Era*, edited by Michaela di Leonardo, pp. 102–139. University of California Press, Berkeley.
Connaway, John M.
  2007 *Fishweirs: a World Perspective with Emphasis on the Fishweirs of Mississippi.* Mississippi Department of Archives and History Archaeological Report No. 33, Jackson.
Connolly, Thomas J.
  1992 *Human Responses to Change in Coastal Geomorphology and Fauna on the Southern Northwest Coast: Archaeological Investigations at Seaside, Oregon.* University of Oregon Anthropological Paper No. 45, Eugene.
  1999 *Newberry Crater: a Ten-Thousand-Year Record of Human Occupation and Environmental Change in the Basin-Plateau Borderlands.* University of Utah Press, Salt Lake City.
Conover, Kathryn
  1978 Matrix Analysis. In *Studies of Bella Bella Prehistory*, edited by James J. Hester and Sarah M. Nelson, pp. 67–99. Department of Archaeology, Simon Fraser University, Publication No. 5, Burnaby, British Columbia.

Corbett, Debra G., Douglas Causey, Mark Clementz, Paul L. Koch, Angela Doroff, Christine Lefevre, and Dixie West

    2008 Aleut Hunters, Sea Otters, and Sea Cows: Three Thousand Years of Interactions in the Western Aleutian Islands, Alaska. In *Human Impacts on Ancient Marine Ecosystems: a Global Perspective*, edited by Torben C. Rick and Jon M. Erlandson, pp. 43–75. University of California Press, Berkeley.

Corr, Lorna T., Michael P. Richards, Colin Grier, Alexander Mackie, and Richard P. Evershed

    2009 Probing Dietary Change of the Kwäday Dän Ts'ìnchi Individual, an Ancient Glacier Body from British Columbia: II. Deconvoluting Whole Skin and Bone Collagen $\delta^{13}C$ Values via Carbon Isotope Analysis of Individual Amino Acids. *Journal of Archaeological Science* 36:12–18.

Coupland, Gary

    1996 The Evolution of Multi-Family Households on the Northwest Coast of North America. In *People Who Lived in Big Houses: Archaeological Perspectives on Large Domestic Structures*, edited by Gary Coupland and E. B. Banning, pp. 121–130. Monographs in World Archaeology No. 27, Prehistory Press, Madison, Wisconsin.

    1998 Maritime Adaptation and Evolution of the Developed Northwest Coast Pattern on the Central Northwest Coast. *Arctic Anthropology* 35(1):36–56.

    2006 A Chief's House Speaks: Communicating Power on the Northwest Coast. In *Household Archaeology on the Northwest Coast*, edited by Elizabeth A. Sobel, D. Ann Trieu Gahr, and Kenneth M. Ames, pp. 80–96. International Monographs in Prehistory, Archaeological Series 16, Ann Arbor.

Coupland, Gary, Terence Clark, and Amanda Palmer

    2009 Hierarchy, Communalism, and the Spatial Order of Northwest Coast Plank Houses: a Comparative Study. *American Antiquity* 74:77–106.

Crockford, Susan J.

    1997 *Osteometry of Makah and Coast Salish Dogs.* Publication No. 22, Archaeology Press, Simon Fraser University, Burnaby, British Columbia.

    2009 *A Practical Guide to* In Situ *Dog Remains for the Field Archaeologist.* Pacific Identifications, Inc., Victoria, British Columbia.

Crockford, Susan J., and Gay Frederick

    2007 Sea Ice Expansion in the Bering Sea During the Neoglacial: Evidence from Archaeozoology. *The Holocene* 17:699–706.

Crockford, Susan J., S. Gay Frederick, and Rebecca J. Wigen

    2002 The Cape Flattery Fur Seal: an Extinct Species of *Callorhinus* in the Eastern North Pacific? *Canadian Journal of Archaeology* 26:152–174.

Croes, Dale R.

    1997 The North-Central Cultural Dichotomy of the Northwest Coast of North America: its Evolution as Suggested by Wet-site Basketry and Wooden Fish-hooks. *Antiquity* 71:594–615.

    2003 Northwest Coast Wet-Site Artifacts: a Key to Understanding Resource Procurement, Storage, Management and Exchange. In *Emerging from the Mist: Studies in Northwest Coast Culture History*, edited by R. G. Matson, Gary Coupland, and Quentin Mackie, pp. 51–75. UBC Press, Vancouver.

Cruikshank, Julie

2005 *Do Glaciers Listen? Local Knowledge, Colonial Encounters, and Social Imagination*. UBC Press, Vancouver, and University of Washington Press, Seattle.

Curtin, A. Joanne

2002 *Prehistoric Mortuary Variability on Gabriola Island, British Columbia*. Archaeology Press, Simon Fraser University, Burnaby, British Columbia.

Cybulski, Jerome S.

1990 Human Biology. In *Northwest Coast*, edited by Wayne Suttles, pp. 52–59. Handbook of North American Indians, Vol. 7, William C. Sturtevant, general editor, Smithsonian Institution, Washington, D.C.

1991 Observations on Labret Wear, Appendix I. In *1989 and 1990 Crescent Beach Excavations, Final Report: the Origins of the Northwest Coast Ethnographic Pattern: the Place of the Locarno Beach Phase*, by R. G. Matson, Heather Pratt, and Lisa Rankin. Permit Report 1989–27, Archaeology Branch, Ministry of Small Business, Tourism and Culture, Victoria, British Columbia.

1992 *A Greenville Burial Ground: Human Remains and Mortuary Elements in British Columbia Coast Prehistory*. Archaeological Survey of Canada Mercury Series Paper No. 146. Canadian Museum of Civilization, Hull, Quebec.

1999 Trauma and Warfare at Prince Rupert Harbour. *The Midden* 31(2): 5–7. Archaeological Society of British Columbia, Vancouver.

2001 Human Biological Relationships for the Northern Northwest Coast. In *Perspectives on Northern Northwest Coast Prehistory*, edited by Jerome S. Cybulski, pp. 107–144. Canadian Museum of Civilization, Hull, Quebec.

2006 Skeletal Biology: Northwest Coast and Plateau. In *Environment, Origins, and Population*, edited by Douglas H. Ubelaker, pp. 532–547. Handbook of North American Indians, Vol. 3, William C. Sturtevant, general editor, Smithsonian Institution, Washington, D.C.

Darby, Melissa

2005 The Intensification of Wapato (*Sagittaria latifolia*) by the Chinookan People of the Lower Columbia River. In *Keeping it Living: Traditions of Plant Use and Cultivation on the Northwest Coast of North America*, edited by Douglas Deur and Nancy J. Turner, pp. 194–217. University of Washington Press, Seattle.

Davis, Stanley D. (editor)

1989 *The Hidden Falls Site, Baranof Island, Alaska*. Aurora: Alaska Anthropological Association Monograph Series V, Anchorage.

de Laguna, Frederica

1960 *The Story of a Tlingit Community: a Problem in the Relationship Between Archeological, Ethnological and Historical Methods*. Smithsonian Institution Bureau of American Ethnology Bulletin 172, Washington, D.C.

1972 *Under Mount Saint Elias: The History and Culture of the Yakutat Tlingit*. Smithsonian Contributions to Anthropology Vol. 7. Smithsonian Institution, Washington, D.C.

Deur, Douglas
    2000 A Domesticated Landscape: Native American Plant Cultivation on the Northwest Coast of North America. Ph.D. dissertation, Louisiana State University, Baton Rouge. University Microfilms, Ann Arbor.
    2005 Tending the Garden, Making the Soil: Northwest Coast Estuarine Gardens as Engineered Environments. In *Keeping it Living: Traditions of Plant Use and Cultivation on the Northwest Coast of North America*, edited by Douglas Deur and Nancy J. Turner, pp. 296–327. University of Washington Press, Seattle.

Deur, Douglas, and Nancy J. Turner
    2005 Introduction: Reassessing Indigenous Resource Management, Reassessing the History of an Idea. In *Keeping it Living: Traditions of Plant Use and Cultivation on the Northwest Coast of North America*, edited by Douglas Deur and Nancy J. Turner, pp. 3–34. University of Washington Press, Seattle.

Dewhirst, John T.
    1980 *The Yuquot Project Volume 1: the Indigenous Archaeology of Yuquot, a Nootkan Outside Village.* History and Archaeology 39, National Historic Parks and Sites Branch, Parks Canada. Environment Canada, Ottawa.

Dickson, James H., and Petra J. Mudie
    2008 The Life and Death of Kwäday Dän Ts'ìnchí, an Ancient Frozen Body from British Columbia: Clues from Remains of Plants and Animals. *The Northern Review* 28:27–50.

Dillehay, Thomas
    2009 Probing Deeper into First American Studies. *PNAS* 106:971–978.

Dixon, E. James
    1993 *Quest for the Origin of the First Americans.* University of New Mexico Press, Albuquerque.
    1999 *Bones, Boats, and Bison: Archaeology and the First Colonization of North America.* University of New Mexico Press, Albuquerque.
    2001 Human Colonization of the Americas: Timing, Technology and Process. *Quaternary Science Reviews* 20:277–299.
    2002 How and When Did People First Come to North America? *Athena Review* 3(2):23–27.
    2008 Bifaces from On Your Knees Cave, Southeast Alaska. In *Projectile Point Sequences in Northwestern North America*, edited by Roy L. Carlson and Martin P. R. Magne, pp. 11–18. Archaeology Press, Publication No. 35, Simon Fraser University, Burnaby, British Columbia.

Dixon, E. James, Timothy H. Heaton, Terence E. Fifield, Thomas D. Hamilton, David E. Putnam, and Frederick Grady
    1997 Late Quaternary Regional Geoarchaeology of Southeast Alaska Karst: a Progress Report. *Geoarchaeology* 12:689–712.

Dombrowski, Kurt
    2002 The Praxis of Indigenism and Alaska Native Timber Politics. *American Anthropologist* 104:1062–1073.

Drucker, Philip

1937 *The Tolowa and their Southwest Oregon Kin*. University of California Publications in American Archaeology and Ethnology 36(4):221–300. Berkeley.

1948 The Antiquity of the Northwest Coast Totem Pole. *Journal of the Washington Academy of Sciences* 38(12):389–397.

1951 *The Northern and Central Nootkan Tribes*. Smithsonian Institution Bureau of American Ethnology Bulletin 144, Washington, D.C.

Dumond, Don E.

1977 *The Eskimos and the Aleuts*. Thames and Hudson, London.

2001 The Archaeology of Eastern Beringia: Some Contrasts and Connections. *Arctic Anthropology* 38(2):196–205.

2009 The "Arctic Maritime" Expansion: a View from the South. In *The Northern World AD 900–1400*, edited by Herbert Maschner, Owen Mason, and Robert McGhee, pp. 58–75. University of Utah Press, Salt Lake City.

Echo-Hawk, Roger C.

1993 Working Together – Exploring Ancient Worlds. *SAA Bulletin* 11(4):5–6.

Ecotrust

2009 Elakha Alliance. Electronic document, http://www.ecotrust.org/nativeprograms/elakha.html, accessed March 10, 2010.

Eldridge, Morley, and Iain McKechnie

2008 (Re)calibrating Regional Chronologies on the North Coast: Data from Prince Rupert Harbour. Paper presented at the 73rd Annual Meeting of the Society for American Archaeology, Vancouver. Millennia Research, Victoria.

Elmendorf, William W., and Alfred L. Kroeber

1992 *The Structure of Twana Culture*. Washington State University Press, Pullman.

Emmons, George T.

1908 Petroglyphs of Southern Alaska. *American Anthropologist* 10:221–230.

1991 *The Tlingit Indians*. Edited with additions by Frederica de Laguna. University of Washington Press, Seattle, Douglas and McIntyre, Vancouver, and American Museum of Natural History, New York.

Erlandson, Jon M., Michael H. Graham, Bruce J. Bourque, Debra Corbett, James A. Estes, and Robert S. Steneck

2007 The Kelp Highway Hypothesis: Marine Ecology, the Coastal Migration Theory, and the Peopling of the Americas. *Journal of Island and Coastal Archaeology* 2:161–174.

Erlandson, Jon M., Douglas J. Kennett, B. Lynn Ingram, Dan A. Guthrie, Don P. Morris, Mark A. Tveskov, G. James West, and Philip L. Walker

1996 An Archaeological and Paleontological Chronology for Daisy Cave (CA-SMI-261), San Miguel Island, California. *Radiocarbon* 38:355–373.

Erlandson, Jon M., Madonna L. Moss, and Mathew Des Lauriers

2008 Living on the Edge: Early Maritime Cultures of the Pacific Coast of North America. *Quaternary Science Reviews* 27:2232–2245.

Etnier, Michael A.
  2002 *The Effect of Human Hunting on Northern Fur Seal* (Callorhinus ursinus) *Migration and Breeding Distributions in the Late Holocene.* Ph.D. dissertation, Department of Anthropology, University of Washington, Seattle.

Fairbanks, Richard G., Richard A. Mortlock, Tzu-Chien Chiu, Li Cao, Alexey Kaplan, Thomas P. Guilderson, Todd W. Fairbanks, Arthur L. Bloom, Pieter M. Grootes, and Marie-Josée Nadeau
  2005 Marine Radiocarbon Calibration Curve Spanning 10,000 to 50,000 Years B.P. Based on Paired $^{230}Th/^{234}U/^{238}U$ and ^{14}C Dates on Pristine Corals. *Quaternary Science Reviews* 24:1781–1796.

Fedje, Daryl W., and Tina Christensen
  1999 Modeling Paleoshorelines and Locating Early Holocene Coastal Sites in Haida Gwaii. *American Antiquity* 64:635–652.

Fedje, Daryl W., Heiner Josenhans, John J. Clague, J. Vaughn Barrie, David J. Archer, and John R. Southon
  2005a Hecate Strait Paleoshorelines. In *Haida Gwaii: Human History and Environment from the Time of Loon to the Time of the Iron People,* edited by Daryl W. Fedje and Rolf W. Mathewes, pp. 21–37. UBC Press, Vancouver.

Fedje, Daryl W., Alexander P. Mackie, Rebecca J. Wigen, Quentin Mackie, and Cynthia Lake
  2005b Kilgii Gwaay: an Early Maritime Site in the South of Haida Gwaii. In *Haida Gwaii: Human History and Environment from the Time of Loon to the Time of the Iron People*, edited by Daryl W. Fedje and Rolf W. Mathewes, pp. 187–203. UBC Press, Vancouver.

Fedje, Daryl W., and Quentin Mackie
  2005 Overview of Cultural History. In *Haida Gwaii: Human History and Environment from the Time of Loon to the Time of the Iron People*, edited by Daryl W. Fedje and Rolf W. Mathewes, pp. 154–162. UBC Press, Vancouver.

Fedje, Daryl W., Quentin Mackie, E. James Dixon, and Timothy H. Heaton
  2004 Late Wisconsin Environments and Archaeological Visibility on the Northern Northwest Coast. In *Entering America: Northeast Asia and Beringia before the Last Glacial Maximum*, edited by David B. Madsen, pp. 97–138. University of Utah Press, Salt Lake City.

Fedje, Daryl W., Quentin Mackie, Duncan McLaren, and Tina Christensen
  2008 A Projectile Point Sequence for Haida Gwaii. In *Projectile Point Sequences in Northwestern North America*, edited by Roy L. Carlson and Martin P. R. Magne, pp. 19–40. Archaeology Press, Publication No. 35, Simon Fraser University, Burnaby, British Columbia.

Fedje, Daryl W., Martin P. R. Magne, and Tina Christensen
  2005c Test Excavations at Raised Beach Sites in Southern Haida Gwaii. In *Haida Gwaii: Human History and Environment from the Time of Loon to the Time of the Iron People,* edited by Daryl W. Fedje and Rolf W. Mathewes, pp. 204–244. UBC Press, Vancouver.

Fedje, Daryl W., and Rolf W. Mathewes (editors)

2005 *Haida Gwaii: Human History and Environment from the Time of Loon to the Time of the Iron People*. UBC Press, Vancouver.

Fedje, Daryl W., Ian D. Sumpter, and John R. Southon

2009 Sea-levels and Archaeology in the Gulf Islands National Park Reserve. *Canadian Journal of Archaeology* 33:234–253.

Feinman, Gary M., and Jill Neitzel

1984 Too Many Types: An Overview of Sedentary Pre-State Societies in the Americas. In *Advances in Archaeological Method and Theory*, vol. 7, edited Michael B. Schiffer, pp. 39–102. Academic Press, Orlando, Florida.

Fisken, Marian

1994 Appendix D: Modifications of Whale Bones. In *Ozette Archaeological Project Research Reports* vol. II *Fauna*, edited by Stephan R. Samuels, pp. 359–377. WSU Department of Anthropology Reports of Investigations 66, Pullman, and National Park Service, Pacific Northwest Regional Office, Seattle.

Fitzhugh, Ben

2003 The Evolution of Complex Hunter-Gatherers on the Kodiak Archipelago. In *Hunter-Gatherers of the North Pacific Rim*, edited by Junko Habu, James M. Savelle, Shuzo Koyama, and Hitomi Hongo, pp. 13–48. National Museum of Ethnology, Osaka, Japan.

Fladmark, Knut R.

1975 *A Paleoecological Model for Northwest Coast Prehistory*. Archaeological Survey of Canada Mercury Series Paper 43, Ottawa.

1982 An Introduction to the Prehistory of British Columbia. *Canadian Journal of Archaeology* 6:95–156.

1986 Lawn Point and Kasta: Microblade Sites on the Queen Charlotte Islands, British Columbia. *Canadian Journal of Archaeology* 10:37–58.

Fladmark, Knut R., D. Erle Nelson, Thomas A. Brown, John S. Vogel, and John R. Southon

1987 AMS Dating of Two Wooden Artifacts from the Northwest Coast. *Canadian Journal of Archaeology* 11:1–12.

Flenniken, J. Jeffrey

1981 *Replicative Systems Analysis: a Model Applied to the Vein Quartz Artifacts from the Hoko River Site*. Laboratory of Anthropology, Washington State University, Report of Investigations No. 59, Pullman.

Frederick, Gay, and Susan Crockford

2005 Appendix D: Analysis of the Vertebrate Fauna from Ts'ishaa Village, DfSi–16, Benson Island, B.C. In *Ts'ishaa: Archaeology and Ethnography of a Nuu-chah-nulth Origin Site in Barkley Sound*, by Alan D. McMillan and Denis St. Claire. Archaeology Press, Department of Archaeology, Simon Fraser University, Burnaby, British Columbia.

Gavin, Daniel G., Linda B. Brubaker, and Kenneth P. Lertzman

2003 Holocene Fire History of a Temperate Rain Forest Based on Soil Charcoal Radiocarbon Dates. *Ecology* 84:186–201.

Gentry, Roger L.
  1998 *Behavior and Ecology of the Northern Fur Seal*. Princeton University Press, Princeton, New Jersey.
Gifford-Gonzalez, Diane, Seth D. Newsome, Paul L. Koch, Thomas P. Guilderson, J. Josh Snodgrass, and Richard K. Burton
  2005 Archaeofaunal Insights on Pinniped–Human Interactions in the Northeastern Pacific. In *The Exploitation and Cultural Importance of Sea Mammals*, edited by Gregory G. Monks, pp. 19–38. Oxbow Books, Oxford.
Gilbert, M. Thomas P., Dennis L. Jenkins, Anders Götherstrom, Nuria Naveran, Juan J. Sanchez, Michael Hofreiter, Philip F. Thomsen, Jonas Binladen, Thomas F. G. Higham, Robert M. Yohe II, Robert Parr, Linda Scott Cummings, and Eske Willerslev
  2008 DNA from Pre-Clovis Human Coprolites in Oregon, North America. *Science* 320:786–789.
Goebel, Ted, Michael R. Waters, and Margarita Dikova
  2003 The Archaeology of Ushki Lake, Kamchatka, and the Pleistocene Peopling of the Americas. *Science* 301:501–505.
Goebel, Ted, Michael R. Waters, and Dennis H. O'Rourke
  2008 The Late Pleistocene Dispersal of Modern Humans in the Americas. *Science* 319:1497–1502.
Goebel, Ted, Michael R. Waters, Ian Buvit, Mikhail V. Konstantinov, and Aleksander V. Konstantinov
  2000 Studenoe–2 and the Origins of Microblade Technologies in the Transbaikal, Siberia. *Antiquity* 74:567–575.
Graesch, Anthony P.
  2006 Archaeological and Ethnoarchaeological Investigations of Households and Perspectives on a Coast Salish Historic Village in British Columbia. Ph.D. dissertation, University of California, Los Angeles. ProQuest http://wwwlib.umi.com/dissertations/search.
  2007 Modeling Ground Slate Knife Production and Implications for the Study of Household Labor Contributions to Salmon Fishing on the Pacific Northwest Coast. *Journal of Anthropological Archaeology* 26:576–606.
Greene, Nancy A.
  2010 Comox Harbour Fish Trap Site. WARP (Wetland Archaeological Research Project) Web Report. Electronic document, http://newswarp.info/wp-content/uploads/2010/03/WARP-web-report.pdf, accessed July 26, 2010.
Grier, Colin
  2003 Dimensions of Regional Interaction in the Prehistoric Gulf of Georgia. In *Emerging from the Mist: Studies in Northwest Coast Culture History*, edited by R. G. Matson, Gary Coupland, and Quentin Mackie, pp. 170–187. UBC Press, Vancouver.
  2007 Consuming the Recent for Constructing the Ancient: The Role of Ethnography in Coast Salish Archaeological Interpretation. In *Be of Good Mind: Essays on the Coast Salish*, edited by Bruce G. Miller, 284–307. UBC Press, Vancouver.

Grier, Colin, Patrick Dolan, Kelly Derr, and Eric McLay
  2009 Assessing Sea Level Changes in the Southern Gulf Islands of British Columbia
  Using Archaeological Data from Coastal Spit Locations. *Canadian Journal of
  Archaeology* 33:254–280.

Gunther, Erna
  1973 *Ethnobotany of Western Washington: the Knowledge and Use of Indigenous Plants
  by Native Americans.* University of Washington Press, Seattle.

Hajda, Yvonne
  1990 Southwestern Coast Salish. In *Northwest Coast*, edited by Wayne Suttles, pp.
  503–517. Handbook of North American Indians, Vol. 7, William C. Sturtevant,
  general editor, Smithsonian Institution, Washington, D.C.

Ham, Leonard C.
  1990 The Cohoe Creek Site: a Late Moresby Tradition Shell Midden. *Canadian
  Journal of Archaeology* 14:199–221.

Ham, Leonard C., Arlene J. Yip, and Leila V. Kullar
  1986 A Charles Culture Fishing Village: the 1982/83 Archaeological Excavations at
  the St. Mungo Site, (DgRr2), North Delta British Columbia. Manuscript on file,
  Heritage Conservation Branch, Government of British Columbia, Victoria.

Hare, P. Gregory, Sheila Greer, Ruth Gotthardt, Richard Farnell, Vandy Bowyer, Charles
  Schweger, and Diane Strand
  2004 Ethnographic and Archaeological Investigations of Alpine Ice Patches in
  Southwest Yukon. *Arctic* 57:260–272.

Hare, P. Gregory, Thomas J. Hammer, and Ruth M. Gotthardt
  2008 The Yukon Projectile Point Database. In *Projectile Point Sequences in Northwestern North America*, edited by Roy L. Carlson and Martin P. R. Magne, pp.
  321–332. Archaeology Press, Publication No. 35, Simon Fraser University, Burnaby, British Columbia.

Harper, John R., Randy Bouchard, Adam Dick, Dorothy I. Kennedy, Donald Mitchell,
  Mary C. Morris, Daisy Sewid-Smith, and Kim Recalma-Clutesi
  2005 *Ancient Sea Gardens: Mystery of the Pacific Northwest*, DVD, 50 minutes. David
  J. Woods, Executive Producer; Diane Woods, Producer; Aaron Szimanski, Director;
  and Tim Horton, Writer. AquaCULTURE Pictures, Inc., Toronto, Ontario, for the
  National Geographic Channel.

Harper, John R., James Haggarty, and Mary C. Morris
  2002 Broughton Archipelago: Clam Terrace Survey. Coastal and Ocean Resources,
  Sidney, British Columbia. Manuscript on file, Land Use Coordination Office, B.C.
  Ministry of Government Services, Victoria.

Hayden, Brian, Gregory A. Reinhardt, Richard MacDonald, Dan Holmberg, and David
  Crellin
  1996 Space Per Capita and the Optimal Size of Housepits. In *People Who Lived in
  Big Houses: Archaeological Perspectives on Large Domestic Structures*, edited by Gary
  Coupland and E. B. Banning, pp. 151–163. Monographs in World Archaeology
  No. 27. Prehistory Press, Madison, Wisconsin.

Hebda, Richard J., and S. Gay Frederick
1990   History of Marine Resources of the Northeast Pacific since the Last Glaciation. *Transactions of the Royal Society of Canada*, series I, vol. I:319–342.
Hebda, Richard J., and Rolf W. Mathewes
1984   Holocene History of Cedar and Native Indian Cultures of the North American Pacific Coast. *Science* 225:711–713.
Heizer, Robert F. (editor)
1978   *California*. Handbook of North American Indians, Vol. 8, William C. Sturtevant, general editor, Smithsonian Institution, Washington, D.C.
Hennon, Paul, David D'Amore, Dustin Wittwer, Adelaide Johnson, Paul Schaberg, Gary Hawley, Colin Beier, Scott Sink, and Glenn Juday
2006   Climate Warming, Reduced Snow and Freezing Injury Could Explain the Demise of Yellow-Cedar in Southeast Alaska, USA. *World Resources Review* 18:427–450.
Hetherington, Renée, Andrew J. Weaver, and Alvaro Montenegro
2007   Climate and the Migration of Early Peoples in the Americas. In *Coastline Changes: Interrelation of Climate and Geological Processes*, edited by Jan Harff, William W. Hay, and Daniel M. Tetzlaff, pp. 113–132. Geological Society of America Special Paper 426, Boulder, Colorado.
Hewes, Gordon W.
1940   Field Notes from Interviews with Indian People of Several Northwest California Tribes, on the Topic of Traditional Fishing Techniques. Unpublished notes on file, Bancroft Library, University of California, Berkeley.
Hill, Beth, and Roy Hill
1975   *Indian Petroglyphs of the Pacific Northwest*. Hancock House, Saanichton, British Columbia.
Hoffecker, John F., and Scott A. Elias
2007   *Human Ecology of Beringia*. Columbia University Press, New York.
Holmes, Charles E., R. Joan Dale, and J. David McMahan
1989   *Archaeological Mitigation of the Thorne River Site (CRG–177), Prince of Wales Island, Alaska*. Office of History and Archaeology Report No. 15. Alaska Department of Natural Resources, Anchorage.
Hunn, Eugene S., Darryll Johnson, Priscilla Russell, and Thomas F. Thornton
2003   Huna Tlingit Traditional Environmental Knowledge, Conservation, and the Management of a "Wilderness" Park. *Current Anthropology* 44(4):S79-S103.
Huelsbeck, David R.
1994   The Utilization of Whales at Ozette. In *Ozette Archaeological Project Research Reports* vol. II *Fauna*, edited by Stephan R. Samuels, pp. 265–303. WSU Department of Anthropology Reports of Investigations 66, Pullman, and National Park Service, Pacific Northwest Regional Office, Seattle.
Hutchings, W. Karl
1996   The Namu Obsidian Industry. In *Early Human Occupation in British Columbia*, edited by Roy L. Carlson and Luke Dalla Bona, pp. 167–176. UBC Press, Vancouver.

Ikawa-Smith, Fumiko

2007   Conclusion: In Search of the Origins of Microblades and Microblade Technology. In *Origin and Spread of Microblade Technology in Northern Asia and North America*, edited by Yaroslav V. Kuzmin, Susan G. Keates, and Chen Shen, pp. 189–198. Archaeology Press, Simon Fraser University, Burnaby.

Ives, John W.

2003   Alberta, Athapaskans and Apachean Origins. In *Archaeology in Alberta, a View from the New Millennium*, edited by Jack W. Brink and J. F. Dormaar, pp. 256–289. The Archaeological Society of Alberta, Medicine Hat, Alberta.

Johnsen, D. Bruce

2004   A Culturally Correct Proposal to Privatize the British Columbia Salmon Fishery. George Mason University School of Law, Working Paper Series, Paper 8. The Berkeley Electronic Press, http://law.bepress.com/gmulwps/gmule/art8.

Jopling, Carol F.

1989   *Coppers of the Northwest Coast Indians: Their Origin, Development, and Possible Antecedents*. Transactions of the American Philosophical Society 79(1):1–164.

Kantner, John

2002   Complexity. In *Darwin and Archaeology: a Handbook of Key Concepts*, edited by John P. Hart and John Edward Terrell, pp. 89–106. Bergin & Garvey, Westport, Connecticut.

Keddie, Grant

1981   The Use and Distribution of Labrets on the North Pacific Rim. *Syesis* 14:59–80.

2007   Labrets in the Collection of the Royal B.C. Museum. Electronic document, http://www.royalbcmuseum.bc.ca/Content_Files/Files/Collections%20and%20Research/HumanHistory/LabretsRBCMCollWebFinalDec20-07.pdf, accessed February 10, 2010.

Kelly, Robert L.

1995   *The Foraging Spectrum: Diversity in Hunter-Gatherer Lifeways*. Smithsonian Institution Press, Washington, D.C.

Kemp, Brian M., Ripan S. Malhi, John McDonough, Deborah A. Bolnick, Jason A. Eshleman, Olga Rickards, Cristina Martinez-Labarga, John R. Johnson, Joseph G. Lorenz, E. James Dixon, Terence E. Fifield, Timothy H. Heaton, Rosita Worl, and David Glenn Smith

2007   Genetic Analysis of Early Holocene Skeletal Remains From Alaska and its Implications for the Settlement of the Americas. *American Journal of Physical Anthropology* 132:605–621.

Kenady, Stephen M., Michael C. Wilson, and Randall F. Schalk

2007   Indications of Butchering on a Late-Pleistocene *Bison antiquus* from the Maritime Pacific Northwest. *Current Research in the Pleistocene* 24:167–170.

Kew, J. E. Michael

1990   History of Coastal British Columbia Since 1849. In *Northwest Coast*, edited by Wayne Suttles, pp. 159–168. Handbook of North American Indians, Vol. 7, William C. Sturtevant, general editor, Smithsonian Institution, Washington, D.C.

Kirk, Ruth

1986 *Tradition and Change on the Northwest Coast: the Makah, Nuu-chah-nulth, Southern Kwakiutl and Nuxalk.* University of Washington Press, Seattle.

Klawock Cooperative Association, and Craig Community Association

2007 Ancient Human Remains Returned to Tlingit Tribes. Press release issued October 18, 2007. Electronic document, www.sealaska.com/object/ancienthuman.html, accessed July 29, 2008.

Knox, Margaret

2000 Ecological Change in the Willamette Valley at the Time of Euro-American Contact ca. 1800–1850. Master's paper, Department of Geography, University of Oregon, Eugene.

Kramer, Stephenie

2000 Camas, Intensification, and Gender: a Case Study of the Kalapuya and their Predecessors, Willamette Valley, Oregon. Master's paper, Department of Anthropology, University of Oregon, Eugene.

Kunibe, Elizabeth

2007 Tracing the Origins of Tlingit Agriculture and Reintroducing Native Cultivars to Today's Gardens. Paper presented at Sharing our Knowledge, a Conference of Tsimshian, Haida and Tlingit Tribes and Clans, Sitka, Alaska.

Lacourse, Terri, and Rolf W. Mathewes

2005 Terrestrial Paleoecology of Haida Gwaii and the Continental Shelf: Vegetation, Climate, and Plant Resources of the Coastal Migration Route. In *Haida Gwaii: Human History and Environment from the Time of Loon to the Time of the Iron People,* edited by Daryl W. Fedje and Rolf W. Mathewes, pp. 38–58. UBC Press, Vancouver.

Langdon, Stephen J.

2006 Tidal Pulse Fishing: Selective Traditional Tlingit Salmon Fishing Techniques on the West Coast of the Prince of Wales Archipelago. In *Traditional Ecological Knowledge and Natural Resource Management,* edited by Charles R. Menzies, pp. 21–46. University of Nebraska Press, Lincoln.

2007 Sustaining a Relationship: Inquiry into the Emergence of a Logic of Engagement with Salmon among the Southern Tlingits. In *Native Americans and the Environment: Perspectives on the Ecological Indian,* edited by Michael E. Harkin and David Rich Lewis, pp. 233–273. University of Nebraska Press, Lincoln.

Langdon, Stephen J., Douglas Reger, and Neil Campbell

1995 Pavements, Pairs, Pounds, Piles and Puzzles: Investigating the Intertidal Fishing Structures in Little Salt Lake, Prince of Wales Island, Southeast Alaska. Paper presented at Hidden Dimensions: the Cultural Significance of Wetland Archaeology conference, University of British Columbia, Vancouver.

La Salle, Marina J.

2008 Beyond Lip Service: an Analysis of Labrets and Their Social Context on the Pacific Northwest Coast of British Columbia. Master's thesis, Department of Anthropology, University of British Columbia, Vancouver.

Lee, Richard B., and Irven DeVore (editors)

1968 *Man the Hunter.* Aldine de Gruyter, Chicago.

Lepofsky, Dana
   2004   Paleoethnobotany in the Northwest. In *People and Plants in Ancient Western North America*, edited by Paul E. Minnis, pp. 367–464. Smithsonian Books, Washington, D.C.

Lepofsky, Dana, Michael Blake, Douglas Brown, Sandra Morrison, Nicole Oakes, and Natasha Lyons
   2000   The Archaeology of the Scowlitz Site, Southwestern British Columbia. *Journal of Field Archaeology* 27:391–416.

Lepofsky, Dana, Douglas Hallett, Ken Lertzman, Rolf Mathewes, Albert McHalsie, and Kevin Washbrook
   2005   Documenting Precontact Plant Management on the Northwest Coast: an Example of Prescribed Burning in the Central and Upper Fraser Valley, British Columbia. In *Keeping it Living: Traditions of Plant Use and Cultivation on the Northwest Coast of North America*, edited by Douglas Deur and Nancy J. Turner, pp. 218–239. University of Washington Press, Seattle.

Lepofsky, Dana, Natasha Lyons, and Madonna L. Moss
   2003   The Use of Driftwood on the North Pacific Coast: an Example from Southeast Alaska. *Journal of Ethnobiology* 23(1):125–141.

Lepofsky, Dana, Madonna L. Moss, and Nastasha Lyons
   2001   The Unrealized Potential of Paleoethnobotany in the Archaeology of Northwestern North America: Perspectives from Cape Addington, Alaska. *Arctic Anthropology* 38(1):48–59.

Lepofsky, Dana, David M. Schaepe, Anthony P. Graesch, Michael Lenert, Patricia Omerod, Keith T. Carlson, Jeanne E. Arnold, Michael Blake, Patrick Moore, and John J. Clague
   2009   Exploring Stó:Lō Coast Salish Interaction and Identity in Ancient Houses and Settlements in the Fraser Valley, British Columbia. *American Antiquity* 74:595–626.

Lepofsky, Dana, and John Welch
   2009   Herring Archaeology in Tla'amin Territory. *The Midden* 41(3):3. Archaeological Society of British Columbia, Vancouver.

Lertzman, Ken, Daniel Gavin, Douglas Hallett, Linda Brubaker, Dana Lepofsky, and Rolf Mathewes
   2002   Long-Term Fire Regime Estimated from Soil Charcoal in Coastal Temperate Rainforests. *Conservation Ecology* 6(2):5. Electronic document, http://www.consecol.org/vol6/iss2/art5, accessed July 13, 2009.

Lightfoot, Ricky Ray
   1989   Cultural Component II. In *The Hidden Falls Site, Baranof Island, Alaska*, edited by Stanley D. Davis, pp. 199–273. Aurora: Alaska Anthropological Association Monograph Series, Anchorage.

Losey, Robert J.
   2010a Archaeology of the Par-Tee Site, Northern Oregon Coast. Electronic document, http://www.ualberta.ca/~rlosey/partee/, accessed January 27, 2010.
   2010b Animism as a Means of Exploring Archaeological Fishing Structures on Willapa Bay, Washington, USA. *Cambridge Archaeological Journal* 20:17–32.

Losey, Robert J., Nancy Stenholm, Patty Whereat-Phillips, and Helen Vallianatos
  2003 Exploring the Use of Red Elderberry (*Sambucus racemosa*) Fruit on the Southern Northwest Coast of North America. *Journal of Archaeological Science* 30:695–707.

Losey, Robert J., and Dongya Y. Yang
  2007 Opportunistic Whale Hunting on the Southern Northwest Coast: Ancient DNA, Artifact, and Ethnographic Evidence. *American Antiquity* 72:657–676.

Luebbers, Roger
  1978 Excavations: Stratigraphy and Artifacts. In *Studies in Bella Bella Prehistory*, edited by James J. Hester and Sarah M. Nelson, pp. 11–66. Department of Archaeology, Simon Fraser University Publication No. 5, Burnaby, British Columbia.

Lundy, Doris
  1974 The Rock Art of the Northwest Coast. Master's thesis, Department of Archaeology, Simon Fraser University, Burnaby, British Columbia.

Lyman, R. Lee
  1988 Zoogeography of Oregon Coast Marine Mammals: The Last 3000 Years. *Marine Mammal Science* 4:247–264.

  1991 *Prehistory of the Oregon Coast*. Academic Press, San Diego.

MacDonald, George F.
  1983a *Haida Monumental Art: Villages of the Queen Charlotte Islands*. UBC Press, Vancouver.

  1983b Prehistoric Art of the Northern Northwest Coast. In *Indian Art Traditions of the Northwest Coast*, edited by Roy L. Carlson, pp. 99–120. Archaeology Press, Simon Fraser University, Burnaby, British Columbia.

McDonald, James
  2005 Cultivating in the Northwest: Early Accounts of Tsimshian Horticulture. In *Keeping it Living: Traditions of Plant Use and Cultivation on the Northwest Coast of North America*, edited by Douglas Deur and Nancy J. Turner, pp. 240–273. University of Washington Press, Seattle.

McGuire, Randall H.
  1996 Why Complexity is Too Simple. In *Debating Complexity*, edited by Daniel A. Meyer, Peter C. Dawson, Donald T. Hanna, pp. 23–29. Proceedings of the 26th Annual Chacmool Conference, Archaeological Association of the University of Calgary, Alberta.

McKenzie, Kathleen H.
  1974 Ozette Prehistory – Prelude. Master's thesis, Department of Archaeology, University of Calgary, Alberta.

McLaren, Duncan
  2008 Sea Level Change and Archaeological Site Locations on the Dundas Island Archipelago of North Coastal British Columbia. Ph.D. dissertation, Interdisciplinary Studies, University of Victoria, British Columbia.

McLaren, Duncan, and Nicole Smith
  2008 The Stratigraphy of Bifacial Implements at the Richardson Island Site, Haida Gwaii. In *Projectile Point Sequences in Northwestern North America*, edited by Roy L.

Carlson and Martin P. R. Magne, pp. 41–60. Archaeology Press, Publication No. 35, Simon Fraser University, Burnaby, British Columbia.

McLaren, Duncan, Rebecca J. Wigen, Quentin Mackie, and Daryl W. Fedje

    2005 Bear Hunting at the Pleistocene/Holocene Transition on the Northern Northwest Coast of North America. *Canadian Zooarchaeology* 22:3–29.

McMillan, Alan D.

    1999 *Since the Time of the Transformers: the Ancient Heritage of the Nuu-Chah-Nulth, Ditidaht, and Makah.* UBC Press, Vancouver.

    2009 A Tale of Two Ethnographies: the Contributions of Edward Sapir and Philip Drucker to Nuu-chah-nulth Archaeology. In *Painting the Past with a Broad Brush: Papers in Honour of James Valliere Wright*, edited by David L. Keenleyside and Jean-Luc Pilon, pp. 617–646. Canadian Museum of Civilization, Gatineau, Quebec.

McMillan, Alan D., and Denis E. St. Claire

    2005 *Ts'ishaa: Archaeology and Ethnography of a Nuu-chah-nulth Origin Site in Barkley Sound.* Archaeology Press, Department of Archaeology, Simon Fraser University, Burnaby, British Columbia.

McNiven, Ian J., and Lynette Russell

    2005 *Appropriated Pasts: Indigenous Peoples and the Colonial Culture of Archaeology.* AltaMira Press, New York.

Mackie, Alexander P., and Ian D. Sumpter

    2005 Shoreline Settlement Patterns in Gwaii Haanas during the Early and Late Holocene. In *Haida Gwaii: Human History and Environment from the Time of Loon to the Time of the Iron People*, edited by Daryl W. Fedje and Rolf W. Mathewes, pp. 337–371. UBC Press, Vancouver.

Mackie, Alexander P., and Laurie Williamson

    2003 Nuu-chah-nulth Houses: Structural Remains and Cultural Depressions on Southwest Vancouver Island. In *Emerging from the Mist: Studies in Northwest Coast Culture History*, edited by R. G. Matson, Gary Coupland, and Quentin Mackie, pp. 105–151. UBC Press, Vancouver.

Mackie, Quentin

    1995 *The Taxonomy of Ground Stone Woodworking Tools.* BAR International Series 613. Archaeopress, Oxford.

    2001 *Settlement Archaeology in a Fjordland Archipelago: Network Analysis, Social Practice and the Built Environment of Western Vancouver Island, British Columbia, Canada, Since 2,000 BP.* BAR International Series 926. Archaeopress, Oxford.

    2003 Location-Allocation Modelling of Shell Midden Distribution on the West Coast of Vancouver Island. In *Emerging From the Mists: Studies in Northwest Coast Culture History*, edited by R. G. Matson, Gary Coupland, and Quentin Mackie, pp. 260–288. UBC Press, Vancouver.

Mackie, Quentin, and Steven Acheson

    2005 The Graham Tradition. In *Haida Gwaii: Human History and Environment from the Time of Loon to the Time of the Iron People*, edited by Daryl W. Fedje and Rolf W. Mathewes, pp. 274–302. UBC Press, Vancouver.

Magne, Martin P.R.

2001   Debitage Analysis as a Scientific Tool for Archaeological Knowledge. In *Lithic Debitage: Context, Form, and Meaning*, edited by William Andrefsky, Jr., pp. 21–31. University of Utah Press, Salt Lake City.

Magne, Martin P.R., and Daryl W. Fedje

2007   The Spread of Microblade Technology in Northwestern North America. In *Origin and Spread of Microblade Technology in Northern Asia and North America*, edited by Yaroslav V. Kuzmin, Susan G. Keates, and Chen Shen, pp. 171–188. Archaeology Press, Simon Fraser University, Burnaby, British Columbia.

Makah Tribal Council and Makah Whaling Commission

2005   The Makah Indian Tribe and Whaling: Questions and Answers. Electronic document, http://www.makah.com/makahwhalingqa.pdf, accessed March 10, 2010.

Malhi, Ripan S., Katherine E. Breece, Beth A. Schultz Shook, Frederika A. Kaestle, James C. Chatters, Steven Hackenberger, and David G. Smith

2004   Patterns of mtDNA Diversity in Northwestern North America. *Human Biology* 76:33–54.

Marshall, Yvonne

1989   The House in Northwest Coast Nuu-chah-nulth Society: the Material Structure of Political Action. In *Households and Communities*, edited by Scott MacEachern, David J. W. Archer, and Richard D. Garvin, pp. 15–21. Proceedings of the 21st Annual Chacmool Conference, Archaeological Association of the University of Calgary, Alberta.

1993   A Political History of the Nuu-chah-nulth People: a Case Study of the Mowachaht and Muchalaht Tribes. Ph.D. dissertation, Department of Archaeology, Simon Fraser University, Burnaby, British Columbia.

2006   Houses and Domestication on the Northwest Coast. In *Household Archaeology on the Northwest Coast*, edited by Elizabeth A. Sobel, D. Ann Trieu Gahr, and Kenneth M. Ames, pp. 37–56. International Monographs in Prehistory, Archaeological Series 16, Ann Arbor.

Martindale, Andrew

2006   Methodological Issues in the Use of Tsimshian Oral Traditions (*Adawx*) in Archaeology. *Canadian Journal of Archaeology* 30:158–192.

Martindale, Andrew, and Kisha Supernant

2009   Quantifying the Defensiveness of Defended Sites on the Northwest Coast of North America. *Journal of Anthropological Archaeology* 28(2):191–204.

Masters, Patricia M., and Ivano W. Aiello

2007   Postglacial Evolution of Coastal Environments. In *California Prehistory: Colonization, Culture, and Complexity*, edited by Terry L. Jones and Kathryn Klar, pp. 35–51. AltaMira, Lanham, Maryland.

Mathews, Darcy

2006   Burial Cairn Taxonomy and the Mortuary Landscape of Rocky Point, British Columbia. Master's thesis, Department of Anthropology, University of Victoria, British Columbia.

Matson, R. G.
1976   *The Glenrose Cannery Site*. National Museum of Man, Mercury Series. Archaeological Survey Paper 52. Ottawa.
2003   The Coast Salish House: Lessons from Shingle Point, Valdes Island, British Columbia. In *Emerging from the Mist: Studies in Northwest Coast Culture History*, edited by R. G. Matson, Gary Coupland, and Quentin Mackie, pp. 76–104. UBC Press, Vancouver.

Matson, R. G., and Gary Coupland
1995   *Prehistory of the Northwest Coast*. Academic Press, San Diego.

Matson, R. G., Heather Pratt, and Lisa Rankin
1991   *1989 and 1990 Crescent Beach Excavations, Final Report: the Origins of the Northwest Coast Ethnographic Pattern: the Place of the Locarno Beach Phase*. Permit Report 1989–27, Archaeology Branch, Ministry of Small Business, Tourism and Culture, Victoria, British Columbia.

Meltzer, David
2009   *First Peoples in the New World: Colonizing Ice Age America*. University of California Press, Berkeley.

Minor, Rick, and Katherine A. Toepel
1986   *The Archaeology of the Tahkenitch Landing Site: Early Prehistoric Occupation on the Oregon Coast*. Heritage Research Associates Report No. 46, Eugene, Oregon.

Mitchell, Donald H.
1971   Archaeology of the Gulf of Georgia, a Natural Region and its Cultural Types. *Syesis 4* (Supplement No. 1).
1988   Changing Patterns of Resource Use in the Prehistory of Queen Charlotte Strait, British Columbia. In *Prehistoric Economies of the Pacific Northwest Coast*, edited by Barry L. Isaac, pp. 245–290. JAI Press, Greenwich, Connecticut.
1990   Prehistory of the Coasts of Southern British Columbia and Northern Washington. In *Northwest Coast*, edited by Wayne Suttles, pp. 340–358. Handbook of North American Indians, Vol. 7, William C. Sturtevant, general editor, Smithsonian Institution, Washington, D.C.

Mitchell, Donald, and David L. Pokotylo
1996   Early Components at the Milliken Site. In *Early Human Occupation in British Columbia*, edited by Roy L. Carlson and Luke Dalla Bona, pp. 65–82. UBC Press, Vancouver.

Mobley, Charles M., and Morely Eldridge
1992   Culturally Modified Trees in the Pacific Northwest. *Arctic Anthropology* 29(2):91–110.

Mobley, Charles M., and W. Mark McCallum
2001   Prehistoric Intertidal Fish Traps from Central Southeast Alaska. *Canadian Journal of Archaeology* 25:28–52.

Monks, Gregory G.
1987   Prey as Bait: the Deep Bay Example. *Canadian Journal of Archaeology* 11:119–142.
2003   The Cultural Taphonomy of Nuu-chah-nulth Whale Bone Assemblages. In *Emerging from the Mist: Studies in Northwest Coast Culture History*, edited by R. G. Matson, Gary Coupland, and Quentin Mackie, pp. 188–212. UBC Press, Vancouver.

Monks, Gregory G., Alan D. McMillan, and Denis E. St. Claire
  2001 Nuu-chah-nulth Whaling: Archaeological Insights into Antiquity, Species Preferences, and Cultural Importance. *Arctic Anthropology* 38(1):60–81.
Montgomery, David R.
  2003 *King of Fish: the Thousand-Year Run of Salmon.* Westview Press, Boulder, Colorado.
Morin, Jesse
  2004 Cutting Edges and Salmon Skin: Variation in Salmon Processing Technology on the Northwest Coast. *Journal of Canadian Archaeology* 28:281–318.
Moss, Madonna L.
  1989 *Archaeology and Cultural Ecology of the Prehistoric Angoon Tlingit.* Ph.D. dissertation, University of California, Santa Barbara. University Microfilms, Ann Arbor.
  1993 Shellfish, Gender, and Status on the Northwest Coast: Reconciling Archeological, Ethnographic, and Ethnohistorical Records of the Tlingit. *American Anthropologist* 95:631–652.
  1999 George Catlin among the Nayas: Understanding the Practice of Labret Wearing on the Northwest Coast. *Ethnohistory* 46:31–65.
  2004a *Archaeological Investigation of Cape Addington Rockshelter: Human Occupation of the Rugged Seacoast on the Outer Prince of Wales Archipelago, Alaska.* University of Oregon Anthropological Paper No. 63, Eugene.
  2004b The Status of Archaeology and Archaeological Practice in Southeast Alaska in Relation to the Larger Northwest Coast. *Arctic Anthropology* 41(2):177–196.
  2004c Island Societies are Not Always Insular: Tlingit Territories in the Alexander Archipelago and the Adjacent Alaskan Mainland. In *Voyages of Discovery: the Archaeology of Islands*, edited by Scott M. Fitzpatrick, pp. 165–183. Greenwood Press, Westport, Connecticut.
  2005 Tlingit Horticulture: an Indigenous or Introduced Development? In *Keeping it Living: Traditions of Plant Use and Cultivation on the Northwest Coast of North America*, edited by Douglas Deur and Nancy J. Turner, pp. 274–295. University of Washington Press, Seattle.
  2007 Haida and Tlingit Use of Seabirds from the Forrester Islands, Southeast Alaska. *Journal of Ethnobiology* 27(1):28–45.
  2008a Islands Coming Out of Concealment: Traveling to Haida Gwaii on the Northwest Coast of North America. *Journal of Island and Coastal Archaeology* 3:35–53.
  2008b Coffman Cove Community Archaeology: Research Questions and Results. Paper presented at the 73rd Annual Meeting of the Society for American Archaeology, Vancouver, British Columbia.
  2010 Pre-Contact Tlingit Warfare: What Do We Really Know? Manuscript on file, Department of Anthropology, University of Oregon, Eugene.
  2011 Fishing Traps and Weirs on the Northwest Coast of North America: New Approaches and New Insights. In *Oxford Handbook of Wetland Archaeology*, edited by Francesco Menotti and Aidan O'Sullivan. Oxford University Press, in press.
Moss, Madonna L., Virginia L. Butler, and J. Tait Elder
  2011 Herring Bones in Southeast Alaskan Archaeological Sites: the Record of Tlingit Use of *Yaaw* (Pacific Herring, *Clupea pallasi*). In *The Archaeology of North Pacific*

Fisheries, edited by Madonna L. Moss and Aubrey Cannon. University of Alaska Press, Fairbanks, in press.

Moss, Madonna L., and Aubrey Cannon (editors)

2011   *The Archaeology of North Pacific Fisheries*. University of Alaska Press, Fairbanks, in press.

Moss, Madonna L., Thomas J. Connolly, Jon M. Erlandson, and Guy L. Tasa

2006a An Early Holocene/Late Pleistocene Archaeological Site on the Oregon Coast? Comments on Hall et al. 2005. *Radiocarbon* 48:237–240.

Moss, Madonna L., and Jon M. Erlandson

1992   Forts, Refuge Rocks, and Defensive Sites: the Antiquity of Warfare along the North Pacific Coast of North America. *Arctic Anthropology* 29(2):73–90.

1998a A Comparative Chronology of Northwest Coast Fishing Features. In *Hidden Dimensions, the Cultural Significance of Wetland Archaeology*, edited by K. Bernick, pp. 180–198. UBC Press, Vancouver.

1998b Early Holocene Adaptations of the Southern Northwest Coast. *Journal of California and Great Basin Anthropology* 20(1):13–25.

2000   Wolf's Lair: Middle and Late Holocene Wooden Artifacts from a Sea Cave on Baker Island, Alaska. *Canadian Journal of Archaeology* 24:107–128.

Moss, Madonna L., Dorothy M. Peteet, and Cathy Whitlock

2007   Mid-Holocene Culture and Climate on the Northwest Coast of North America. In *Climate Change and Cultural Dynamics: a Global Perspective on Mid-Holocene Transitions*, edited by David G. Anderson, Kirk A. Maasch, and Daniel H. Sandweiss, pp. 491–529. Elsevier, Amsterdam.

Moss, Madonna L., Dongya Y. Yang, Seth D. Newsome, Camilla F. Speller, Iain McKechnie, Alan D. McMillan, Robert J. Losey, and Paul L. Koch

2006b Historical Ecology and Biogeography of North Pacific Pinnipeds: Isotopes and Ancient DNA from Three Archaeological Assemblages. *Journal of Island and Coastal Archaeology* 1:165–190.

Mudie, Petra J., Sheila Greer, Judy Brakel, James H. Dickson, Clara Schinkel, Ruth Peterson-Welsh, Margaret Stevens, Nancy J. Turner, Mary Shadow, and Rosalie Washington

2005   Forensic Palynology and Ethnobotany of *Salicornia* Species (Chenopodiaceae) in Northwest Canada and Alaska. *Canadian Journal of Botany* 83:111–123.

Murdock, George P.

1968   The Current Status of the World's Hunting and Gathering Peoples. In *Man the Hunter*, edited by Richard B. Lee and Irven DeVore, pp. 13–20. Aldine, Chicago.

Oliver, Jeff

2007   Beyond the Water's Edge: Towards a Social Archaeology of Landscape on the Northwest Coast. *Canadian Journal of Archaeology* 31:1–27.

Olson, Ronald L.

1936   The Quinault Indians. *University of Washington Publications in Anthropology* 6(1):1–190.

Orchard, Trevor J.
  2007 Otters and Urchins: Continuity and Change in Haida Economy during the Late Holocene and Maritime Fur Trade Periods. Ph.D. dissertation, Department of Anthropology, University of Toronto.

Patenaude, Valerie
  1985 The Pitt River Archaeological Site DhRq 21: a Coast Salish Seasonal Camp on the Lower Fraser River (volumes 1 & 2). Heritage Conservation Branch, Victoria, British Columbia.

Pauketat, Timothy R.
  2007 *Chiefdoms and Other Archaeological Delusions*. AltaMira Press, New York.

Paul, Frances
  1944 *Spruce Root Basketry of the Alaska Tlingit*. USDI, Bureau of Indian Affairs, Washington, D.C.

Pegg, Brian
  2000 Dendrochronology, CMTs, and Nuu-chah-nulth History on the West Coast of Vancouver Island. *Canadian Journal of Archaeology* 24:77–88.

Pegg, Brian, Gail Wada, and Andrew Mason
  2007 Archaeological Mitigation of DkSb–30, Saltery Bay, B.C., Telus North Island Ring Project. Heritage Conservation Act Permit 2004–120. Golder Associates, Ltd., for Telus Corporation, Burnaby, B.C. Report on file, Archaeology Branch, Victoria, British Columbia.

Pitulko, Vladimir V., Pavel A. Nikolsky, Evgeny Yu. Girya, Alexander E. Basilyan, Vladimir E. Tumskoy, Sergei A. Koulakov, Sergei N. Astakhov, Elena Yu. Pavlova, Mikhail A. Anisimov
  2004 The Yana RHS Site: Humans in the Arctic Before the Last Glacial Maximum. *Science* 303:52–56.

Pluciennik, Mark
  2004 The Meaning of "Hunter-Gatherers" and Modes of Subsistence: a Comparative Historical Perspective. In *Hunter-Gatherers in History, Archaeology, and Anthropology*, edited by Alan Barnard, pp. 17–29. Berg, Oxford.

Potter, Ben A.
  2008 A First Approximation of Holocene Inter-Assemblage Variability in Central Alaska. *Arctic Anthropology* 45(2):89–113.

Powers, W. Roger
  1990 The Peoples of Eastern Beringia. *Prehistoric Mongoloid Dispersals* 7:53–74. University of Tokyo.

Pratt, Heather
  1992 The Charles Culture of the Gulf of Georgia: a Re-evaluation of the Culture and its Three Sub-Phases. Master's thesis, Department of Anthropology, University of British Columbia, Vancouver.

Price, T. Douglas
  1981 Complexity in 'Non-Complex' Societies. In *Archaeological Approaches to the Study of Complexity*, edited by Sander Van der Leeuw, pp. 53–97. Institut voor Pre- en Protohistorie, Amsterdam.

Rahemtulla, Farid
2003   The Use of Large Terrestrial Mammal Bone on the Northwest Coast. In *Archaeology of Coastal British Columbia, Essays in Honour of Philip M. Hobler*, edited by Roy L. Carlson, pp. 61–64. Archaeology Press, Simon Fraser University, Burnaby, British Columbia.

Rasic, Jeffrey, and William Andrefsky, Jr.
2001   Alaskan Blade Cores as Specialized Components of Mobile Toolkits: Assessing Design Parameters and Toolkit Organization through Debitage Analysis. In *Lithic Debitage: Context, Form, and Meaning*, edited by William Andrefsky, Jr., pp. 61–79. University of Utah Press, Salt Lake City.

Reuther, Joshua R., Robert J. Speakman, Peter M. Bowers, Michael D. Glascock, Ben A. Potter, and John D. Cook
2007   Recent Obsidian Analysis in Alaska. Poster presented at the 72nd Annual Meeting of the Society of American Archaeology, Austin, Texas.

Richards, Michael P., Sheila Greer, Lorna T. Corr, Owen Beattie, Alexander Mackie, Richard P. Evershed, Al von Finster, and John Southon
2007   Radiocarbon Dating and Dietary Stable Isotope Analysis of Kwaday Dan Ts'inchi. *American Antiquity* 72:719–733.

Riches, David
1979   Ecological Variation on the Northwest Coast: Models for the Generation of Cognatic and Matrilineal Descent. In *Social and Ecological Systems*, edited by Philip Burnham and Roy F. Ellen, pp. 145–166. Academic, New York.

Rick, Torben C., Jon M. Erlandson, Todd J. Braje, James A. Estes, Michael H. Graham, and René L. Vellanoweth
2008   Historical Ecology and Human Impacts on Coastal Ecosystems of the Santa Barbara Channel Region, California. In *Human Impacts on Ancient Marine Ecosystems: a Global Perspective*, edited by Torben C. Rick and Jon M. Erlandson, pp. 77–101. University of California Press, Berkeley.

Rousseau, Jerome
2006   *Rethinking Social Evolution: the Perspective from Middle-Range Societies*. McGill-Queen's University Press, Montreal.

Rowley-Conwy, Peter
2001   Time, Change, and the Archaeology of Hunter-Gatherers: How Original is the 'Original Affluent Society'? In *Hunter-Gatherers: an Interdisciplinary Perspective*, edited by Catherine Painter-Brick, Robert Layton, and Peter Rowley-Conwy, pp. 39–72. Cambridge University Press, Cambridge.

Samuels, Stephan R.
1991   Patterns in Ozette Floor Middens: Reflections of Social Units. In *Ozette Archaeological Project Research Reports*, vol. I, *Household Structure and Floor Midden*, edited by Stephan R. Samuels, pp. 175–270. WSU Department of Anthropology Reports of Investigations 63, Pullman, and National Park Service Pacific Northwest Regional Office, Seattle.
2006   Households at Ozette. In *Household Archaeology on the Northwest Coast*, edited by Elizabeth A. Sobel, D. Ann Trieu Gahr, and Kenneth M. Ames, pp. 200–232. International Monographs in Prehistory, Archaeological Series 16, Ann Arbor.

Samuels, Stephan R., and Richard D. Daugherty
　1991　Introduction to the Ozette Archaeological Project. In *Ozette Archaeological Project Research Reports,* vol. I, *Household Structure and Floor Midden,* edited by Stephan R. Samuels, pp. 1–27. WSU Department of Anthropology Reports of Investigations 63, Pullman, and National Park Service Pacific Northwest Regional Office, Seattle.

Schaepe, David M.
　2003　Validating the Maurer House. In *Archaeology of Coastal British Columbia: Essays in Honour of Professor Philip M. Hobler,* edited by Roy L. Carlson, pp. 113–152. Archaeology Press, Publication No. 30, Simon Fraser University, Burnaby, British Columbia.

Schalk, Randall F., and Greg C. Burtchard
　2001　The Newskah Creek Fish Trap Complex, Grays Harbor, Washington. Report submitted to U.S. Army Corps of Engineers, Seattle District (Contract No. DACW67–97–D–1010) by International Archaeological Research Institute, Honolulu, and Cascadia Archaeology, Seattle.

Schalk, Randall F., Stephen M. Kenady, and Michael C. Wilson
　2007　Early Post-Glacial Ungulates on the Northwest Coast: Implications for Hunter-Gatherer Ecological Niches. *Current Research in the Pleistocene* 24:182–185.

Schiffer, Michael B.
　1986　Radiocarbon Dating and the "Old Wood" Problem: the Case of the Hohokam Chronology. *Journal of Archaeological Science* 13:13–30.

Schneider, Alan L.
　2002　Kennewick Man: The Three Million Dollar Skeleton. Electronic document, http://www.friendsofpast.org/kennewick-man/news/021128–3mil.html, accessed July 29, 2008.

Sealaska Heritage Institute
　2005　*Kuwóot yas.éin: His Spirit is Looking Out From the Cave.* Documentary film available from http://www.sealaskaheritage.org/shop/video%20Kuw%C3%B3ot%20yas.%C3%A9in.htm, Juneau, Alaska.
　2008　Press Release: DNA Links Native Alaskans to Ancient Man Found in Glacier. May 2, 2008. Electronic document, http://www.sealaskaheritage.org/news/news_article_Alaskans_related_to_Long_Ago_Person_Found.htm, accessed March 17, 2010.

Shaw, Jennie Deo
　2008　Driftwood as a Resource: Modeling Fuelwood Acquisition Strategies in the Mid- to Late Holocene Gulf of Alaska. Ph.D. dissertation, Department of Anthropology, University of Washington, Seattle.

Sheehan, Michael S.
　2004　Ethnographic Models, Archaeological Data, and the Applicability of Modern Foraging Theory. In *Hunter-Gatherers in History, Archaeology, and Anthropology,* edited by Alan Barnard, pp. 163–173. Berg, Oxford.

Singh, Ram Raj Prasad
　1966　*Aboriginal Economic System of the Olympic Peninsula Indians, Western Washington.* Sacramento Anthropological Society Papers 4. Sacramento, California.

Skinner, Craig T.
2009   Lost and Found in British Columbia: Central Coast A. Electronic document, http://sourcecatalog.blogspot.com/, accessed January 20, 2010.

Smith, Bruce
2005   Low-Level Food Production and the Northwest Coast. In *Keeping it Living: Traditions of Plant Use and Cultivation on the Northwest Coast of North America*, edited by Douglas Deur and Nancy J. Turner, pp. 37–66. University of Washington Press, Seattle.

Smith, Jane L.
2006   Fish Traps and Weirs in Central Southeast Alaska. Poster presented at the 33rd Annual Meeting of the Alaska Anthropological Association, Kodiak, Alaska.

Smith, Marian
1940   *The Puyallup-Nisqually.* Columbia University Contributions to Anthropology 32, New York.

Steffen, Martina Lianne
2006   Early Holocene Hearth Features and Burnt Faunal Assemblages at the Richardson Island Archaeological Site, Haida Gwaii, British Columbia. Master's thesis, Department of Anthropology, University of Victoria, Victoria, British Columbia.

Stein, Julie K.
1992   *Deciphering a Shell Midden.* Academic Press, San Diego.

Stein, Julie K., Jennie N. Deo, and Laura S. Phillips
2003   Big Sites—Short Time: Accumulation Rates in Archaeological Sites. *Journal of Archaeological Science* 30:297–316.

Stein, Julie K., Kimberly D. Kornbacher, and Jason L. Tyler
1992   British Camp Shell Midden Stratigraphy. In *Deciphering a Shell Midden,* edited by Julie K. Stein, pp. 95–134. Academic Press, San Diego.

Stevenson, Ann
1998   Wet-Site Contributions to Developmental Models of Fraser River Prehistory. In *Hidden Dimensions, the Cultural Significance of Wetland Archaeology*, edited by Kathryn Bernick, pp. 220–233. UBC Press, Vancouver.

Stewart, Hilary
1977   *Indian Fishing: Early Methods on the Northwest Coast.* University of Washington Press, Seattle.
1990   *Totem Poles.* University of Washington Press, Seattle.

Stryd, Arnoud H., and Morley Eldridge
1993   CMT Archaeology in British Columbia: The Meares Island Studies. *BC Studies* 99:184–234.

Sullivan, Gregg Matthew
1993   Postdepositional Leaching of Shell in Two Northwest Coast Shell Middens. Master's thesis, Department of Archaeology, Simon Fraser University, Burnaby, British Columbia.

Sutherland, Patricia D.
2004   *Variability, Historical Contingency, and Cultural Change in Northern Archaeological Sequences.* Ph.D. dissertation, University of Alberta, Edmonton.

Suttles, Wayne

1951 The Early Diffusion of the Potato among the Coast Salish. *Southwestern Journal of Anthropology* 7(3):272–288.

1968 Coping with Abundance: Subsistence on the Northwest Coast. In *Man the Hunter*, edited by Richard B. Lee and Irven DeVore, pp. 56–68. Aldine, Chicago.

1974 *The Economic Life of the Coast Salish of Haro and Rosario Straits*. Garland, New York.

1990b Environment. In *Northwest Coast*, edited by Wayne Suttles, pp. 16–29. Handbook of North American Indians, Vol. 7, William C. Sturtevant, general editor, Smithsonian Institution, Washington, D.C.

Suttles, Wayne (editor)

1990a *Northwest Coast*. Handbook of North American Indians, Vol. 7, William C. Sturtevant, general editor, Smithsonian Institution, Washington, D.C.

Thom, Brian

1992 Investigation of Interassemblage Variability within the Gulf of Georgia Phase. *Canadian Journal of Archaeology* 16:24–31.

1995 The Dead and the Living: Burial Mounds and Cairns and the Development of Social Classes in the Gulf of Georgia Region. Master's thesis, Department of Anthropology, University of British Columbia, Vancouver.

Thomas, David Hurst

2000 *Skull Wars: Kennewick Man, Archaeology, and the Battle for Native American Identity*. Basic Books, New York.

Thompson, Laurence C., and M. Dale Kinkade

1990 Languages. In *Northwest Coast*, edited by Wayne Suttles, pp. 30–51. Handbook of North American Indians, Vol. 7, William C. Sturtevant, general editor, Smithsonian Institution, Washington, D.C.

Thornton, Thomas, Virginia Butler, Fritz Funk, Madonna Moss, Jamie Hebert, and Tait Elder

2010 *Herring Synthesis: Documenting and Modeling Herring Spawning Areas within Socio-Ecological Systems Over Time in the Southeastern Gulf of Alaska*. North Pacific Research Board Project #728. Electronic document, http://herringsynthesis. research.pdx.edu/, accessed October 1, 2010.

Troffe, Peter M., Donga Yang, Al von Finster, and Camilla Speller

2008 Identification of Salmon from the Kwäday Dän Ts'ìnchi site. Abstract, Kwäday Dän Ts'ìnchi Symposium Topics and Speakers, April 25–26, 2008. Electronic document, http://www.kdtsymposium.bc.ca/KDTSymposium/about.aspx, accessed March 17, 2010.

Turner, Nancy J., and Sandra Peacock

2005 Solving the Perennial Paradox: Ethnobotanical Evidence for Plant Resource Management on the Northwest Coast. In *Keeping it Living: Traditions of Plant Use and Cultivation on the Northwest Coast of North America*, edited by Douglas Deur and Nancy J. Turner, pp. 101–150. University of Washington Press, Seattle.

Turner, Nancy J., Robin Smith, and James T. Jones

2005 "A Fine Line Between Two Nations": Ownership Patterns for Plant Resources among Northwest Coast Indigenous Peoples. In *Keeping it Living: Traditions of Plant*

Use and Cultivation on the Northwest Coast of North America, edited by Douglas Deur and Nancy J. Turner, pp. 151–178. University of Washington Press, Seattle.

Turner, Nancy J., and Roy L. Taylor
1972   A Review of the Northwest Coast Tobacco Mystery. *Syesis* 5:249–257.

U. S. Department of Commerce, National Oceanic and Atmospheric Administration
2009   Endangered and Threatened Wildlife and Plants: Proposed Threatened Status for Southern Distinct Population Segment of Eulachon. *Federal Register* 74(48): 10857–10876. Electronic document, http://edocket.access.gpo.gov/2009/E9-5403.htm, accessed March, 2010.

Upham, Steadman
1987   A Theoretical Consideration of Middle Range Societies. In *Chiefdoms in the Americas*, edited by Robert Drennan and Carlos A. Uribe, pp. 345–368. University Press of America, Lanham, Maryland.

Valentine, Kim, Deborah Duffield, Lorelei E. Patrick, David R. Hatch, Virginia L. Butler, Roberta Hall, and Niles Lehman
2008   Ancient DNA Reveals Genotypic Relationships among Oregon Populations of the Sea Otter (*Enhydra lutris*). *Conservation Genetics* 9:933–938.

Wakeman, Pauline
2008   *Taxidermic Signs: Reconstructing Aboriginality*. University of Minnesota Press, Minneapolis.

Ward, Brent C., Michael C. Wilson, David W. Nagorsen, D. Erle Nelson, Jonathan C. Driver, and Rebecca J. Wigen
2003   Port Eliza Cave: North American West Coast Interstadial Environment and Implications for Human Migrations. *Quaternary Science Reviews* 22:1383–1388.

Waters, Michael R., and Thomas W. Stafford
2007   Redefining the Age of Clovis: Implications for the Peopling of the Americas. *Science* 315:1122–1126.

Wessen, Gary C.
1990   Prehistory of the Ocean Coast of Washington. In *Northwest Coast*, edited by Wayne Suttles, pp. 412–421. Handbook of North American Indians, Vol. 7, William C. Sturtevant, general editor, Smithsonian Institution, Washington, D.C.

Whitlock, Cathy, and Margaret A. Knox
2002   Prehistoric Burning in the Pacific Northwest. In *Fire, Native Peoples and the Natural Landscape*, edited by Thomas R. Vale, pp. 195–231. Island Press, Washington, D.C.

Wilson, Michael C.
2009   Come to the Islands: Early Postglacial Paleobiogeography, Insular Megafauna, and Community Succession in the Pacific Northwest. Paper presented at the CANQUA–CGRG Biennial Meeting, Simon Fraser University, Burnaby, British Columbia.

Worl, Rosita F.
1990   History of Southeastern Alaska Since 1867. In *Northwest Coast*, edited by Wayne Suttles, pp. 149–158. Handbook of North American Indians, Vol. 7, William C. Sturtevant, general editor, Smithsonian Institution, Washington, D.C.

Index

Coffman Cove, AK, 113, 124
Cohoe Creek site, BC, 76, 79, 84
coppers, 24
Coupland, Gary, 49, 119–20
Crescent Beach site, BC, 85, 98, 103
crescents, 54–55
cultural complexity, 29–32
culturally modified trees, 135, 136
Curtin, A. Joanne, 125
Cybulski, Jerome S., 124

Daax Haat Kanadaa, AK, 114
Daisy Cave, CA, 54
The Dalles, OR, 35
deer, 11, 60, 78, 81–82, 100, 102–3, 108, 134, 135
de Laguna, Frederica, 133–34
Denali industry, 55
dentalium, 100–102, 120, 125
Developed Northwest Coast Pattern, 74, 79, 119
Developmental Stage, 47, 49, 132
Deur, Douglas, 39–41
Dionisio Point, BC, 120
Dixon, E. James, 2–3, 61
dogs, 45–46, 60, 78, 81, 82, 123, 134
dolphins, 81–82, 94n3
Douglas fir, 10, 41, 74, 135
DNA: of elk, 142; of herring, 141; of Kwaday Dan Ts'inchi, 143–145; of northern fur seal, 138; of salmon, 35, 78; of sea otters, 139; of Shuka' Kaa, 4, 35, 53
Drucker, Philip, 24, 142
Dundas Islands, BC, 68, 76, 94n2

Early Graham tradition, 110
Early Holocene, 43, 50, 61, 63–72, 76, 80, 82–84, 86, 88–89, 91–92, 96–97, 109–10, 132
Early Moresby tradition, 66, 110
elites, 8, 15, 18, 103, 129, 130, 131n15
elk, 10, 11, 81, 85, 102, 114–15, 135, 142
English Camp, WA, 42, 87, 106, 131n8
Erlandson, Jon M., 51, 54, 70
ethnography, archaeological uses of, 5, 22–26, 29, 31, 38–40, 60, 74–75, 95, 107, 119–20, 122–23, 142

eulachon, 12, 28, 35, 38, 42, 126, 128, 139

Far West Point, BC, 68, 76
Fedje, Daryl W. et al., 64, 109, 110
Fifield, Terry, 1
fires, 10, 63, 74, 135
fishing: Late Holocene, 126–27; as primary way of life, 27, 28; weirs and traps, 35, 37–38, 91–92, 126–27; women and children and, 38. *See also* salmon
Fladmark, Knut R., 47, 75–76
Foliate Biface tradition, 61
Forrester Islands, AK, 140–41
Fraser River, BC, 118, 134–35
Fraser Valley Fire Period, 135
fur seal, 137–38

Gaadu Din, BC, 52, 59, 60
gender roles and relations, 13, 18, 21, 24, 29, 38, 41–42, 106, 121–22, 131n5
Gifford-Gonzalez, Diane et al., 138
Glenrose site, BC, 35, 43, 85, 88, 92
Graesch, Anthony P., 105
Gray's Harbor, WA, 38
Greenville Burial Ground, BC, 124
Grier, Colin, 26
Groundhog Bay II site, AK, 68
ground stone tools, 88–89, 104–5
Gulf of Georgia, 88–89, 98–107, 125, 129
Gulf of Georgia phase, 106
Gwaii Haanas, 111

Haida, 40, 111, 140–41
Haida Gwaii, 59, 60; Early Holocene sites on, 63–67; Middle-Late Holocene sites on, 109–12; sea level rise on, 63
Haplogroup A, 53
Haplogroup B, 53, 54
Haplogroup D, 4, 53, 54
Harper, John R., 43
Heaton, Tim, 2
herring, 35, 38, 78, 79, 81, 82, 126, 141
Hidden Falls, AK, 68, 113–14
Hobler, Philip M., 84–85
Hoko River, WA, 42, 105
Holocene time periods, 50

level changes at, 76; shell midden at, 76; reliance on salmon at, 35, 39, 78, 79, 84
Nenana industry, 55
Neoglacial, 138
nephrite, 104
Netarts Sandspit Village, OR, 42
Northwest Coast: archaeological localities on, 47, 48; complex hunter-gatherer stereotype of, 27–34, 45–46; contact and colonialism on, 16–22; cultural groups on, 7–8, 12–13, 14–15; first people of, 59; geographic context of, 8, 10–11, 14; glacial refugia in, 57–59; linguistic map of, 9; most sites on as palimpsests, 74; perishable materials of, 64; potential for zooarchaeology on, 137–42; resource management ideology on, 34; sea-level histories of, 56–59; travels to interior of, 143–45
Nuu-chah-nulth, 24–25, 40, 41, 142

obsidian, 4, 61, 69, 71, 102, 108, 109, 113, 119, 133
Obsidian Culture, 108
Old Cordilleran complex, 60, 88
On Your Knees Cave, AK, 1, 52, 61, 71
Oregon, 19–20. *See also* names of specific sites
Ozette, WA, 23, 42, 64, 90, 97, 115–16, 118, 120, 121, 131n11, 140

Pacific Period, 49
Paisley Caves, OR, 53–54
Par-Tee site, OR, 114–15, 142
Paulina Lake, OR, 117
Paul Mason site, BC, 119
Peace River fluted points, 62
Pebble Tool Tradition, 60, 67, 68, 88
Pender Canal, BC, 103, 123
Pender Island, BC, 84–85
Pitt River, BC, 98, 103
plant cultivation, 39–43
potatoes, 17–18, 42
Pribilof Islands, AK, 137–38
Price, T. Douglas, 29
Prince of Wales Archipelago, 57, 67
Prince Rupert Harbor, BC, 85, 88, 112, 124, 128

Qithyil site, BC, 118
Queen Charlotte Strait Culture, 108–9

Rahemtulla, Farid, 102
Rainbow Mountains obsidian, 109
redcedar, 10, 73–74, 91, 110–11, 135
Richardson Island site, BC, 66–67, 74
rock art, 126, 127
rockfish, 35, 38, 64, 66–68, 71, 78, 81–82, 91, 94n2
Rocky Point Cemetery, BC, 126
Rousseau, Jerome, 32–33
Rowley-Conwy, Peter, 31–32

St. Mungo site, BC, 85
salmon: butchery, 105; DNA analysis of, 35, 78; lack of evidence for intensification of, 39; as most important resource, 75; occasional failure of, 78, 79; ownership of, 39; reliance at Namu on, 35, 39, 78, 79, 84; sea level change and, 83–84
Saltery Bay site, BC, 81–82, 84, 94n3
Scowlitz site, BC, 125–26
seabirds, 140–41
sea otters, 17, 139
seals, sea lions, 2, 27, 42, 64, 68, 70, 78, 81–82, 108, 120, 127, 137–38, 142
seascapes, 134
Sheehan, Michael S., 26
shellfish, 24, 28, 43–45, 54, 64, 80, 84–88; at Namu, 78–79; poisoning, 128
shell middens: as built environments, 123–24; burials and, 123–24; dating of, 75–76; Early Holocene, 76; explanation of, 86–87, 132–133; low temporal resolution of, 74; Middle Holocene, 84–86, 88
Shoemaker Bay I, BC, 119
Silverhole basket, 90
Shuká Kaa, 3–4, 35, 53, 70
silverweed, 40
slate tools, 89, 98, 100–2, 104–5, 108, 110, 113–15, 131n6, 133
Smith, Bruce, 33
Somenos Creek, BC, 124
specialization, 97, 105
Stafford, Jim, 80